Innovation in University-Based Intensive English Programs

NEW PERSPECTIVES ON LANGUAGE AND EDUCATION
Founding Editor: Viv Edwards, *University of Reading, UK*
Series Editors: Phan Le Ha, *University of Hawaii at Manoa, USA* and Joel Windle, *Monash University, Australia.*

Two decades of research and development in language and literacy education have yielded a broad, multidisciplinary focus. Yet education systems face constant economic and technological change, with attendant issues of identity and power, community and culture. What are the implications for language education of new 'semiotic economies' and communications technologies? Of complex blendings of cultural and linguistic diversity in communities and institutions? Of new cultural, regional and national identities and practices? The New Perspectives on Language and Education series will feature critical and interpretive, disciplinary and multidisciplinary perspectives on teaching and learning, language and literacy in new times. New proposals, particularly for edited volumes, are expected to acknowledge and include perspectives from the Global South. Contributions from scholars from the Global South will be particularly sought out and welcomed, as well as those from marginalized communities within the Global North.

All books in this series are externally peer-reviewed.

Full details of all the books in this series and of all our other publications can be found on http://www.multilingual-matters.com, or by writing to Multilingual Matters, St Nicholas House, 31-34 High Street, Bristol, BS1 2AW, UK.

NEW PERSPECTIVES ON LANGUAGE AND EDUCATION: 116

Innovation in University-Based Intensive English Programs

From Start to Future

Edited by
Jason Litzenberg

MULTILINGUAL MATTERS
Bristol • Jackson

DOI https://doi.org/10.21832/LITZEN4440
Library of Congress Cataloging in Publication Data
A catalog record for this book is available from the Library of Congress.
Names: Litzenberg, Jason, editor.
Title: Innovation in University-Based Intensive English Programs: From Start to Future/Edited by Jason Litzenberg.
Description: Bristol; Jackson: Multilingual Matters, 2023. | Series: New Perspectives on Language and Education: 116 | Includes bibliographical references and index. | Summary: 'This book considers innovation in US-based Intensive English Programs (IEPs), which provide international students with an immersion-style environment for learning academic English, prior to matriculating into a full-time degree program. The chapters demonstrate the ways that IEPs influence the wider fields of Applied Linguistics and TESOL' – Provided by publisher.
Identifiers: LCCN 2023028592 (print) | LCCN 2023028593 (ebook) | ISBN 9781800414433 (paperback) | ISBN 9781800414440 (hardback) | ISBN 9781800414457 (pdf) | ISBN 9781800414464 (epub)
Subjects: LCSH: English language – Study and teaching (Higher) – Foreign speakers. | Educational innovations.
Classification: LCC PE1128.A2 I55 2023 (print) | LCC PE1128.A2 (ebook) | DDC 428.0071/1 – dc23/eng/20230817
LC record available at https://lccn.loc.gov/2023028592
LC ebook record available at https://lccn.loc.gov/2023028593

British Library Cataloguing in Publication Data
A catalogue entry for this book is available from the British Library.

ISBN-13: 978-1-80041-444-0 (hbk)
ISBN-13: 978-1-80041-443-3 (pbk)

Multilingual Matters
UK: St Nicholas House, 31-34 High Street, Bristol, BS1 2AW, UK.
USA: Ingram, Jackson, TN, USA.

Website: https://www.multilingual-matters.com
Twitter: Multi_Ling_Mat
Facebook: https://www.facebook.com/multilingualmatters
Blog: https://www.channelviewpublications.wordpress.com

Copyright © 2024 Jason Litzenberg and the authors of individual chapters.

All rights reserved. No part of this work may be reproduced in any form or by any means without permission in writing from the publisher.

The policy of Multilingual Matters/Channel View Publications is to use papers that are natural, renewable and recyclable products, made from wood grown in sustainable forests. In the manufacturing process of our books, and to further support our policy, preference is given to printers that have FSC and PEFC Chain of Custody certification. The FSC and/or PEFC logos will appear on those books where full certification has been granted to the printer concerned.

Typeset by Riverside Publishing Solutions.

The existence of this volume is indebted to the talents and skills of its contributors, without whom this project would not be possible. Their insights are invaluable, providing a nuanced view of Intensive English Programs, an important yet often overlooked area of applied linguistics and TESOL.

None of this work, however, could have been realized without contributors' affiliation with educational institutions located in the geographies of Turtle Island and Abya Yala, the continents also known as North America and South America, respectively. The topic of the volume and its contents originate as a consequence of settler colonial histories that have shaped English into the global lingua franca it is today. Modern practitioners inherit and benefit from this legacy, but they also contribute to the future directions of their fields.

This volume is dedicated to the original stewards of the land upon which the institutions represented herein are located.

Contents

	Contributors	ix
	Introduction: Understanding Innovation in University-Based Intensive English Programs *Jason Litzenberg*	1
1	The First IEP: The English Language Institute at the University of Michigan *Diane Larsen-Freeman*	20
2	ELI, ELP or IEP? Tracing the Growth of an Industry *Jason Litzenberg and Minjin Kim*	34
3	Founding the Modern Era: A Conversation Among Former IEP Directors *Sharon Cavusgil, Martyn J. Miller, Rebecca Smith-Murdock and Betty Soppelsa*	51
4	Employment Trends in English Language Programs *Jeremy D. Slagoski*	69
5	Beyond Revenue: IEP Service to the University and Community *Sarah Arva Grosik*	85
6	Multilingualism, Multiculturalism and Advocacy: How Intensive English Language Programs can Impact Campus Culture *Michael E. Anderson and LeeAnne Berger Godfrey*	101
7	Behold-Remold: Navigating and Innovating Liminal Spaces as an IEP Practitioner-Administrator-Scholar (PAS) *Nikki Mattson and Jacqueline M. Gianico*	116
8	The Missing Puzzle Piece: Racism and Native-Speakerism Scholarship *JPB Gerald*	132

9 The Other Side of Community Engagement Projects: Benefits to the Community? 144
James M. Perren

10 Mind the Gap! Voices of Brazilian English Language Teachers in a Continuing Education Intensive English Program in the United States 159
Kleber Aparecido da Silva, Dllubia Santclair, Lauro Sérgio Machado Pereira, Silvia Penna and Oseas Bezerra Viana-Jr

11 Over a Decade of Third-Party Pathway Programs in the United States 175
Carter A. Winkle

12 Brave New Classrooms: On the Role of Technology in IEPs 192
Ekaterina Arshavskaya and Marta Halaczkiewicz

13 Where to From Here? Continuing to Innovate, Respond and Reform in IEPs 208
Crystal Bock Thiessen

Index 225

Contributors

Michael Anderson, PhD, is the Executive Director of College Pathways in the College of Continuing and Professional Studies at the University of Minnesota – Twin Cities. He has taught English in France and the United States, has been the director of an intensive English program for over 15 years and has served on the board of University and College Intensive English Programs (UCIEP). He works in teacher development with instructors within the Minnesota English Language Program (MELP) and also teaches a practicum course for students in the MA TESOL program. His research interests include programming for multilingual students, language teacher education and language assessment.

Kleber Aparecido da Silva is an Associate Professor in the Department of Linguistics, Portuguese and Classical Languages at the Institute of Letters of the University of Brasília (UnB), where he teaches subjects in the Brazilian Portuguese Language Course as a Second Language and in the Program of Post-Graduation in Linguistics at UnB, in the Post-Graduate Program in Literature: Culture, Education and Languages at the State University of Southwest Bahia and in the Post-Graduate Program in Literature at the Federal University of Tocantins – Campus de Porto Nacional. He has a degree in English from the Federal University of Ouro Preto, an MA in Applied Linguistics from UNICAMP and a PhD in Linguistic Studies from UNESP. He is the coordinator of the Group for Critical and Advanced Studies in Languages (GECAL) at UnB. His areas of interest in research include gender, race and language education; language, discourse and identity practices; (multi)literacies and critical education of language teachers; critical theories and pedagogies and decolonial practices in the production of knowledge.

Ekaterina Arshavskaya, PhD, is an Associate Professor in the intensive English program at Utah State University (USU). She is also in charge of the international teaching assistants' training program and currently co-directs the MA Second Language Teaching program at the same university. She advises PhD students in the Teacher Education and Leadership (TEAL) program at USU. Her research and teaching interests include intercultural learning, multilingual literature, computer-assisted language learning (CALL), critical pedagogy and L2 teacher education. She is actively engaged with Intermountain TESOL and International TESOL (ITA- and CALL-IS). She has served the TESOL ITA-IS as a community events organizer and a newsletter editor and has published in *System*, *TESOL Journal* and *Teaching Education*.

Sharon Cavusgil is a Senior Lecturer in the Department of Applied Linguistics & ESL at Georgia State University, where she teaches undergraduate and graduate courses, primarily for speakers of English as a second language. She also serves in various administrative roles, most recently as director of the department's undergraduate program and director of ESL for graduate students. Sharon is passionate about helping others achieve their academic and professional goals as they relate to language development and cultural understanding. In addition to the diverse population she serves in the United States, she has presented and conducted workshops on academic communication and English language pedagogy in South America, Asia, Europe and the Middle East.

JPB Gerald is a graduate of the EdD program in Instructional Leadership from CUNY – Hunter College. He works in adult education and professional development for a national nonprofit, teaches a course on whiteness and language teaching at Adelphi University in New York, and also writes about language, whiteness and disability. His most recent work is *Antisocial Language Teaching: English and the Pervasive Pathology of Whiteness*, available from Multilingual Matters (2022). He lives on unceded Munsee Lenape and Canarsie territory – better known as Queens, NY, USA – with his dog, wife and toddler.

Jacqueline M. Gianico has taught adult and post-secondary international students since 2006. She holds an MA degree in Italian from Middlebury College and an MA degree in Applied Linguistics from Teachers College, Columbia University. Her career in IEPs began as an adjunct instructor for the programs at Columbia University and New York University, eventually serving nine years at the Intensive English Communication Program (IECP) at The Pennsylvania State University (PSU). She is currently Associate Teaching Professor of Applied Linguistics at PSU, teaching undergraduate courses in both the departments of Applied Linguistics and Communication Arts and Sciences in the College of the Liberal Arts. Her research interests include the intersection of performance and pedagogy, and she is involved in her local improvisational theatre group.

LeeAnne Berger Godfrey, PhD, is a Teaching Specialist in the Minnesota English Language Program (MELP) at the University of Minnesota – Twin Cities. She teaches courses in the academic English program and serves as the Faculty Liaison. As Faculty Liaison she supports faculty and staff across campus in better serving international/multilingual students. LeeAnne has been involved in language teaching or language teacher education for nearly 20 years and has lived and taught in France, Poland, China, Korea and Minnesota. Her interests include inclusion of and access for multilingual learners across the curriculum, second language acquisition, multilingualism, language teacher education and play in higher education.

Sarah Arva Grosik, EdD, is the Director of Programs at the University of Pennsylvania English Language Programs, where she oversees and teaches a wide variety of English language courses and programs for international students. In addition to teaching ESL courses, Sarah also serves as a lecturer in the Educational Linguistics division of the University of Pennsylvania's Graduate School of Education. Prior to her current role, Sarah taught EFL abroad, elementary ESL in Philadelphia, adult ESL classes at Bucks County Community College and teacher education courses at Temple University and Lehigh University. Her research and teaching interests include international students' preparation for, access to and equity in postsecondary education.

Marta Halaczkiewicz, PhD, is a Principal Lecturer in the World Languages and Cultures Department and the Director of the Intensive English Language Institute at Utah State University (USU). She teaches English to multilingual and international students at USU and in partnerships with several universities in China. She also teaches Learning Theory and Games and Learning courses at the Instructional Technology and Lending Sciences Department at USU. She advises and mentors pre-service ESL and EFL teachers in the MA Second Language Teaching program at USU. Her research interests span from creative writing pedagogy, collaborative peer-review spaces and game-based and gameful instruction to computer-assisted language learning (CALL). She has contributed extensively to the CALL Interest Section of *TESOL International* as a presenter, volunteer, officer and chair. Her articles have appeared in *TESOL Journal* and *TESL Electronic Journal*.

Minjin Kim is a PhD candidate in the Department of Applied Linguistics and a research assistant in the Center for Language Acquisition at Pennsylvania State University. Her research interests include corpus linguistics, natural language processing, second language acquisition, computer-assisted language learning and English for Academic Purposes. She has primary interests in second language learners' linguistic development in L2 production, genre-based approaches to academic writing research and pedagogy and stance construction in academic speech. She has over 10 years of English teaching experience in various educational settings in South Korea and the United States, and taught academic writing and grammar in the Intensive English Communication Program of Pennsylvania State University in 2020–2021.

Diane Larsen-Freeman began teaching English as a Peace Corps Volunteer in Malaysia in the 1960s. In the 1970s, she pursued graduate study at the University of Michigan, earning her PhD in Linguistics in 1975. During her study at Michigan, she was a Teaching Assistant at the English Language Institute and also taught evening courses for adult students in the Ann Arbor community. She was appointed a tenure track position at the University of California, Los Angeles. She later left UCLA and joined the graduate faculty at the School for International Training in Brattleboro, Vermont. In 2002, she returned to the University of Michigan to direct its English Language Institute and take up professorial appointments. She is currently Professor of Linguistics Emerita, Professor of Education Emerita, Research Scientist Emerita at the University of Michigan and Professor Emerita at the School for International Training and Visiting Faculty member at the University of Pennsylvania. From 2000 to 2005, Larsen-Freeman edited the journal *Language Learning* and subsequently served as Chair of its Board of Directors.

Jason Litzenberg has a PhD in Applied Linguistics and ESL from Georgia State University; he has over 20 years of experience teaching English and language education in Ecuador, Germany, the UAE and the United States. Jason is Teaching Professor of Applied Linguistics at The Pennsylvania State University, where he is affiliated faculty of the Rock Ethic's Institute and full-time Director of the Intensive English Communication Program (IECP). He is currently Vice President of Three Rivers TESOL in Pennsylvania and Vice-President of UCIEP. His academic/research interests include phonetics and phonology, sociolinguistics, linguistic landscapes, language ideologies, English as a Lingua Franca (ELF), program administration and decolonial scholarship.

Nikki Mattson has been a faculty member at the Intensive English Communication Program (IECP) at The Pennsylvania State University (PSU) since 2009. She currently serves as the Coordinator of Strategic Initiatives (CSI) for the IECP in addition to being a Teaching Professor. She holds her MA in Linguistics and a Certificate of Graduate Study in TESOL from the University of South Carolina. Nikki is dedicated to supporting campus internationalization efforts as well as global engagement in the classroom, on campus and beyond. She is the founder and advisor for the PSU Living-Learning Community, the Global Engagement Community. She also serves as a Global Learning Coordinator (GLC) for PSU's Experiential Digital Global Engagement (EDGE) Program. Her research interests include intensive English program oral placement test validation, evaluating computer-assisted language learning (CALL) usage in second language (L2) classrooms and internationalization in higher education.

Martyn J. Miller holds graduate degrees in fantasy and medieval English Literature from The University of Georgia and a BA degree in English Literature and teaching diploma in English as a Foreign Language from the American University of Beirut (AUB). Miller is an Arab-American who grew up in Syria and Lebanon and has lived in the United States since graduating from AUB. Miller is currently the Assistant Vice President for International Services and Cultural Activities at Temple University, where he oversees the Center for American Language and Culture (TCALC), the Center for Chinese Language Instruction (CCLI), International Student Affairs (ISA) and International Student and Scholar Services (ISSS). Miller also assists with Indian subcontinent and MENA student recruiting and partnership development. Before joining Temple in 1999, Miller was Department Head of The University of Georgia American Language Program.

Silvia Penna is a Professor at the Federal Institute of Minas Gerais (IFMG-OP) in Ouro Preto, Minas Gerais, Brazil. She has a degree in Language teaching – English and Portuguese – from the Federal University of Ouro Preto (UFOP), she has a TESOL certificate from Beloit College, Beloit, Wisconsin (US) and a MA in Literature, from the Federal University of Minas Gerais (UFMG). She is currently enrolled in the Linguistics PhD program at the University of Brasília (UnB). Her professional experience includes teaching English on high school level technical courses, college-level courses and teaching Portuguese as a Foreign Language to exchange students. Her areas of interest in research include: (multi)literacies and critical education of language teachers; critical theories and pedagogies; decolonial practices; and internationalization.

Lauro Sérgio Machado Pereira is a Professor at the Federal Institute of Northern Minas Gerais (IFNMG), in Janaúba, Minas Gerais, Brazil. With a degree in English Language from the State University of Montes Claros (UNIMONTES), he obtained his MA in Applied Linguistics from the University of Brasília (UnB) and is currently a doctoral candidate in the Postgraduate Program in Linguistics at the same institution. He was an inaugural member of the SETEC-CAPES/NOVA Training Program for English Teachers of the Federal Network for Vocational, Scientific, and Technological Education. His professional experience includes open language courses and basic, vocational and higher education teaching. His research interests are critical-reflective practice, English teacher education, collaborative action-research, internationalization, language policy, translingual practices and critical applied linguistics (CAL).

James M. Perren is a Professor at Alliant International University in San Diego, California. James earned his EdD in Curriculum, Instruction, and Technology in Education at Temple University, PA, and a BA Degree in Spanish and an MA TESOL Degree from San José State University in California. Most recently, James received an MBA from University of the People. James is a language teacher, teacher educator, editor and author. He has taught in Japan and the US. James' disciplinary scholarship has examined educational technology, technology in English language education, service learning in applied linguistics, intercultural communication, ESL/EFL teaching methodology, materials development, teacher training and critical SLA theory. When taking a break from doing what he loves as an educator, he races his bicycle as a masters level competitor and plays guitar as much as he possibly can. James also grows his own vegetables and is known to make a very delicious organic salad directly from the garden.

Dllubia Santclair is an associate teacher in Basic Education, from the Education Department of the State of Goiás (Seduc-GO), Brazil. She is part of the team of the Center for Studies, Research, and Professionals Education in Goiás (CSRPE – GO). She graduated in Arts Portuguese–English from the State University of Goiás (UEG – Campus Porangatu); she obtained her interdisciplinary MA degree in Education, Language, and Technologies from the State University of Goiás (UEG - Anápolis) and is currently pursuing a PhD in Linguistics from the University of Brasília (UnB).

Jeremy D. Slagoski is the Assistant Dean of the School of Humanities and Social Sciences and Director of the Applied Language Institute (ALI) at the University of Missouri Kansas City (UMKC). In 1998, he started his career as an English language teacher in Japan. Since then, he has taught English learners and trained English teachers in South Korea, Russia, China and the US. In 2014, he earned his PhD in Teaching and Learning from the University of Iowa. Since then, he has been awarded grants to design and facilitate programs for 24 teachers around the world in the English Access Microscholarship Program and for 40 innovative leaders of various binational centers throughout Brazil. During the pandemic, he coordinated virtual exchange programs at UMKC and is developing an online and hybrid competency-based English language learning program to complement the ALI's long-standing intensive English program. He lives in Shawnee, Kansas with his wife, daughter and two cats. The pandemic has prolonged their settling into life in the Kansas City metro region, but they enjoy the many varieties of KC barbecue.

Rebecca Smith-Murdock has a PhD in English Literature from University of Alberta, Canada, an MA in English Literature, University of Arkansas and an RSA TEFL Certificate, London, UK. Between 1970 and 2011, she taught English in the US, England, Canada, China and Thailand. Rebecca has held faculty positions at University of Alberta, University of Prince Edward Island and Pacific Lutheran University, and she served for over two decades as director of Intensive English Programs at the University of Arkansas at Little Rock (1979–1989) and the University of North Texas (1989–2001). Throughout her career, she has presented more than 40 times at professional conferences, completed more than 30 funded proposals and served as a consultant for the governments of Jordan, Thailand and multiple universities in Saudi Arabia. Rebecca was an ESL program evaluator for the Oklahoma State Regents and she has served as CEA site reviewer, Commission member and chair, site-visit representative, employee and staff consultant. Rebecca has served in various roles in UCIEP, EnglishUSA (AAIEP), TESOL and NAFSA.

Betty Soppelsa first taught English as a US Peace Corps volunteer in West Africa. She continued in the field for 40 years, teaching and serving as Assistant Director of the English Language Program at Ohio State University, Director of The Applied English Center at the University of Kansas and as an educational consultant in the US and abroad. She published articles in the *Journal of Intensive English Studies* and *TESOL Quarterly* and a chapter on faculty empowerment in *The Administration of English Language Programs* (Stoller & Christison, eds.). Following her years in TESL, Soppelsa served as Deputy Executive Director of NAFSA: Association of International Educators, oversaw the management of the annual conference and developed programs for faculty to support infusion of global awareness into their curricula. For teacher education, Soppelsa initiated the development of My Cultural Awareness Profile, an online instrument, and co-authored 'InTASC as a Framework: Viewing the InTASC Standards through a Global Preparation Lens'.

Crystal Bock Thiessen is a PhD candidate in education and an ESL lecturer at the University of Nebraska-Lincoln where she works in the intensive English program and with undergraduate and graduate multilingual learners of English. She has MA-TESL and BA degrees in photography and Spanish. Her research interests include sociocultural connections between university domestic and international students, the sociolinguistic development of international multilingual learners of English on campus and arts-based language teaching and learning. She has taught English in Japan and in Ukraine at the secondary and post-secondary levels, respectively, and has conducted teacher training as a U.S. Department of State English Language Specialist in Ukraine, Russia, Belarus, Moldova, Georgia, Azerbaijan, Pakistan and Vietnam. Her passions include photography, language learning and travel (she just visited her 51st country this winter).

Oseas Bezerra Viana Júnior is a Professor at the Federal University of the Agreste of Pernambuco, in Garanhuns, Pernambuco, Brazil. He graduated in English Language from the State University of Paraiba (UEPB) and has obtained his Master's and doctoral degrees in Applied Linguistics from the Federal University of Bahia (UFBA). His professional experience includes the teaching of English at various public universities of Brazil as well teaching in private institutions. Grounded in critical applied linguistics, critical discourse analysis, cultural studies and sociolinguistics. Anchored in critical/decolonial perspectives, his areas of interests include the use and acquisition of the English language in formal contexts of learning, focusing on how it is influenced/attached by different glocal social processes, such as race, social class and gender.

Carter A. Winkle (he/him/his) serves as an Associate Dean for the Adrian Dominican School of Education, Leadership, and Human Development at Barry University. An Associate Professor of Education, he also facilitates doctoral and graduate courses across a variety of programs in the school. Beyond research in the area of matriculation pathway programs for international ESL students in university settings, Winkle explores reflexivity and positionality in doctoral research education through self-study research practices. A practitioner of arts-based research methods and methodologies – in particular, ethnodrama and other narrative genres – he additionally examines research questions related to second-language teaching and learning through a social justice or advocacy lens.

Introduction: Understanding Innovation in University-Based Intensive English Programs

Jason Litzenberg

Setting the Scene

We are, supposedly, surrounded by innovation. We oft times use the term indiscriminately as a way of emphasizing some novel aspect of a product or service. In such instances, innovation operates as a generic, comprehensive term for new ideas and practices (White *et al.*, 2008). At other times, however, we apply the concept of innovation intentionally and calculatedly. For example, an employee may seek advancement by promoting themselves as an innovator, or an online MA TESOL program may recruit students by promoting its 'innovative curriculum'. Indeed, innovation and change have been an important subject in language education since the early days of the field (Hyland & Wong, 2013), driven in large part by a desire to find new, better ways to teach and learn languages. The field of applied linguistics arose in large part from this innovative drive to improve the acquisition and development of second and foreign languages (Howatt & Widdowson, 2004).

In 1941, Charles C. Fries at University of Michigan opened what is widely recognized as the first Intensive English Program, or IEP (see Larsen-Freeman, this volume, for a historical overview of the development of this program). As Fries (1948: 12) posits in the inaugural issue of the journal *Language Learning*, curricular innovations were a central component of the program; he lists core principles underlying the work of University of Michigan's IEP as 'satisfactory basic materials' and 'the selection and sequence of the materials to be studied'. IEPs have proliferated across the United States and around the world since the opening of the first program in the early 1940s. In the 1980s and 1990s, the footprint of IEPs expanded exponentially as higher education institutions in North America began viewing these programs as sources of revenue and as ways to increase international student populations on their campuses. IEPs experienced historical levels of student populations in 2014 and 2015, subsequently followed by several years of declining enrollments up until – and naturally, throughout – the early stages of the Covid pandemic, a time during which this publication was being assembled. Throughout the entirety of this history of IEP growth, development and changes, programs have continually and consistently been associated with innovation.

The field of applied linguistics continues to maintain a symbiotic relationship with IEPs, with programs serving as sites of research, teacher training and curriculum development, among other affinities. Yet IEPs must frequently struggle for recognition, with many in the field viewing IEPs as not 'particularly worthy of their notice, time, and effort' (Litzenberg, 2021). Indeed, the majority of publications involving IEPs primarily utilize these programs as sites of research, with little consideration of the logistics and mechanisms required for sustaining such programs. Book length publications on IEPs tend to be similarly limited in scope, focusing more upon the administrative aspects of program operations and therefore orienting toward administrators or students interested in future program administration. One of the earliest books on IEPs is *The Administration of Intensive English Language Programs* (Barret, 1982), a short and somewhat informal collection of essays that serves as early acknowledgement of IEPs as a distinct field of professional engagement. Later publications include *Building Better English Language Programs* (Pennington, 1991), *Management in English Language Teaching* (White et al., 1991), *A Handbook for Language Program Administrators* (Christison & Stoller, 1997), *Service, Satisfaction and Climate: Perspectives on Management in English Language Teaching* (Walker, 2010) and *English Language Program Administration: Leadership and Management in the 21st Century* (Christison & Stoller, 2023), as well as the slightly slimmer texts from Dimmit and Dantas-Whitney (2002) and Orlando (2016). Perhaps the most influential of IEP-related texts is Christison and Stoller (1997), which was subsequently updated and reissued in 2012. The original book implicitly equates *language program* with IEPs while the second edition works from more nuanced distinctions among language program types, with specific chapters in the final section of the book focusing on adult education programs, binational centers, IEPs, international schools, K-12[1] and private schools. Other important works that consider language programs more generally look at assessment practices (Kiely & Rea-Dickins, 2005; Lynch, 1996), program revitalization and renewal (Rice & Graupensperger, 2007) and language program leadership (Christison & Murray, 2009; Lord, 2014; White et al., 2008).

Acknowledging the important contributions of these works to understanding the synergy of innovation in language programs, the present book assumes a broader stance toward innovation. More specifically, while the contributions of this book consider IEPs and

IEP practices, they also attempt to expand outward and assess the impact of IEP innovations beyond the traditional boundaries of the programs themselves. At the same time, however, the IEPs discussed in this book represent a limited range of program types – namely, those affiliated with institutions of higher education in the United States. This approach is not without reason. Murray (2013) describes the variety and complexity of educational initiatives, emphasizing the importance of contextualization, which, by necessity, requires a bounded scope. In addition, a limited context of discussion provides for more 'nuanced description' (Pennycook & Makoni, 2020: 123) of the frameworks for which we seek to expand our perspectives and create alternatives. Thus, rather than being a disadvantage, the limited range of program types and program locations considered in this book is an advantage because one is able to focus on the contextual subtleties of these IEPs. Moreover, this orientation does not preclude relevancy to other types of language programs, program administrators, researchers and applied linguists around the world, who will find many overlaps to their own work. The hope is that readers, regardless of location or point of engagement in the field, are able to find similarities to and insight and inspiration from the contexts and innovations described herein.

The next section further delineates the types of IEPs considered in this volume, followed by a section that seeks to define innovation as understood in previous language program and IEP literature. Using these earlier conceptualizations of innovation as a foundation, the third section briefly orients this collection of chapters within language policy and planning research, arguing for a re-envisioning – or perhaps even, if readers would so kindly permit, re-innovating – of how we conceptualize and engage with innovation. The fourth and final section of this chapter lays out the trajectory of the book and provides an overview of the contributions.

Sites of Innovation: Intensive English Programs

The present volume focuses specifically on IEPs that are affiliated with and administered by higher education institutions. 'IEP' frequently serves as an overarching term for any type of program that provides the legally mandated minimum hours of study for international students on a language study visa. For instance, academic units operating under titles such as English Language Institute or English Language Program may all be considered IEPs (see Litzenberg & Kim, this volume). IEPs are centers that serve 'full-time English language students who seek to develop their English skills rapidly in an immersion setting' (Hamrick, 2016: 321) in which the core purpose of the IEP is 'to design, develop, and successfully deliver a curriculum and overall positive educational experience to help ESL [English as a Second language] students acquire English language skills necessary for higher education academic success' (Orlando, 2016: 12).

IEPs are frequently (but unofficially) assigned 'outsider' status at their host institutions. Most programs are self-supporting units, so even though they may be affiliated with a university or college, they receive limited or no support from the institution. In addition, the majority of programs do not provide degrees, so the courses they offer are non-credit. In the case of my own institution, this situation prevents our courses from being indexed among the main university course listings and restricts our ability to access certain enrollment and course management tools. IEPs may be located in out-of-the-way areas (e.g. off campus, basements, etc.), and their faculty viewed as non-traditional in comparison to collogues of other campus units. Other challenges faced by IEPs include budget fluctuations, staffing challenges and dynamic student/teacher ratios. At the same time, however, IEPs align with campus internationalization efforts because they serve as a gateway for bringing international students – and the higher tuition rates they incur – to an institution. IEPs often advise their host institutions on issues related to international students, such as language proficiency entrance requirements, language accommodations or fostering campus multiculturality. IEPs may also support education, foreign/modern language and linguistics departments by providing services such as practicum opportunities, workshops and professional development opportunities and serving as sites of linguistic research.

The administration of an IEP may occur through various types of campus units, such as international admissions offices, academic departments, student affairs units, continuing education programs or international programming offices. Literature on IEPs and on language programs tend to position program directors as the core facilitators of innovation within a program, although Stoller (2014) also attributes IEP innovation to their outsider status. Dimmit and Dantas-Whitney (2002: 4), for example, point out that IEPs are able to 'to experiment with new courses without having to go through university curriculum committees' and that teachers are able to 'try out new ideas and teaching methods'. Program directors are responsible for demonstrating the impact – regardless of whether positive or negative – of the innovations the programs foster. Directors must be nimble and innovative, envision the need for innovations, manifest dynamism and flexibility, encourage 'buy-in', engage collaborators, anticipate challenges, communicate effectively, ensure resources, assess program effectiveness and demonstrate purpose beyond program (Lord, 2014; Moyer & Gonglewski, 2014; Stoller, 1994, 2014).

Why Innovation?

Empirical research of innovation in the field of TESOL is a 'rare bird' (Markee, 2013). In IEPs, innovation research is limited primarily to Stoller (1994), who investigates the role of perceived attributes of innovations in IEP contexts. In a study involving 43 IEPs administered by colleges or universities, Stoller identified *curriculum* as the most common example of innovation, followed by *personnel, technology, policy and planning, community/campus liaison, faculty development, student placement/evaluation, student orientation/advising, student recruitment/program promotion* and others. Participants were also asked to evaluate the degree to which 13 attributes (i.e. *originality, complexity/difficulty, explicitness, visibility, practicality, flexibility, trialability/pilotability, improvement over past practices, feasibility, usefulness, dissatisfaction with past practices, improved status of the IEP* and *compatibility with past practices*) may impact innovations. Stoller (1994: 314) concluded, among other things, that 'favorable attitudes develop toward an innovation when potential adopters view the innovation as sufficiently divergent but not too divergent from current practices'. The 'zone of innovation' (Figure I.1), in other words, has a limited range for implementation before it becomes viewed as too simple or too complex by stakeholders.

While recognition of the zone of innovation is important for advocates of change in gaining support from potential adopters, Stoller suggests that the complexity of an innovation should not be a deterrent. The inherent problem-solving ability of IEPs reduces the complexity of obstacles, making them less formidable.

IEPs are intrinsically bound with innovation – in fact, Stoller (1995, 2009) challenges readers to imagine a language program lacking change and innovation. Numerous publications on IEPs and language programs

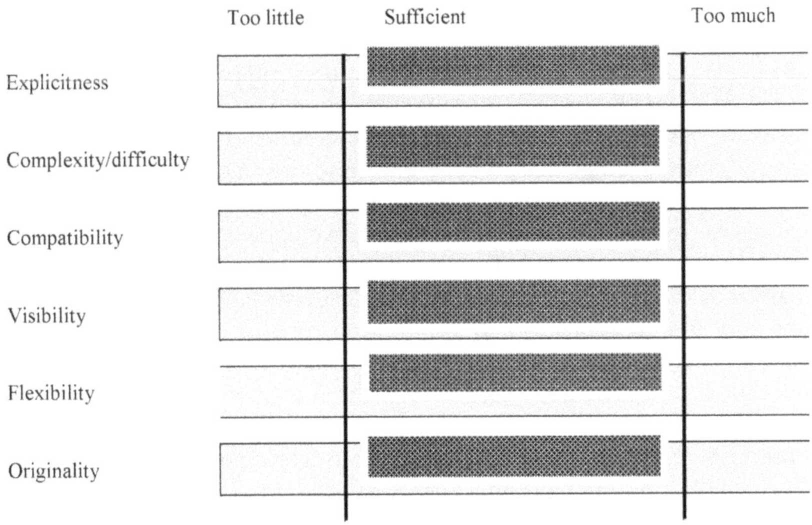

Figure I.1 The Zone of Innovation, which motivates individuals to support innovation (adapted from Stoller 1994: 314; see also Sebolai & Stoller, 2023: 96)

have chapters that deal specifically with the theme of innovation (Dimmit & Dantas-Whitney, 2002; Lord, 2014; White *et al.*, 1991, 2008). In a piece published in *International Educator*, Ladika (2018) describes the challenges faced by IEPs because of ebbing enrollments. She discusses the ways several institutions 'innovate and adapt' in order to 'successfully weather the long-term changes in the field' (2018: 42–43) – e.g. translating websites into various languages; launching of transition programs; engaging language assistants; initiating community engagement projects; short-term and professional programs; and optimizing the identity of a program. The opportunity for innovation is one that language programs should embrace (Lord, 2014).

Naturally, the concept of innovation is not exclusive to IEPs and has been widely applied elsewhere in English Language Teaching (ELT). Innovation is an integral part of educational endeavors, such as teacher preparation, curriculum design, textbook writing and classroom pedagogies (Lo Bianco, 2013). Such innovations are frequently situated within the broader discourse of globalization (Lo Bianco, 2013), an orientation that may dilute the value of the lexeme. In fact, Gramling (2019: 32) describes innovation as a 'pragmatically sedimented lexeme' based upon the presumption that 'we all know what it means'. The term itself prohibits 'reasonable impromptu objection' (2019: 26). Gramling critiques the adoption of the understandings and usages of innovation from the field of business into ELT, suggesting that practitioners in applied linguistics should engage cautiously with the concept of innovation. Commenting on a collection of essays about creativity and innovation in language education, Gramling laments that few of the contributions actively consider innovation. He observes: 'innovation appears either undefined or otherwise spirited into a catalog alongside other terms' (2019: 21). Gramling simultaneously comments upon a lack of interest in the field for theorizing or embodying innovation, while never really clarifying his own understanding of the term and leaving *innovation* equally spirited away. Supposedly, one must assume, Gramling is able to comment upon innovation (or lack of innovation) because he knows it when he sees it and because, of course, we know what he means. The point here is not to criticize Gramling – his thesis provides valuable analysis of the history of innovation – instead, the point is to demonstrate how easy it is to conflate innovation into a concept of convenience even when a critique of such usages is the exact subject of discussion. We use innovation to frame our discourses without ever defining the concept itself. For this reason, we should engage cautiously with the term; we must understand our relationship to it, its conceptual history, current conceptualizations and our imagination of what innovation can become.

While occasionally used interchangeably, most researchers and language program practitioners interested in innovation distinguish between *change* and *innovation*. Experiencing both change and innovation can elicit discomfort and resistance among stakeholders, but only change is inevitable. It occurs without intention or intervention, and it is a 'stable feature of organizational life' but does 'not necessarily ensure improvements' (Stoller, 2009: 73). Change is the natural difference that arises between any two points in time (White *et al.*, 2008). On the other hand, innovation is the *intentional* introduction of ideas and practices that are perceived as new by a population (White *et al.*, 2008). It requires motivation and deliberate effort, and it is intended to bring about improvements (Stoller, 2014). Yet the boundary between change and innovation is also nebulous. For example, (Watson Todd, 2006) considers the *continuation* stage – that is, the stage of innovation following initial implementation – of curricular innovation of a task-based curriculum at a university in Thailand. Following changes to the curriculum during the four-year period of the continuation stage, Watson Todd observes that even when teachers were dissatisfied with some of the changes arising from the innovation, they nevertheless had control over what took place in their classrooms. However, practitioners were making changes in the classroom that were not envisioned as part of the original innovation; these interventions lacked systematicity and direction and were therefore not viewed as innovation. On the other hand, the changes the teachers implemented were intentional, with the aim of bringing about improvements, and in this way not dramatically different from innovation (the stages of which are non-linear). Why, then, does Watson Todd not consider these teacher-implemented changes to be part of the original innovation? Why classify these actions as changes rather than innovation – simply because they were not part of the original design? The boundary is unclear. Indeed, change can transition into innovation, although this metamorphosis is unidirectional: Innovation may *beget* change, but innovation does not *transition into* change. When the subsequent outcome of a change is true improvement, it may become understood as innovation (Stoller, 2009). In hindsight, perhaps some of the changes Watson-Todd (2006) discusses are, in fact, innovations.

Defining innovation is clearly problematic. Gramling (2019) criticizes the sloganization of innovation. He describes the term as underspecified, conflated and suppressed with certain aspects of neoliberal innovation discourse. Influences from the field of business are evident in descriptions of innovation in IEPs and language programs. 'Thinking outside the box' and 'the next new tool' (Lord, 2014: 155) reflect a business-oriented ideology for describing innovation in IEPs. Litzenberg (2020) describes the subtle neoliberal orientations of IEPs; several of the anecdotes presented in this article could quite easily be fit into the rubric of innovation. In defending the neoliberal orientations of IEPs, Walker (2010) lists innovation, customer satisfaction and retention, number of complaints, and staff satisfaction as non-financial measures that ultimately contribute to a program's bottom line. Since explicit definitions of innovation are infrequent, one must look at descriptions and examples provided by researchers and practitioners in order to understand how they envision the concept. Examples of innovation in Lord (2014: 166) include activities such as 'researching language teacher training, exploring connections between language and acquisition, theories and classroom pedagogies, writing textbooks, and other work'. Innovation disrupts the status quo; it introduces new practices and new ways of thinking, and requires adjustments to attitudes and behaviors (Stoller, 2009).

In sum, innovation requires change, and this change requires a disruption of the status quo. The disruption – that is, the innovation – may be either internally or externally inspired. Internal motivations tend to arise from some initial dissatisfaction with the status quo, such as perceptions of workplace professionalism, unsatisfactory curriculum, a redefining of responsibilities and so forth. External factors are also motivated by a desire to change the status quo, but they generally come in the form of mandates from authorities, such as higher administration, governing boards, federal agencies or standards issued by respected professional organizations redefined (Lord, 2014; Stoller, 2009). Innovation is rarely linear, it requires continual readjustment and adaptation. These constant adjustments and adaptations are disruptive; they can temporarily increase workloads, require retraining and cost time, energy and resources (Stoller, 2014), and such uncertainty elicits discomfort and resistance, even when the motivation was internal and even with systems and measures in place. Regardless of the motivation, innovation disrupts the status quo and, therefore, as Lord (2014: 159) states 'should not be undertaken lightly or without plenty of planning and considerable time to implementation'.

Quite clearly, defining innovation is not easy or straightforward. It is an amorphous concept. While we all seem able to recognize innovation when we see it, we nevertheless seem unable to define it. Complicating the matter is that an innovation in one context may be 'old hat' in another context. For instance, a new method in an IEP for assigning faculty substitution duties may have been standard practice for years in another IEP. Perhaps, then, we are merely less able to recognize innovation in unfamiliar contexts. So, how can one study what we cannot reliably define or even agree upon as to what it is? I do not wish to argue that one should or shouldn't study innovation, but I do argue that innovation is clearly of importance to ELT and, in particular, to IEPs. Innovation is a core quality of IEP identity, and this observation alone makes IEP innovation – its conceptualizations among practitioners, its genesis, motivations, examples, ideals and potential – worthy of our attention. By focusing on the theme of innovation, this volume provides a nuanced view of an industry and its relation to a concept. It demonstrates the ways in which our understanding innovation has propelled us and how it has developed and looks at the ways in which our drive to innovate influences current industry practices as well as where innovation may take us.

The Variables of Innovation

The processes of innovation consist of three stages: the initiation stage, the implementation stage and the continuation/diffusion stage. The stages require successive cycles of long-term involvement, commitment and support in order to be successful, and they do not occur in a linear fashion. Stoller (2014) describes a set of four interacting variables that can either facilitate or inhibit innovation (Figure I.2). The variables include those associated with the language program (e.g. faculty, staff, facilities, etc.) and the home institution (e.g. policies, resources, etc.) as well as external variables (e.g. society, culture, economy, etc.) and innovation variables (e.g. qualities of the innovation, clarity of objectives, etc.).

Another way to envision this relationship comes from language policy and planning research. The variables described by Stoller are not unlike the multilayered onion described by Ricento and Hornberger (1996). External variables, for instance, correspond to the outer layers of the onion (e.g. legislation and political processes), home institution variables correspond to the middle layers (e.g. regional agencies and institutions) and language program variables correspond to the center of the onion. In this case, the center represents the internal processes and structures of language programs. Innovation runs through each of these layers, a network woven throughout the onion. Innovation in Stoller's (2014) model is unlike the other variables: it is a concept, an idea for which no part – at least as used in the model – has or can have a physical form. As we have seen, innovation itself is seldom defined. Thus, the advantage of the onion imagery is that it demonstrates the hierarchical relationship among the three similar variables as they are permeated by innovation.

Pennington and Hoekje (2010) consider language programs from an ecological perspective. They portray language programs as ecological organizations that emphasize 'the multiplicity of interconnected components or resources and their mutual relationships and dependencies' (2010: 214). An ecological orientation provides an integrative, holistic and dynamic manner for understanding the social contexts in which language use and language policy are situated. Pennington and Hoekje

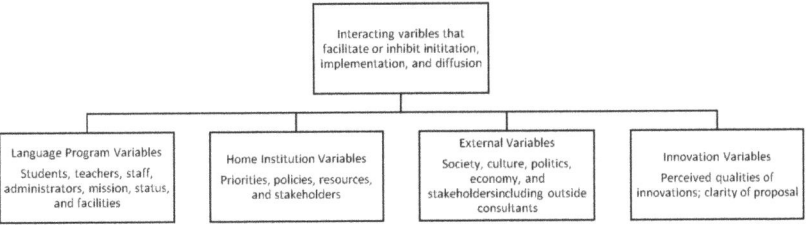

Figure I.2 Factors that interact to facilitate or inhibit innovation diffusion process (Adapted from Stoller, 2014: 46)

describe language programs as unique combinations of tangible and intangible assets that link and interact with one another and with external factors. Tangible assets include fiscal resources, physical resources (e.g. facilities and equipment) and human resources; intangible assets include a program's mission, values, curriculum, professional interpersonal relationships, climate, reputation, image and potential for innovation. The combined program resources make up the ecological context within which innovation is possible: Innovation weaves in and out of the layers and among the variables. Each program has a unique set of characteristics and resources. These qualities provide for an ecology that forms the basis of a program's *innovation potential* – i.e. its ability to progressively develop and improve itself in response to circumstances – and this potential belongs to the larger part of a program's *evolution potential*, i.e. its ability to continually develop its resources and its capacity to survive and thrive in a changing world.

The curriculum is perhaps the most commonly discussed innovation of language programs. Participants in Stoller (1994) identified the curriculum as a site for innovation more than personnel and technology combined, the two most cited types of innovation after curriculum. Dimmit and Dantas-Whitney (2002) dedicate three chapters to curricular change and innovation in IEPs. The curriculum is undoubtedly a critical feature of any pedagogical program, so it is perhaps unsurprising that the curriculum is so frequently considered in discussions of innovation, and it is perhaps equally unsurprising that these curricular changes are looked at for improvements in student performance. Language programs and the changes enacted within a program, however, represent only the innermost layers of the onion. An ecological perspective informs us that the influence of language programs extends beyond the boundaries of the program itself; innovations inevitably impact other variables as well, such as those within the home institution, language program administration, applied linguistics and applied linguistics research or even national language policy, among other areas. As with any set of integrated processes, a single innovation or change is likely to have a notable impact in other areas of the system. For instance, a curricular innovation that improves student performance on a program's exit criteria could accelerate the number of students moving through a program and thus increase the number of international students applying to an institution or, conversely, decrease the number of international students in a region as IEP students depart after completing their language studies. In addition, the potential impact extends across time and space, such as when international students exposed to social justice-based curricula return to their home countries and engage themselves in local politics. While measuring the impact of innovations upon all variables with any sort of confidence is inherently challenging (and most likely impossible), the reach of some innovations can be easier to identify than others. Extensive IEP recruiting in a particular region of the world, for instance, could lead to increased representation of students from that region at a program's host institution. Indeed, IEPs can have an impact beyond their walls. Litzenberg (2021: 13) suggests that IEPs possess the 'social and political capital within an institution' to provide them 'with the reputability and leverage for re-orienting campus discussions of internationalization, multiculturality, and diversity'. A natural question, then, is: Where else can we identify the impact of IEP innovations? How far do they extend? How long?

Applied linguists, TESOL professionals and IEP practitioners have a responsibility to understand the impact of their actions – or, in this case, their 'innovations' – as much as possible. Pennington and Hoekje (2010: 226) point out that program innovation and development decisions require 'a high degree of attention to a wide range of relevant factors' in order to understand 'potential impacts on current and future resources'. While the resources referred to in this observation seem to refer to those internal to a program, this same logic extends to other layers of the onion as well, to other variables such as the impact upon the host institution itself, the local community, professional organizations, national language policy and so forth. Such an endeavor is seldom easy or straightforward, and in some cases the insights gleaned may be undesirable. Yet understanding the significance of our actions in different arenas allows us – the professionals involved in the decision-making processes of initiation stage, implementation phase and the continuation/diffusion of innovations – to more appropriately and skillfully shape desired outcomes. Or, in other words, knowledge about the impact of our innovations can help us be better innovators.

Gramling (2019: 38) claims that scholars have become 'weary of the cycle of innovation and its promises' and suggests that 'it may be time for language education discourse and applied linguistics to go "beyond innovation" – or to forgo it'. Yet for IEPs, the suggestion to forego innovation seems to require innovation, at least as it has thus far been envisioned by practitioners: innovation requires new perspectives and approaches, adjustments to attitudes and a willingness to challenge the status quo. We are, then, not necessarily trying to forego innovation, but rather we are trying to be more conscientious of how we engage with and use the concept. Re-envisioning innovation requires us to eschew the impulse toward accelerated change and to evaluate success beyond enrollments and dividends; it requires us to draw upon 'alternate historical sensibilities around newness, novelty and invention' (Gramling, 2019: 38). Over the past several decades, decolonial theory and approaches have gained increasing recognition in ELT and related fields (DeGraff, 2019; Kumaravadivelu, 2003, 2008, 2016; Macedo, 2019; Siqueira & Alves Rocha, 2019). The decolonial option provides practitioners a route for envisioning the alternate sensibilities required for conscientious innovation. We must, according to Domínguez

(2019), 'find ways to innovate by thinking of the world differently, being decolonial in intention and practice, and asking uncomfortable questions about ours and our novices' place in the world, while we consider what knowledges, ways of being, and definitions of success we value, and are privileging in our praxis in radically different ways' (2019: 47).

The decolonial option is not the only way forward for IEP innovation, and practitioners need not necessarily ascribe to all facets of decolonial approaches or even agree with each other about the most appropriate way forward. The point is that language programs are well-situated to engage in essential questions of language teaching and the wider context to which they belong (Lord, 2014) – i.e. the variables in the inner, middle and outer layers of the onion. For practitioners, the most appropriate innovations may not always be the most comfortable, but disruptions to the status quo are seldom uncomplicated and painless. Indeed, innovation – and, in particular, conscientious innovation – is tedious, interminable and challenging. At the same time, however, innovation is empowering and rewarding; innovation allows programs and personnel to develop new paths, test novel ideas, and experience the benefits of their efforts (Stoller, 2014). Indeed, as Stoller comments, '[i]f we truly believe in the innovation that we are advocating, the benefits should outweigh the difficulties without manipulation' (2014: 50).

Tracing the History of Innovation: Content of the Volume

The chapters in this volume approach innovation from a range of different levels of professional engagement in IEPs. While they do not adhere to a single conceptualization of innovation, the contributions demonstrate the authors' interpretations toward this theme and how they engage with the concept. In some ways, then, these contributions are qualitative expressions of how practitioners interpret innovation. The volume is organized in such a way that the first three chapters of this volume focus on the historical aspects of innovation in IEPs; the latter chapters consider current operations and practices, with an eye toward the future: What are the future needs of IEPs? Of language programming? How may the industry be shaped and evolve?

The first chapter of this volume, the appropriately titled 'The First IEP: The English Language Institute at the University of Michigan' by Larsen-Freeman, chronicles the establishment of the English Language Institute (ELI) at the University of Michigan in 1941. It describes the sociopolitical, psychological and linguistic contexts of the time that led to the innovative founding a language institute. The chapter traces the various expressions of innovation throughout the ELI's history – these include the Oral Approach; the publication of *Language Learning* (the world's first English language journal in applied linguistics);

language tests; language teaching books; the development of teacher training materials for US Peace Corps volunteers, ESL/EFL teachers, and international graduate teaching assistants; the development of a suite of EAP courses; the construction of language corpora; teacher credentialing; and research on second language acquisition.

In Chapter 2, 'ELI, ELP or IEP? Tracing the Growth of an Industry', Litzenberg and Kim look at the impact of IEPs in applied linguistics. They conduct a corpus analysis of three key journals from the field (*Language Learning*, *Modern Language Journal* and *TESOL Quarterly*) to evaluate the role that IEPs have played in supporting applied linguistics research. The chapter reviews the development of the first IEPs into the industry that they are today. The chapter connects developments and changes in IEPs to trends in applied linguistics, emphasizing how these trends are reflected in the work of IEPs as well as how the unique context of IEPs has supported innovations in research, teacher development, understandings of multiculturality and so forth. This consideration of IEP/applied linguistics symbiosis provides a nuanced look at an oft-neglected relationship of the field and provides a historical basis for understanding current and future trends in the field.

The next chapter (Chapter 3), 'Founding the Modern Era: A Conversation Among Former IEP Directors', presents an edited conversation with four former IEP professionals who managed programs during the 'midlife' of the field – namely, from the 1980s through the early 2000s. The conversation is engaging, insightful and, at times, even funny as the former directors relate anecdotes and experiences from their years as IEP professionals. For these former directors, innovation impacted the curriculum, administration and 'everything from the carpets to the filing cabinets' (p. 59). Their descriptions emphasize the connection between innovation and flexibility (a common theme for many current IEP professionals), as Betty Soppelsa describes in the chapter: '[S]ome of the things that were significant in terms of innovation ... you have to be flexible in Intensive English Programs ... to be able to change, and to deploy resources in new ways if the need arises' (p. 62). Indeed, the conversation brings the concept of innovation to the fore and provides a backdrop for understanding current approaches toward innovation in the field.

As these first three more historically oriented chapters indicate, the 'first' IEPs arose from the influence of higher education institutions in the United States, and even though ELT has in arguably become a global industry (with schools around the world describing themselves as providing intensive instruction and even using the name 'IEP') the United States continues to be the region most commonly associated with the term. For instance, the US-based professional organization, International TESOL, has an interest section dedicated to Intensive English Programs, and the US federally recognized accreditation body, Commission on English Language Program

Accreditation (CEA), refers to 'intensive English program[s]'. On the other hand, the British Council, an accrediting body in the United Kingdom, refers to 'ELT Programmes in Universities', and in Australia, the English Language Intensive Courses for Overseas Students (ELICOS) industry categorizes these same types of tertiary English language courses as English for Specific Purposes (ESP). Examples continue, but the point is that the term 'IEP' is inherently US-centric. Nevertheless, the US IEP industry has a global impact, as Chapter 10 by da Silva, Santclair, Pereira, Penna and Viana-Jr in this volume demonstrates. In this chapter, 'Mind the Gap! Voices of Brazilian English Language Teachers in a Continuing Education Intensive English Program in the United States' considers the impact of IEPs beyond their national boundaries. The authors look at the experiences of two co-author participants in a continuing education program supported by the Brazilian and US government organizations – a program that relied upon US-based IEPs as the service providers and what eventually became colloquially referred to in IEP circles as 'the Brazilian teachers' program'. Using a decolonial perspective as the analytical lens, the authors suggest that an imbalance in the perceptions of the program participants (both those from Brazil as well as the United States) resulted in a unidirectional professional 'exchange'.

Other contributions in this volume also consider the influence of IEPs beyond the physical boundaries of their location. As a way of integrating student populations into their local communities, many IEPs incorporate service-learning or civic engagement components into their curricula. While most literature describes these types of projects as providing authentic learning environments for IEP students as well as opportunities for both IEP students and practitioners to develop positive interactions with their local communities, the impact of such initiatives extends beyond the IEPs and IEP students. In Chapter 9, Perren reviews extant literature on service-learning projects in IEPs, considering their benefits, limitations and potential for participants and stakeholders outside of the IEP environment. He argues that equitable and bilateral communication among stakeholders are essential for the development of long-term and sustainable community projects. Such recognition is fundamental for educators who wish to align their practices with the changing needs of society.

In Chapter 11, Winkle pulls apart the relationship between university or college-governed IEPs and proprietary providers of pathway programs. In 'Over a Decade of Third-Party Pathway Programs in the United States', the author elaborates and reflects upon the findings of his 2013 book, *University Partnerships with the Corporate Sector: Faculty Experiences with For-Profit Matriculation Pathway Programs* (Winkle, 2013). The chapter provides an in-depth review of the development of the third-party pathway program industry: an overview of results from Winkle's 2013 study as well as more contemporary data collected from administrators, faculty and students at institutions with corporate-sector pathway partnerships. Winkle's analysis is both insightful and inspiring, encouraging IEP practitioners to engage in collaborative efforts with their host institutions so that they may lead the development of innovative applications of IEP services. IEPs are well positioned to influence institutional change and development.

Within the host institutions themselves, the influence of IEPs can be remarkable. In Chapter 5, 'Beyond Revenue: IEP Service to the University and Community', Grosik explores the possibility of re-envisioning IEPs as university service units through the pursuit of instructional and pedagogical opportunities that are not necessarily focused on the generation of revenue. Such a reorientation, Grosik argues, would allow programs to continue to serve their institutions and departments while providing new opportunities for students and educators. Many IEP professionals, according to Grosik, 'tend to be passionate about using language instruction as a vehicle for expanding educational access and opportunity to populations worldwide' (p. 97), yet they find themselves engaged in a field that creates barriers to education access by commodifying the resource of language. Yet when IEPs are reconceived in broader terms – such as that of an English Language Program (ELP) – programs are better positioned to provide educational access and support.

Anderson and Godfrey (Chapter 6, 'Multilingualism, Multi-culturalism and Advocacy: How Intensive English Language Programs can Impact Campus Culture') expand on this differentiation between ELP and IEP. The authors argue that for services beyond traditional non-credit, non-degree English language programming that IEPs offer – such as ongoing support services and helping students 'in being more critical consumers of English' – ELP may be a more appropriate or 'broader term to describe these centers' (p. 105). They describe the amorphous nature of IEPs as well as their overlap and synergy with ELPs, with one type of program often evolving into the other. Nevertheless, regardless of how such campus units may be identified, they can serve as centers of expertise in language and intercultural development that can be core to university missions of internationalization and diversity, equity, and inclusion efforts. This positive vision is an encouraging one, and may hint at a natural development of an industry trying to understand its place within the era of late capitalism.

Another component of the global ELT industry to which IEPs belong is the academic field of teacher preparation, which in many ways also operates as an industry similar to IEPs, as both require students to remain financially defensible. Graduates continue to walk away with degrees in TEFL, TESL, ESL and so forth, and these newly minted professionals need jobs. In Chapter 4, 'Employment Trends in English Language Programs', Slagoski provides an overview of employment trends in ELT and applied linguistics in the United States since 2010. He compares these trends to IEP student enrollment data and considers how these fluctuations may impact opportunities for recent graduates in the field. How do IEPs compare to other areas of professional activity that require an MA TESOL or similar degree? How can IEPs and IEP professionals best inoculate themselves against the fluctuating demand for English? As Slagoski points out, 'IEPs are particularly vulnerable ... [to the] [i]solationism, nationalism, technology, and global pandemics [that] rapidly change the demands on and for the TESOL profession' (p. 75). The author considers a range of innovations aimed at providing greater stability for IEPs and IEP practitioners. Many of these innovations blur the boundaries traditionally separating IEPs from their host universities and their partner programs overseas, allowing for more accessible immersion into languages and cultures, with students as transceivers of intercultural knowledge and skills. IEP professional may attempt to safeguard themselves against the more egregious changes of the field by teaching remotely, gaining accreditation to teach in K-12 schools, or even earning a PhD, but the English language teaching job market in the United States remains 'tenuous'.

For the ELT professionals who do attain successful employment in IEPs, their academic and professional identities interact proactive and reactive ways. In Chapter 7, 'Behold-Remold: Navigating and Innovating Liminal Spaces as an IEP Practitioner-Administrator-Scholar (PAS)', Mattson and Gianico examine instances of pedagogical and administrative innovation – from inception to implementation – in a university-based IEP, problematizing the theory-practice framework that underpins the education of IEP instructors and influences their role(s) in the IEP classroom and within an academic department. The authors position themselves as practitioner-administrator-scholars (PAS) in the periphery of the academy who primarily serve marginalized populations, a tension that is not uncommon among IEP faculty. The authors take an autoethnographic approach to investigating the ways in which their work during the past decade has involved negotiating the theoretical and the practical to enact and sustain innovative practices, policies and pedagogies to varying degrees of efficacy within the IEP. The chapter provides a critical reflection on the interplay between conceptual, contextual and institutional parameters for innovation necessitated by economic and political fluctuations that affect international education.

Finally, two additional contributions to this volume look at IEPs from a wider sociohistorical lens. Chapter 8 presents an essay from Gerald, who condenses as well as expands on some of the ideas from his recently published book, *Antisocial Language Teaching: English and the Pervasive Pathology of Whiteness* (Gerald, 2022). He looks at how the concept of 'native speaker' has been taken up by three major contributors to the field, namely, Rampton (1990), Widdowson (1994) and Bonfiglio (2013). While Gerald generally supports the arguments against native speakerism, he posits that any discussion of the concept of native speaker that fails to incorporate race (and, more centrally, Whiteness) as part of the discussion is ignoring a central component of the ideologies behind the term. The chapter concludes with suggestions of how the field may better serve students, professionals and other stakeholders: members of the field of ELT must ask 'the right questions' and 'make the hard choices' necessary to ensure that 'discussions of nativeness and race are a standard part of' (p. 142) language education in IEPs and within teacher training and education programs.

In the penultimate chapter of this volume, Arshavskaya and Halaczkiewicz look at the role of technology in IEPs, a feature of the ELT ecology whose influence is unlikely to wane. The chapter sits between the present and the future: it first considers the role of technology in modern IEP classrooms and provides suggestions for facilitating the successful integration of technology. The chapter then looks at the ways technology may continue to influence English language classrooms, offering warnings as well as suggestions for moving forward that help practitioners 'not to lose sight of our bigger goals in education and our humanity' (p. 205). The book finally rounds out with a contribution from Bock Thiessen (Chapter 13) – a reflective and forward-thinking piece that summarizes the volume and poses critical questions for future directions of IEPs and ELT as whole.

IEPs are a critical component of applied linguistics, TESOL and, more broadly, ELT. They are a unique industry with a unique history, and they are positioned to influence the academy through the pedagogies they employ, and the discipline and profession through their support of research and pre-service teacher experience. Simultaneously, IEPs operate as both revenue-generating businesses and service units for their host institutions, local communities, or international partners. IEPs deserve a bit more attention than they have received over the past couple of decades. This volume is a tiny step in the right direction.

Acknowledgements

I would like to thank all of the colleagues whose work has inspired and provided a foundation for my own. And, of course, an enormous hug of appreciation and love to my family, who has patiently supported me throughout this project and by now is very, very tired of hearing me talk about IEPs.

Note

(1) K-12 refers to Kindergarten through 12th Grade of the United States primary and secondary educational system.

References

Barret, P. (1982) *The Administration of Intensive English Language Programs*. Washington, DC: NAFSA.
Bonfiglio, T. (2013) Inventing the native speaker. *Critical Multilingualism Studies* 1 (2), 29–58.

Christison, M. and Murray, D. (2009) *Leadership in English Language Education: Theoretical Foundations and Practical Skills for Changing Times*. New York, NY: Routledge.

Christison, M. and Stoller, F.L. (1997) *A Handbook for Language Program Administrators*. Palm Springs, CA: Alta English.

Christison, M. and Stoller, F.L. (eds) (2023) *English Language Program Administration: Leadership and Management in the 21st Century*. Cham: Springer.

DeGraff, M. (2019) Foreword. In D. Macedo (ed.) *Decolonizing Foreign Language Education: The Misteaching of English and Other Colonial Languages* (pp. ix–xxxii). New York, NY: Routledge.

Dimmit, N. and Dantas-Whitney, M. (2002) *Intensive English Programs in Postsecondary Settings*. Alexandria, VA: TESOL.

Domínguez, M. (2019) Decolonial innovation in teacher development: Praxis beyond the colonial zero-point. *Journal of Education for Teaching* 45 (1), 47–62.

Fries, C.C. (1948) As we see it. *Language Learning* 1 (1), 12–16.

Gerald, J.P.B. (2022) *Antisocial Language Teaching: English and the Pervasive Pathology of Whiteness*. Bristol: Multilingual Matters.

Gramling, D. (2019) We innovators. In B. Schmenk, S. Breidbach and L. Küster (eds) *Sloganization in Language Education Discourse: Conceptual Thinking in the Age of Academic Marketization* (pp. 19–41). Bristol: Multilingual Matters.

Hamrick, J. (2016) Intensive English programs. In M. Christison and F.L. Stoller (eds) *A Handbook for Language Program Administrators* (2nd edn., pp. 321–328). Palm Springs, CA: Alta English.

Howatt, A.P.R. and Widdowson, H.G. (2004) *A History of English Language Teaching* (2nd edn). Oxford: Oxford.

Hyland, K. and Wong, L.L.C. (2013) Introduction: Innovation and implementation of change. In K. Hyland and L.L.C. Wong (eds) *Innovation and Change in English Language Education* (pp. 1–10). New York, NY: Routledge.

Kiely, R. and Rea-Dickins, P. (2005) *Program Evaluation in Language Education*. New York, NY: Palgrave.

Kumaravadivelu, B. (2003) A postmethod perspective on English language teaching. *World Englishes* 22 (4), 539–550.

Kumaravadivelu, B. (2008) *Cultural Globalization and Language Education*. New Haven, CT: Yale University Press.

Kumaravadivelu, B. (2016) The decolonial option in English teaching: Can the subaltern act? *TESOL Quarterly* 50 (1), 66–85. https://doi.org/10.1002/tesq.202.

Ladika, S. (2018) Weathering the storm: How intensive English programs are responding to declining enrollments. *International Educator* July/August, 38–43.

Litzenberg, J. (2020) "If I don't do it, somebody else will": Covert neoliberal policy discourses in the decision-making processes of an intensive English program. *TESOL Quarterly* 54 (4), 823–845. https://doi.org/10.1002/tesq.563.

Litzenberg, J. (2021) Innovation, resiliency, and genius in intensive English programs: Decolonializing recruitment and contradictory advocacy. *Applied Linguistics* 42 (5), 905–923. https://doi.org/10.1093/applin/amab015.

Lo Bianco, J. (2013) Innovation in language policy and planning: Ties to English language education. In K. Hyland and L.L.C. Wong (eds) *Innovation and Change in English Language Education* (pp. 139–154). New York, NY: Routledge.

Lord, G. (2014) *Language Program Direction: Theory and Practice*. Upper Saddle River, NJ: Pearson.

Lynch, B.K. (1996) *Language Program Evaluation: Theory and Practice*. New York, NY: Cambridge.

Macedo, D. (2019) *Decolonizing Foreign Language Education: The Misteaching of English and Other Colonial Languages*. New York, NY: Routledge.

Markee, N. (2013) Context of change. In K. Hyland and L.L.C. Wong (eds) *Innovation and Change in English Language Education* (pp. 28–43). New York, NY: Routledge.

Moyer, A. and Gonglewski, M. (2014) Surviving the leap from graduate student to Language Program Director: Issues, challenges, rewards. *ADFL Bulletin* 30 (1), 52–58.

Murray, D. (2013) Higher education constraints on innovation. In K. Hyland and L.L.C. Wong (eds) *Innovation and Change in English Language Education* (pp. 186–199). New York, NY: Routledge.

Orlando, R.D. (2016) *Teaching English in US University Intensive English Programs*. Alexandria, VA: TESOL Press.

Pennington, M.C. (1991) *Building Better English Language Programs*. Washington, DC: NAFSA.

Pennington, M.C. and Hoekje, B.J. (2010) Language program as ecology: A perspective for leadership. *RELC Journal* 41 (3), 213–228. https://doi.org/10.1177/0033688210380556.

Pennycook, A. and Makoni, S. (2020) *Innovations and Challenges in Applied Linguistics from the Global South*. New York, NY: Routledge.

Rampton, M. (1990) Displacing the 'native speaker:' Expertise, affiliation, and inheritance. *ELT Journal* 44 (2), 97–101.

Rice, A. and Graupensperger, J. (2007) *Revitalizing an Established Program for Adult Learners*. Alexandria, VA: TESOL.

Ricento, T.K. and Hornberger, N.H. (1996) Unpeeling the onion: Language planning and policy and the ELT professional. *TESOL Quarterly* 30 (3), 401. https://doi.org/10.2307/3587691.

Siqueira, S. and Alves Rocha, A. (2019) Curriculum and materials development in language teacher education in contemporary times: Are we ready for change? In G.Y. Ekşi, L. Guerra, D. Werbińska and Y. Bayyurt (eds) *Research Trends in English Language Teacher Education and English Language Teaching* (pp. 37–58). Évora: University of Évora.

Stoller, F.L. (1994) The diffusion of innovations in intensive ESL programs. *Applied Linguistics* 15 (3), 300–327. https://doi.org/10.1093/applin/15.3.300.

Stoller, F.L. (1995) Innovation in a non-traditional academic unit: The intensive English program. *Innovative Higher Education* 19 (3), 177–195. https://doi.org/10.1007/BF01191218.

Stoller, F.L. (2009) Innovation as the hallmark of effective leadership. In M. Christison and D.E. Murray (eds) *Leadership in English Language Teaching and Learning* (pp. 73–84). New York, NY: Routledge.

Stoller, F.L. (2014) Catalyst for innovation. In M. Christison and F.L. Stoller (eds) *A Handbook for Language Program Administrators* (pp. 37–55). Palm Springs, CA: Alta English.

Walker, J. (2010) *Service, Satisfaction and Climate: Perspectives on Management in English Language Teaching*. Leiden: Emerald Group Publishing Limited.

Watson Todd, R. (2006) Continuing change after the innovation. *System* 34 (1), 1–14. https://doi.org/10.1016/j.system.2005.09.002.

White, R., Martin, M., Stimson, M. and Hodge, R. (1991) *Management in English Language Teaching*. Cambridge: Cambridge University Press.

White, R.V., Hockley, A., van der Horst Jansen, J. and Laughner, M.S. (2008) *From Teacher to Manager: Managing Language Teaching Organizations*. Cambridge: Cambridge University Press.

Widdowson, H.G. (1994) The ownership of English. *TESOL Quarterly* 28 (2), 377–389.

Winkle, C. (2013) *University Partnerships with the Corporate Sector: Faculty Experiences With For-Profit Matriculation Pathway Programs*. Leiden: Brill.

1 The First IEP: The English Language Institute at the University of Michigan[1]

Diane Larsen-Freeman

Introduction

This chapter begins with an historical account of the establishment of the first English Language Institute (ELI) in the United States. It also describes the prevailing sociopolitical climate at the time of its founding. In addition, the chapter seeks to clarify the theoretical underpinnings of what has come to be called the 'Michigan Method'. The chapter goes on to trace subsequent innovations that were motivated from its beginning by the needs and opportunities of the day both to generate knowledge (i.e. to draw on experiential knowledge and to conduct research) and to use it (i.e. in service).

Early History

The English Language Institute was established by action of the Regents of the University of Michigan at their June meeting in 1941. Professor Charles C. Fries, an English language specialist in the Department of English, was appointed its first Director. The charge to the ELI (as it soon became known) was twofold: to conduct research (generate knowledge) in teaching English as a foreign language and to develop scientifically based materials (use that knowledge) for teaching. Fries and his colleagues soon inaugurated a full-time intensive course in ESL, the first ever offered on a university campus in the United States. Its mission was to develop language and cultural programs for Latin American students and professionals. Michigan was chosen to set up the special language institute as part of President Franklin D. Roosevelt's 'Good Neighbor Policy'. Support for the institute and development of its original textbook series came from the State Department and the Rockefeller Foundation. The choice of the target audience was calculated, of course, taking advantage of the 'soft power' that language confers. Indeed, the politics of the moment were informed by Roosevelt's Policy, which called for cooperation, non-intervention and trade instead of military force. This call was realized in part by responding to the demand for English instruction in Latin American countries as part of cultural exchange programs just before and during the time of the US's involvement in World War II.

In Albert Marckwardt's words:

> This was a time when war clouds were gathering and our own entanglement in the struggle was not far off. The United States was becoming concerned over the cultural penetration by totalitarian powers into various Latin American countries. The teaching of Italian and German was an important element in this cultural effort. As a country, our response to this was the development of English teaching in these same countries. We had to begin this by preparing materials for teaching. (Norris, 1966: 2, as cited in Morley *et al.*, 1984: 177)

Backtracking in time a little, Morley *et al.* (1984: 178) report that

> [b]y 1939, the concern of the U.S. Department of State for the teaching of English in Puerto Rico and Latin America had reached crisis proportions. The result was a crucial invitational conference held on the Ann Arbor campus of the University of Michigan in the fall of 1939.

In Harold Allen's words:

> The purpose of the conference was to decide upon the ideological basis for such teaching – as it turned out, to decide between the Basic English with pictures proposed by I.A. Richards and a linguistically-based approach advocated by Fries. The upshot of the conference was a grant to Fries to develop teaching materials for the intensive course in English that was experimentally offered in the trial summer program for Latin American students at Michigan in the summer of 1941. By 1943, the ELI offered continuous eight-week intensive English courses throughout the entire calendar year. The first courses offered four hours of classroom instruction per day, with one hour of laboratory study soon added. (Allen, 1979: 2, cited in Morley *et al.*, 1984: 178)

In the first year of the institute there were 13 students; however, by 1945, that number had grown to 80, and by 1946, 750 students had passed through the ELI.

When Fries (1945: v) turned his attention to the development of English texts for Spanish speakers, he characterized his work as an 'attempt to interpret, in a practical way for teaching, the principles of modern linguistic science and to use the results of scientific linguistic research'. The reigning linguistics theory was structuralism, and famed University of Michigan linguists Harold King, Albert Marckwardt and Kenneth Pike were members of the ELI 'family', the latter two becoming ELI directors at a later point in time. Fries called himself a 'descriptive structural linguist', believing in 'a careful sociolinguistic descriptivism in which appropriateness to a given situation was paramount' (Anthony, 1989: 7). Fries defined language as 'a set of habits for oral production and reception', thus embodying not only linguistic concepts but psychological concepts as well (Fries, 1945: 6) because for Fries 'habit and thought were closely intertwined' (Peter Fries, personal communication, 26 March 2022).

> Learning a language was believed to involve making the basic patterns of arrangement of the language – the grammatical forms – matters of automatic habit. (Fries, 1945: 3). (Morley et al., 1984: 180)

Initially, habits were to be built through oral-aural practice.

'The Michigan Method' (Fries himself called it an 'Oral Approach') then began with very intensive training through oral practice – choral drills initially, soon followed by more individualized practice – and accompanied by equally intensive practice in the essentials of English sentence structure. Only after oral practice were the students introduced to reading or writing activities. Although Fries' approach has often been categorized as behaviorist, because of his emphasis on the need to establish habits, in fact, Fries was not a behaviorist. For one thing, in the approach Fries advocated, meaning was always central[2]:

> The same patterns must become matters of habit productively and receptively. They must function automatically when the attention is centered wholly upon meaning and not at all upon the mechanics of the language. (Fries, 1945: 36)

As Fries and Fries (1961: 251) later put it:

> a language cannot be learned in a meaning vacuum. Nor can structures *be mastered for use* through any amount of mere mechanical manipulation of 'empty' sentences that have, for the learning pupil, no real context or social meaning.

This position seems to be in keeping with contemporary thinking.

Another innovation, which Fries pioneered and which has resonance today, is his notion that foreign language teaching is always a matter of teaching a specific 'foreign' language to students who have specific 'native' language background (Fries, 1945: vi). Thus, it followed that:

> The most efficient materials are those that are based upon a scientific description of the language to be learned, carefully compared with a parallel description of the native language of the learner. (Fries, 1945: 9)

For this reason, the materials that were developed rested principally on contrastive analyses between the language spoken by the students and the target language.

Before moving on from the early days of the ELI, an additional key practice deserves mention: It was clear to Fries that learning a language was not just something that took place in the classroom; the learning process had to go beyond the classroom into the use of language in *real-life communicative situations*. The result was a highly immersive experience for students. Early on, some instructors were housed with the students in dormitories, and were expected to interact with students at meals, in the evenings, and at other times outside of classes. There were also gatherings on Friday evenings, with students giving talks on aspects of their home cultures (on which they had worked to prepare earlier in the week (with guidance from an instructor)). There were also skits and films, singing and dancing.

From its early beginnings, many other innovations followed. One of them was the launching of a journal – one with a title that would prove prescient given what subsequently transpired. In 1948, the first English language journal in the world in applied linguistics, *Language Learning: A Journal of Applied Linguistics* was published. Archivists in the field, such as A.P.R. Howatt (1984: 313) credit Michigan with being the first institution to use the term, 'applied linguistics', which subsequently spread throughout the world, and which in more recent times has evolved into a thriving discipline. *Language Learning* has been published continuously since 1948 under the auspices of the University of Michigan and enjoys considerable stature as a journal of research in language studies to this day.

By the late 1950s, the ELI had international language development programs in countries on five continents. One of the most extensive was the Southeast Asian Regional English Project, with a budget of nearly 2 million dollars under contract to the United States Agency for International Development. Three centers were established in Thailand, Vietnam and Laos.

Fries remained director until 1956, and during these 15 years, established the premier role of Michigan's ELI in North American ESL, especially for its Intensive Program, its textbooks (e.g. the 'Rainbow' series for its volumes of different colors, published by the University of Michigan Press: *Oral Pattern Practice, Lessons in Vocabulary*, and *English Sentence Patterns*), its development of English language proficiency tests, and its summer activities in ESL teacher-training. The cohering forces behind all this were Fries' pioneering efforts to base a description of contemporary American English on authentic data, which he himself compiled from a variety of sources. Indeed, today Fries would be considered a corpus linguist.

Soon, programs began springing up all over the country in imitation of Michigan's English Language Institute and its renowned teaching method. In fact, programs at Georgetown, the University of California, Los Angeles, the University of Pittsburgh, the University of Minnesota, to name a few, were all founded by leaders who had been associated with ELI/Michigan.

The other key figure in the early years was Robert Lado, who obtained his PhD at Michigan and later became a Professor of English. His main areas of expertise were in language testing and in contrastive linguistics (the comparison of phonological and structural differences between languages in an effort to establish areas of special difficulty for speakers of certain languages). The testing program under Lado began in 1946, and in the 1950s, following a contract with the United States Information Agency (USIA), expanded to include the Examination for the Certificate of Proficiency in English (ECPE) for use abroad. Lado became ELI Director in 1956, and later became Dean of the School of Languages and Linguistics at Georgetown.

The Middle Years

In 1961, the ELI was selected for participation in the US government Peace Corps training program. In fact, the first announcement of his intention to create the Peace Corps was made in 1960 on the steps of the University of Michigan Union by John F. Kennedy during a stop in his presidential campaign. The responsibility for training young Americans to be Peace Corps Volunteer EFL Teachers fell to knowledgeable, experienced faculty at the ELI. One manifestation of their influence was that the foreign language classes the trainees took featured team teaching with an ELI teacher who planned the lessons and presented information about the structure and phonology of the language, working alongside a native speaker of the language who presented the in-class model for language practice.

In 1964, phonetician Ian Catford was appointed as director of the English Language Institute. Professor Catford came from the University of Edinburgh, where he had founded the first School of Applied Linguistics, bringing with him to Michigan an interest in both applied linguistics and phonetics and contributing to the growing interest and expertise in the former. In fact, Catford continued to serve as Chairman of the Board of Directors of *Language Learning* for many years, and in 1998 he gave the keynote address, 'History of Applied Linguistics and Language Learning', at the 50-year Jubilee meeting of the journal.

The next ELI director was the sociolinguist, Ronald Wardhaugh, who recognized that ELI faculty possessed considerable knowledge, but little time to put it to use apart from the demanding job of teaching intensive courses. Therefore, an innovation under Wardhaugh's directorship was a scheme whereby a member of the ELI could obtain release time to shape ESL teaching materials into a suitable textbook format, which would be published by the University of Michigan Press, while, in exchange, the institute would receive an agreed percentage of the royalties. Director Wardhaugh's scheme remained effective for the next 30 years. In this way, textbooks tended to actually get finished, while the institute received a discretionary income of an origin and substance that is very rare for ESL operations. The first person to receive release time was Joan Morley, who became the Press' best-selling author, with total book sales in excess of 500,000, and became particularly well known for her work in developing materials for pronunciation and aural comprehension. Other highly successful textbooks to have originated at the ELI include *Writing as a Thinking Process* by Mary Lawrence, *Readers' Choice* by Sandra Silberstein, Barbara Dobson and Mark Clarke, who were graduate students and ESL teachers at the institute at the time of the first edition in 1977, and which is now in its sixth edition, and *Academic Writing for Graduate Students* by John Swales and Christine Feak, first published in 1994, with subsequent editions in 2004 and 2012. A further positive aspect of the ELI's close involvement with the Press is that Michigan's list of ESL publications has been of considerable financial advantage to the press.

Succeeding Wardhaugh as director in 1976 was Acting Director, H. Douglas Brown, under whose leadership a masters of arts in TESOL program was founded. The MA in TESOL degree was co-sponsored by the Linguistics Department and the School of Education. It thrived with scores of graduate students earning TESOL degrees, including some of the leading figures in the field today. One of the other highlights at this time was a series of annual conferences in applied linguistics, several of which brought to campus leading figures, such as S. Pit Corder, a pioneer in the early days of the subfield that became known as second language acquisition (SLA).

Building further on its applied linguistics base, in 1977, Larry Selinker, who was a well-known specialist in second language acquisition for his transformative concept of 'interlanguage', was appointed as director. The dean at the time gave Selinker the mandate 'to make the ELI a research unit' (Selinker, personal communication, 19 March 2022). During his tenure, an approach to communicative language teaching that became known as 'task-based learning' was promoted. During this period, the Intensive Program was brought up to date methodologically and its students were frequently participants in various kinds of SLA research projects.

By the mid-1980s the ELI's Intensive English Program (IEP) was struggling somewhat, partly because many other universities had set up IEPs, often based on the Michigan model, and partly because of what was known as the 'pre-admission issue'. The major student-sponsoring agencies, typically at that time the US cultural attachés of OPEC countries, were increasingly insisting that they would only send students to a university's IEP if that university would guarantee that students would have a place in one of its own degree programs once they had successfully completed their English language preparation. Michigan would not agree to this.

The final challenge in 1985 involved what was known at that time as 'the foreign teaching assistant problem'. Every so often, the President of the University and various deans would be deluged with angry letters or emails from parents complaining that their children had failed basic math or science courses because they had been taught by 'incomprehensible' international teaching assistants (ITAs). Often the ITA was by no means the real cause of the failure; nevertheless, the upshot was the development of a new course (in collaboration with Michigan's Center for Research on Learning and Teaching), *ELI 994 College Teaching in the US: Pedagogy, Culture and Language*, which was created for international students who were destined to become instructors (at Michigan, no longer called 'teaching assistants', but now renamed Graduate Student Instructors (GSIs)). Course assignments included video-recorded practice teaching and feedback, office hour role-plays, and observations. Participants received feedback from instructors, from experienced GSIs, and from current University of Michigan undergraduates.

Also ongoing for some time and continuing to this day, in service to both domestic and international audiences, was the ELI's Conversation Partners, now called Conversation Circles, where Michigan students or staff met weekly with interested international students to exchange cultural information and to enjoy each other's company.

In More Recent Times: A Metamorphosis

Following Selinker, John Swales, who was a specialist in English for Academic Purposes, was brought in as Acting Director and Visiting Professor in 1985, positions that would be regularized two years later. In late 1985/early1986, the dean expressed a concern to Swales. He said, 'I don't understand why your institute spends all its time on helping strangers when we have so many of our own students who need help'. The dean went on to say that he wanted the IEP closed down so that the ELI's resources could be devoted to enrolled students. The dean further explained that he wanted a professional English for Academic Purposes (EAP) operation for international students that was to be largely run through well-trained lecturers, rather than teaching assistants; that the classes could be relatively small; they could be labor intensive because they would likely require materials created in house; and that the ELI courses shouldn't carry such a high credit load that international students would have to drop some of their degree courses to meet their English language requirements.

In response, building on Swales' genre approach and the knowledge of ELI instructors, the ELI developed a suite of six 20-hour one-credit

300-level courses covering all four skill areas. Carolyn Madden became course coordinator (and later Associate Director for Curriculum), Professor Joan Morley took charge of the pronunciation courses, Professor Swales the writing courses, and lecturers were responsible for the materials development of the rest. The result of all this effort was that the ELI provided in effect a 'longitudinal' syllabus whereby students would be able to take a series of one-credit mini-courses synchronized with the increasing communicative demands that they would encounter throughout their time at Michigan.

During the 1990s and subsequent years the institute continued to expand its course offerings, including several courses that accrued graduate credit, such as Research Paper Writing (522), Dissertation Writing and Writing for Publication (620), Discussion and Oral Argumentation (534) and Speaking in Research Contexts (601). Special summer pre-MBA (taught by ELI lecturer Roann Altman), pre-law (taught by ELI lecturer Susan Reinhart, who had a law degree herself), EAP and courses for architectural students (taught by ELI lecturer Theresa Rohlck) were also initiated.

Meanwhile, the ELI's testing programs had also been expanding in size and scope, particularly after the creation of the Examination for the Certificate in Competency in English (the ECCE) in 1993. Aware of the new but growing field of corpus linguistics, Sarah Briggs of the Testing Division urged that some of the new test-fee income be invested in order to generate new knowledge. In particular, a corpus of academic speech would be valuable, not only for tests of academic listening comprehension, but also to help international students engage with oral academic discourse. As a result, the Michigan Corpus of Academic Spoken English (MICASE) was born, and as intended, it provided a resource for the continuing development and refinement of Michigan tests and EAP courses. In addition, the MICASE team created an archival version of the corpus sound files. Also generating knowledge was the construction of The Michigan Corpus of Undergraduate Student Papers (MICUSP). This collection of 'A' papers, written by undergraduate students representing a number of disciplines, has proven to be valuable for teachers and researchers as they search for the distinctive features of high-quality writing by undergraduates.

In 1988, the digital services unit of the Graduate Library agreed to fund the development of a 'Web-based search interface so that MICASE would be available not only to researchers at Michigan but to students, teachers, and researchers around the world' (https://lsa.umich.edu/eli/language-resources/micase-micusp.html). It was decided to make the 1.8-million-word corpus available to everybody for free. The construction, distribution and use of MICASE would have greatly pleased the ELI's founding director, Charles Fries, whose classic 1952 volume, *The Structure of English*, was based on 50 hours of transcribed telephone conversations.

The other innovation at this time, consonant with the theme of knowledge generation, was the establishment of the Morley Scholarship Endowment fund to celebrate Joan Morley's 40-year career at the university. The fund covered travel expenses to Ann Arbor and gave scholars a stipend. The scholarships were designed mainly for scholars overseas, especially those from developing countries. Morley scholars made use of the ELI's library resources, such as 'The Genre Archive', a collection of approximately one thousand papers dealing with non-literary genres. They also worked with ELI faculty on research projects related to second language theory and pedagogy. In addition, in recognition of Mary Spaan's contributions to the field of language assessment for more than three decades, Spaan Fellowships were established to provide financial support for anyone wishing to carry out research projects related to second or foreign language assessment and evaluation. A requirement of the fellowship was for fellows to write a research report based on their project. Spaan Fellow Working Papers were subsequently edited and published by the ELI.

Starting at this time, several other changes of note took place. First of all, the Testing Division, under the direction of Barbara Dobson, had expanded considerably. The Division had become increasingly taxed by the growth in international test takers of the 'Michigan Tests'. In addition to creating and working with partners all over the world to administer the ECCE and ECPE to tens of thousands of individuals, the Testing and Certification Division was also responsible for the development and administration of the Assessment of Academic English (AEE) for entering University of Michigan students, the GSI test for graduate student instructors, who had not had an English-medium undergraduate education, and the MELAB (Michigan English Language Assessment Battery) for applicants to the University of Michigan and other North American universities. The staff was clearly stretched thin, so under the direction of the new ELI Director, Diane Larsen-Freeman, who arrived in 2002, and with the support of the Dean's office, a number of new staff were recruited, trained, and integrated into the Division.

As indicated earlier, at this point in time the core of ELI's English for Academic Purposes offerings consisted of a full range of credit-bearing courses for international students. In addition, with coordination by ELI lecturer, Elizabeth Axelson, ELI faculty began teaching focused workshops, aiming to improve targeted communication skills in English for international members of the campus community. Topics such as 'job interview skills' and 'formulaic expressions in academic speech' proved enormously popular, and it soon became clear that bigger and bigger rooms would be needed to accommodate the 'standing-room-only' audience. The workshops have continued to this day and recent topics include 'poster presentations: interacting with your audience', 'mindful listening: stress reduction strategies for international students', 'writing effective email' and 'planning your English self-study program for spring and summer'.

Other extracurricular activities that had been begun some years earlier, complementing the courses and workshops, included services such as the ELI Speaking Clinic and the ELI Writing Laboratory, featuring one-on-one speaking and writing support for international undergraduate students (now called Speaking and Writing Studios). An innovation during this period responded to an expressed wish by international scholars that the ELI implement an EAP course for visiting international scholars, researchers and post-docs. In addition, ELI lecturer Judy Dyer created a special section for writing for generation 1.5 undergraduate students who were born in the US, but whose home language was not English. It was found that these students needed support in writing, but support which was different from that given to international students, the traditional population at the ELI. Another innovative course was one inaugurated by Nick Ellis, whose graduate students constructed their own corpora, collecting research articles and digitizing them, which subsequently became the student's own individualized EAP texts, for which ELI faculty facilitated exploration and instruction.

In the interest of service, lecturers also built new technological resources. Funded by the College of Literature, Sciences and Arts, the Undergraduate Instructional Events Digital Video Project archived a library of digital video recordings of undergraduate students in instructional contexts for the purpose of providing authentic materials for GSI training and orientation. Later, a team led by ELI lecturer Brenda Imber adapted Praat software, with its spectral analysis feature, which served as an instructional tool to provide the visual feedback that would enhance the teaching as well as the learning of pausing, linking and stress placement. To practice listening, an ELI lecturer, Julia Salehzadeh, created a text, *Lecture Listening: A Strategy Guide*, with CD-ROM accompanying the text including video selections and short audio selections of academic speech from MICASE, which provided EAP students ample and realistic lecturer listening material. Still later, a website to connect university students to high-quality interactive language learning sites and resources worldwide was developed. Curated online self-study e-resources, 'English Learning Links', extended opportunities for informal language practice and cultural engagement.

Tapping into and expanding its knowledge base, the ELI faculty has continued all along to offer teacher education courses. These courses (Community-Engaged Learning in ESL Teaching Contexts and Teaching English Internationally) include a balance of theory and practice, as well as a strong emphasis on community engagement and service learning principles. Students in the courses gain practical life skills and learn how to successfully interact with individuals across cultures.

Drawing on its teacher training experience, the ELI also collaborated with the university's Residential College to build a migrant worker program, coordinated by ELI lecturer Deborah Des Jardins. Michigan undergraduate students receive a semester of teacher training and then venture forth in the summer to migrant worker camps working on farms in a nearby county to offer supervised ESL lessons in the evening to workers and their families, who openly expressed their interest and appreciation. For many Michigan undergraduates, this proved to be an eye-opening experience in helping them to have a cross-cultural experience close to home.

The ELI also responded (in service) to another need in the state of Michigan, i.e. to support public school teachers who had English language learners (ELLs) in their classrooms – in the case of many teachers for the first time. Adapting knowledge that the ELI had accrued from its years of ESL teacher training courses, Larsen-Freeman, in collaboration with ELI faculty and colleagues at the School of Education, created a new ESL Endorsement Program. Approved by the Department of Education of the State of Michigan in February 2004, the new program was structured around six, later seven, graduate courses that aimed to prepare graduate students to work with English language learners in K-12 public schools. The program was designed for students who were enrolled in a Master's degree program, and who were also receiving teaching certification, so that they would be ready to welcome ELLs into their classrooms the following year. The program proved popular, and many teachers elected to add the ESL endorsement credential to their teacher certification. The productive alliance between the ELI and School of Education faculty has helped address the needs of ELLs, in which the state of Michigan, especially the southeastern portion, has experienced incredible growth.

Complementing this program, the ELI began to convene annual conferences, which brought area educators together with ESL Endorsement students for a one-day symposium where they could share experiences. Moreover, maintaining the tradition introduced earlier, a number of other small conferences were organized. A partial list includes an invitational conference for those colleagues from other universities who worked with international graduate student instructors, the ELI's co-sponsorship (with International Computer Archive of Modern and Medieval English (ICAME)) of the first symposium in the United States to address corpus linguistics, the ELI's hosting MITESOL, the state affiliate of the international TESOL organization and later LTRC (Language Testing Research Colloquium), under the auspices of Michigan Language Assessment (see below).

Also, 2004 saw an earlier research direction being renewed at the ELI. Larsen-Freeman, who had long been researching second language acquisition, felt that a systematic investigation of SLA, was a natural complement to the ELI's corpus research and its ongoing teaching and testing activities. To this end, she worked with colleagues in the Psychology Department to jointly appoint Professor Nick Ellis. His knowledge of second language acquisition and formulaic language reinforced the ELI's strengths. By 2005, Ellis had set up a lab at the institute that was very productive. Among other projects, Ellis and Rita Simpson produced an academic formulas list. Both Ellis and Larsen-Freeman are former Editors of *Language Learning*, and they maintained the Michigan connection of this distinguished journal with Ellis taking over the duties as General Editor of *Language Learning*, and Larsen-Freeman as Chair of the Board. Together, they promoted a conceptual understanding of language as a complex system, the theme of a conference held at the famed Santa Fe Institute in New Mexico, with support from John Holland of the Center for Complex Systems at Michigan, who was also a trustee at the Santa Fe Institute. Later, an anthology compiled of papers delivered at the conference, *Language as Complex System*, edited by Ellis and Larsen-Freeman, was published.

The next ELI director that the college appointed was Steven Dworkin, a historical romance linguist, to administer the institute from 2008–2013. This period was one of severe retrenchment for the institute. The new dean initiated a process which would eventually result in the Testing Division merging with the larger Cambridge University ESL testing operation under the banner of CaMLA (Cambridge Michigan Language Assessment – now Michigan Language Assessment) and becoming an 'auxiliary unit' of the university. In addition, The ESL Endorsement Program reverted to the School of Education. Further, a national search was held for a new director, but this would be, for the first time in its history, an administrative and not an academic appointment. In keeping with this directive, the ELI would become a service, rather than an academic unit, and would report to a different associate dean.

The international search culminated in the appointment of Angelo Pitillo, who had extensive experience leading ESL programs both domestically and overseas. Under the leadership of the new director several innovations transpired. Even before the pivot to online teaching was made necessary due to the Covid pandemic, versions of ELI's graduate EAP courses were made available online, beginning in 2015, in collaboration with University of Michigan's Office of Academic Innovation. ELI 210, Academic Vocabulary Building, was the very first online course for undergraduates to be approved by the Curriculum Committee and this course, like its graduate predecessor ELI 510, follows a 'gaming' approach that allows students to customize their learning experience by selecting from a menu of tasks and activities that they complete asynchronously. A subsequent development was an online pre-arrival course for University of Michigan students. This course aims to prepare international students to succeed at Michigan by introducing them to campus life and culture. Course components include information on university resources as well as strategies to support their speaking interactively and writing academically. Additionally, students co-construct a Personal Engagement Plan, where they are able to track their progress and set goals. The idea behind this flexible, asynchronous course is also to encourage international students to make friends and establish an early support network before they arrive on campus. More recently and motivated similarly, a MOOC for general audiences via Coursera was created by ELI lecturer, Pamela Bogart. The course will soon enroll its 20,000th student.

Heeding recent calls to decolonize education, ELI faculty have taken on a more active advocacy role on behalf of international and other second-language students as part of the University's diversity, equity and inclusion (DEI) efforts, and they have begun integrating DEI and antiracist pedagogies into the EAP curriculum. Most recently, a new course, Culture and Communication in the United States (592), has been offered, a course where students learn to make connections across cultures and talk about their own culture in English and explore their own identity and culture in relation to others so that they can participate in campus conversations about DEI.

At the 75th anniversary of the ELI in October 2016, a celebration of its history of innovation and engagement with the world was held. Having just past 80 years of age in the fall of 2021, the ELI remains committed to knowledge generation and to service as its mission statement makes clear:

> The mission of the English Language Institute is to provide language, academic, and intercultural instruction which enables all members of the University of Michigan community, regardless of the language in which they were raised or educated, to fully participate in the life of the University, and to excel in their scholarly, instructional, and professional endeavors throughout their academic careers. In the firm belief that this effort enriches the educational experience of domestic and international students alike, the ELI strives to collaborate with units across the University to foster an open, welcoming climate and to connect the Ann Arbor campus with the world. (ELI, 2023)

Notes

(1) In preparing this chapter, I have drawn extensively (with permission from the University of Michigan) from Swales and Larsen-Freeman's (2015) *English Language Institute*, copyrighted by the Regents of the University of Michigan for the bicentennial of the University of Michigan (2017). I have also excerpted from Morley *et al.* (1984). I am also grateful for the feedback from Peter Fries, Angelo Pitillo, Larry Selinker and John Swales on an earlier draft of this chapter.
(2) This is not the place to engage in a long discussion of why Fries' approach was not behaviorist. (See contributions to Norris and Strain (1989) for a more in-depth analysis).

References

Allen, H.B. (1979) *The Teaching of English as a Second Language and U.S. Foreign Policy.* Washington, DC: TESOL.

Anthony, E.M. (1989) The theoretical framework underlying Fries' 'oral approach.' In W.E. Norris and J.E. Strain (eds) *Charles Carpenter Fries: His 'Oral Approach' for Teaching and Learning Foreign Languages* (pp. 6–10). Washington, DC: Georgetown University Press.

ELI (2023) ELI mission. See https://lsa.umich.edu/eli/about-us/eli-mission.html (accessed June 2023).

Fries, C.C. (1945) *Teaching and Learning English as a Foreign Language.* Ann Arbor, MI.: The University of Michigan Press.

Fries, C.C. (1952) *The Structure of English.* New York, NY: Harcourt, Brace & World, Inc.

Fries, C.C. and Fries, A.C. (1961) *Foundations of English.* Tokyo: Kenkyusha Ltd. for the English Language Exploratory Committee, Tokyo, Japan.

Howatt, A.P.R. (1984) *A History of English Language Teaching.* Oxford: Oxford University Press.

Morley, J., Wallace Robinett, B., Selinker, L. and Woods, D. (1984) ESL theory and the Fries legacy. *JALT Journal* 6 (2), 171–207.

Norris, W. (1966) *A Casual Chronology* [Internal Document]. Ann Arbor, MI: The English Language Institute, The University of Michigan.

Norris, W.E. and Strain, J.E. (eds) (1989) *Charles Carpenter Fries: His 'Oral Approach' for Teaching and Learning Foreign Languages.* Washington, DC: Georgetown University Press.

Swales, J. and Larsen-Freeman, D. (2015) English Language Institute. *The University of Michigan: An Encyclopedic Survey.* Ann Arbor, MI: University of Michigan. http://hdl.handle.net/2027/spo.13950886.0002.032.

2 ELI, ELP or IEP? Tracing the Growth of an Industry

Jason Litzenberg and Minjin Kim

Introduction

Intensive English Programs (IEPs) have a symbiotic relationship with research. They are critical, yet often-overlooked, components of applied linguistics and TESOL research, and, in turn, research is 'fundamental to the quality and longevity' of IEPs (Jensen & Soppelsa, 1996: 1). IEPs are important sites of action research and often serve as mechanisms for introducing new professionals to research in the field. As Margaret Thomas, a history of linguistics professor, states, many applied linguists 'entered the field through teaching ESL at universities' (de Bot, 2015: 19). Indeed, IEPs have a distinct connection to applied linguistics and TESOL.

Smith (2016: 72) describes the need for 'principled historical research in and into the field of linguistics, or of "linguistic ideas"'. Similarly, Canagarajah (2016: 9) argues that the subfield of English Language Teaching (ELT) is in need of 'disciplined historiography'. This chapter follows these calls, presenting a nuanced view into the relationship between IEPs and research in applied linguistics. It does so by considering how IEPs have supported research published in three major journals of the field – namely, *Language Learning*, *Modern Language Journal* and *TESOL Quarterly*. For the purposes of the present discussion, applied linguistics and TESOL are considered as a single field, while acknowledging that often clear distinctions exist. In this sense, the term 'applied linguistics' is used to refer to both applied linguistics and TESOL. This approach aligns with that of Smith (2016) who describes 'Applied Linguistic Historiography' as having a broader base than 'Historiography of Applied Linguistics', as the former includes language teaching and learning.

Positioning the Journal Review

According to Smith (2016), understanding historical evidence can provide a basis for constructing appropriate reform efforts. Or, in the case of the present chapter, historical evidence can provide a basis for informing future innovation in IEPs. Understanding the extent to which IEPs support research within applied linguistics and TESOL, for instance, provides insight into the ways in which such programs benefit their host institutions and may impact the allocation of institutional and programmatic resources. Smith (2016: 74) claims that the paucity of research into histories of the field has been countered by recent stirrings of interest that demonstrate 'a certain "coming of age" in the fields of [applied linguistics] and language didactics'. A problem with more recent historical overviews of applied linguistics, according to Smith, is that they have frequently been short and over-reliant upon secondary sources. Moreover, Smith claims that others, such as Phillipson (1992) and Pennycook (1998), tend to be 'propagandistic' in that they 'cite rather selectively for the purposes of argument, offering insufficient context for sources' (Smith, 2016: 75). On the other hand, Smith describes both Mitchell (1997), who traces a 30-year history of British Association of Applied Linguistics (BAAL) from 1967 to 1997, and de Bot (2015), who traces trends and influences within applied linguistics based on 40 interviews and almost 70 questionnaires with professionals in the field, as well-focused. In addition to de Bot, Ellis (2016) provides another book-length historiography (published the same year as Smith's call for historiographies), a collection of 10 autobiographical stories of applied linguists relating their progression into and within the field.

Two historiographies that use journals – specifically, *TESOL Quarterly* – to trace developments in the field are Liu and Berger (2015) and Canagarajah (2016). Liu and Berger (2015) conduct a thematic analysis of *TESOL Quarterly* articles from 1967 to 2011. One of the features of articles they consider is language context – namely, English as a Foreign Language (EFL), English as a Second Language (ESL) and English as a Lingua Franca (ELF). Divided into sets of roughly four decades, Liu and Berger identify among the articles an upward trend for EFL contexts and a downward trend for ESL contexts. The representation of tertiary institutions and programs, however, has remained relatively stable since the 1978–1988 period. Among the research themes, Liu and Berger identify SLA, teachers and teacher development, curriculum and materials, methodology, assessment, and language skills as themes losing representation within the journal, and language use/sociolinguistics, policy/standards, and learners and language learning as gaining representation. Canagarajah (2016), as part of a *TESOL Quarterly* anniversary issue, looks at 50 years of the journal's issues as part of a content analysis based on thematic trajectories, research methods, publishing genres, authorship and location. The analysis revealed a consistent US-dominant orientation to research published in the journal during this time. Even though research in inner circle contexts began to decline around 1995 (and are completely overtaken by outer circle contexts during the five-year period prior to Canagarajah's study) this trend represents a shift in context of *focus* rather than *location* of authorship. US-based authors continued to dominate the pages of the journal but, Canagarajah suggests, are reporting on research conducted at locations outside of the US 'in order to understand pedagogical concerns more diverse settings' (2016: 28). Canagarajah's findings corroborate those of Liu and Berger.

The Journals

The three journals selected for this analysis were *Language Learning*, *Modern Language Journal* and *TESOL Quarterly* (listing alphabetical). Since the object of focus was US-based IEPs, three US journals were selected. These journals represent three of the six journals identified as relevant to the professional lives of applied linguists by (de Bot, 2015), the other journals being *Applied Linguistics*, *Bilingualism: Language and Cognition* and *Studies in Second Language Acquisition*. The purpose of the present inquiry was to evaluate the involvement of US-based IEPs in applied linguistics research; the three journals were selected because they are published in the US, have histories of 50+ years, and have missions that align with opportunities for research afforded by IEPs. The initial audience for the *Modern Language Journal*, for instance, was US-based, as evidenced by the US-centric membership of the organizational founders as well as the editor's praise for the fortitude of the 'American teacher' in the lead article of the inaugural issue (Kayser, 1916). Similarly, the formation of TESOL was 'largely defined according to the language teaching needs of the United States' (Canagarajah, 2016: 26). The data in this article range from 1967, the first publication date of *TESOL Quarterly* and the latest first publication date of the three journals, to 2020.

The 'birth' of *Language Learning* in 1948 was 'an extremely important landmark in the history of applied linguistics' (Catford, 1998: 465). The original title of the publication was *Language Learning: A Quarterly Journal of Applied Linguistics*; it was the first journal in the world to use the term 'applied linguistics' as part of its title and is largely seen as being responsible for the popularization of the term. The journal was inspired into existence by the Research Club in Language Learning, a group of graduate students who were motivated by their work in the English Language Institute (ELI) at the University of Michigan and 'the exciting new ideas about language and language learning that they were receiving from their professors' (Catford, 1998: 481). One of those graduate students (and founding editorial member as well as subsequent editor and co-editor of the journal from 1951 to 1953), Betty J. Wallace Robinett, describes the members of the Research Club, in a personal communication with Catford (1998), as 'starry-eyed neophytes in linguistics' who loved their work and wanted to share ideas with others; they decided that 'a journal would be the best way to disseminate all the wonderful things' they were discussing among their group (1998: 481). Wallace Robinett later became the founding editor of *TESOL Quarterly*

(1967–1972). Over the decades, *Language Learning* has experienced a six-fold increase in publication pages, starting from a 'slim' average of 34 pages to over 210 pages in more recent issues (Catford, 1998). In its inaugural issue, David W. Reed (1948: 1–2), a member of the editorial board, contrasts the focus and intent of the journal to other journals of the era, describing the focus of *Language Learning* as 'descriptive rather than historical linguistics ... [t]he present journal ... will present only those linguistic articles which, at least implicitly, contribute to the improvement of foreign language learning and teaching ... [and] pedagogical articles only when the subject matter involved is language'. The journal's website (Language Learning, 2022) describes the current aim and scope of the journal as 'dedicated to the understanding of language learning broadly defined' and 'concerned with fundamental theoretical issues in language learning'.

The *Modern Language Journal* has the longest history of the three journals considered here; it celebrated its Golden Jubilee in 1966, one year before *TESOL Quarterly* was launched. The journal began in 1916 as a publication of the Modern Language Association, an organization that united 'in a federation the various and state modern language associations of the East and Middle West and South [of the United States] for the purpose of bringing out a federation organ which was to be a journal of, by, and for the teachers of modern languages' (Kayser, 1916: 1). The *Modern Language Journal* describes its current editorial mission as 'devoted to research and discussion about the teaching and learning of foreign and second languages', and it 'is particularly committed to publishing high quality work in non-English languages' (*Modern Language Journal*, 2022). In 2016, then-editor Heidi Byrnes described the journal's mission to investigate languages beyond lingua franca English as an 'unmistakable ... seemingly resurgent' need (Byrnes, 2016: 4).

TESOL Quarterly began publication in 1967 as an initiative of the contemporary organization TESOL (Teaching English to Speakers of Other Languages, Inc.), which had been established only a year prior in 1966. As the title suggests, *TESOL Quarterly* is more focused on the profession of TESOL than the other two journals. The inaugural editor of the journal, Betty Wallace Robinett (1967), described the journal as broadly focused on 'practical matters' that encourage readers 'to search a little more deeply into the "why" of certain drills and the "wherefore" of certain techniques'. Robinett also acknowledges language programs and language program administration as distinct areas of concentration within the wider field. Early innovators in the field, according to Canagarajah (2016: 11), were 'on a mission to discover the acquisition process typical of all learners, regardless of their location and diversity ... early articles in *TQ* were marked by ... self-assuredness, optimism, and progressivism ... We knew what we wanted to know, and we were going to find it systematically'. *TESOL Quarterly* currently describes itself as a publication representing a variety of both theoretical and practical cross-disciplinary interests 'of significance to individuals concerned with English language teaching and learning and standard English as a second dialect' (*TESOL Quarterly*, 2022).

Methodology

The purpose of this research was to identify how US-based IEPs (i.e. sites of postsecondary pre-matriculated academic English language instruction for international students) have supported research in applied linguistics and TESOL over approximately the past 50 years. The three journals of focus were *Language Learning*, *Modern Language Journal*, *TESOL Quarterly*. Articles were batch downloaded via Text and Data Mining (TDM) service offered by Wiley Online Library. Lists of Digital Object Identifiers (DOIs) for each article were extracted using CrossRef API, the largest DOI registration agency where publishers can deposit DOIs with associated metadata. DOIs were then encoded with their Uniform Resource Locator (URL), and Python scripts looping through codes for the automatic bulk-downloading of articles were created. Some volumes were not available through the Wiley API service (e.g. *TESOL Quarterly* prior to 1981 and *Modern Language Journal* prior to 2001); in such cases, articles were retrieved manually or provided through former editors of the journal.

Articles were downloaded in PDF format and converted to text files so that they could be imported into the text analysis software, AntConc (Anthony, 2020). The concordance software was used to extract the frequency of the terms that represent pre-matriculated academic English programs. Initial search terms included: English Language Institute, English Language Program, Intensive English Program, American Language Institute, Center for English Language Training, Intensive English as a Second Language Program and so forth, as well as acronyms for each of the above. Other searches used truncated forms of these terms such as 'intensive English', 'English program', 'intensive language' and so forth, which identified additional contributions such as 'intensive English courses', 'intensive English as a second language programming' and 'intensive ESL program'. Each term was counted only one time per article; for example, if 'English Language Program' or 'ELP' occurred multiple times in a single contribution, it was counted only once. A few articles included more than one search term; the first occurrence of each was counted. Articles were included if a search term was identified in the main body of the text, abstract, author affiliation, footnote/endnote or spelled out as part of a unique citation within the text; bibliographic entries were not included. Finally, the IEPs considered here are exclusively US-based units providing postsecondary pre-matriculated academic English, so K-12 contexts as well as programs located outside of the United States were excluded. Authors' home institution and in-text descriptions of the research were used to identify program location.

In their analysis of *TESOL Quarterly*, Liu and Berger (2015) focused exclusively on the main articles. The current research expanded this pool slightly, including also Research Notes, Brief Reports, Forum, response articles and similar research- or position-oriented contributions that are typically shorter than full-length articles; the title and focus of these sections naturally varied depending on the journal. These shorter contributions were included because, despite their length, they nevertheless represent current research or discussion in the field. The following types of journal contributions were excluded from the data set: conference announcements, lists of contributors, instructions for contributors, academic reports, book reviews, newsletters, advertisements, publications received, degrees granted, position statements, bibliographies and so forth. Following Canagarajah (2016: 10), special issues were also excluded, as 'the themes and discourses of special topic issues are atypical ... [their] purpose is to highlight new and promising developments in the field'. Articles were manually checked to ensure compliance with the inclusion/exclusion criteria, and article counts were completed by both authors.

Results

Results for each of the three journals are organized in three-year intervals from 1967 to 2020. Three years seemed a reasonable interval for 'uncluttering' the data presentation, as the period is not so broad as to erase observable changes in the number of articles published, and it allowed the data to be easily divided into 18 equal units. Naturally, however, compressing the years under review in this manner also removes a certain level of detail from the data (e.g. a change within an interval from 20 publications in one year to two publications the next year is washed out through the averages), and shifting the intervals backwards or forwards one year would elicit slight changes to the results. Nevertheless, the data are a valuable indicator of the publishing trends throughout the entirety of the 54-year period under consideration. Table 2.1 shows the number of articles in which IEPs were represented (i.e. articles that met the search criteria described above), the total number of articles, and the percentage of IEP representation within the total number of articles for each interval. Percentages were used in order to create a more equal basis for comparison among the journals. For the purposes of the subsequent discussion, 'IEP' is used to represent the four main types of tertiary language programming – i.e. English Language Institute (ELI), English Language Program (ELP), Intensive English Program (IEP) and American Language Institute (ALI) as well as other program designations that offered pre-matriculated academic English as

40 Innovation in University-Based Intensive English Programs

Table 2.1 IEPs as sites of research in three journals: *Language Learning*, *Modern Language Journal*, *TESOL Quarterly*

Year	Language Learning			Modern Language Journal			TESOL Quarterly			All Journals		
	IEP*	# of Articles	% of Articles	IEP*	# of Articles	% of Articles	IEP*	# of Articles	% of Articles	IEP*	# of Articles	% of Articles
1967–1969	4	57	7.0%	2	138	1.4%	11	119	9.2%	17	314	5.4%
1970–1972	8	52	15.4%	1	141	0.7%	14	92	15.2%	23	285	8.1%
1973–1975	7	54	13.0%	0	90	0.0%	12	101	11.9%	19	245	7.8%
1976–1978	12	66	18.2%	0	91	0.0%	20	118	16.9%	32	275	11.6%
1979–1981	6	66	9.1%	1	105	1.0%	26	131	19.8%	33	302	10.9%
1982–1984	13	74	17.6%	0	83	0.0%	32	146	22.6%	46	303	15.2%
1985–1987	10	77	13.0%	0	73	0.0%	32	151	21.2%	42	301	14.0%
1988–1990	1	54	1.9%	1	69	1.4%	14	126	11.1%	16	249	6.4%
1991–1993	2	48	4.2%	3	76	3.9%	15	129	11.6%	20	253	7.9%
1994–1996	3	61	4.9%	2	77	2.6%	4	98	4.1%	9	236	3.8%
1997–1999	10	61	16.4%	1	61	1.6%	2	100	2.0%	13	222	5.9%
2000–2002	6	56	10.7%	2	61	3.3%	6	91	6.6%	14	208	6.7%
2003–2005	1	53	1.9%	2	57	3.5%	8	111	7.2%	11	221	5.0%
2006–2008	4	60	6.7%	4	129	3.1%	5	125	4.0%	13	314	4.1%
2009–2011	6	113	5.3%	4	131	3.1%	3	103	2.9%	13	347	3.7%
2012–2014	3	96	3.1%	3	123	2.4%	10	108	9.3%	16	327	4.9%
2015–2017	2	86	2.3%	2	125	1.6%	8	109	7.3%	12	320	3.8%
2018–2020	0	87	0.0%	6	128	4.7%	8	135	5.9%	14	350	4.0%
Total	97	1221	7.9%	34	1758	1.9%	230	2093	11.0%	361	5072	7.1%

* Includes all program designations that offered pre-matriculated academic English as understood through the content of the articles, e.g. ELI, ELP, IEP, American Language Institute (ALI), Center for English Language Training (CELT), Intensive English as a Second Language Program, 'intensive English coursework' and so forth.

ELI, ELP or IEP? Tracing the Growth of an Industry   41

understood through the content of the articles (e.g. Center for English Language Training, Intensive English as a Second Language Program, 'intensive English coursework' and so forth).

The same information from Table 2.1 is presented in chart form in Figures 2.1 and 2.2. Both figures trace the percentage of IEP representation within the total number of articles for each three-year interval. Figure 2.1 shows results for each journal separately; Figure 2.2 combines the results into a single trendline.

From 1967 to 2020, articles that were in some way supported by IEPs totaled 368 out of 5072 total articles, or 7.3%. *TESOL Quarterly*

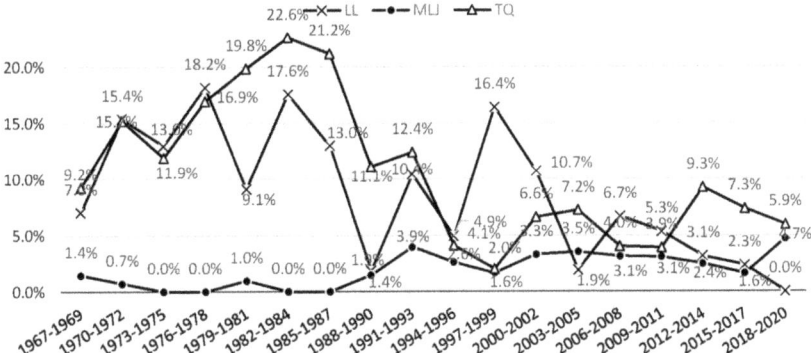

Figure 2.1 Percentage of articles supported by IEPs* for each of the three journals individually

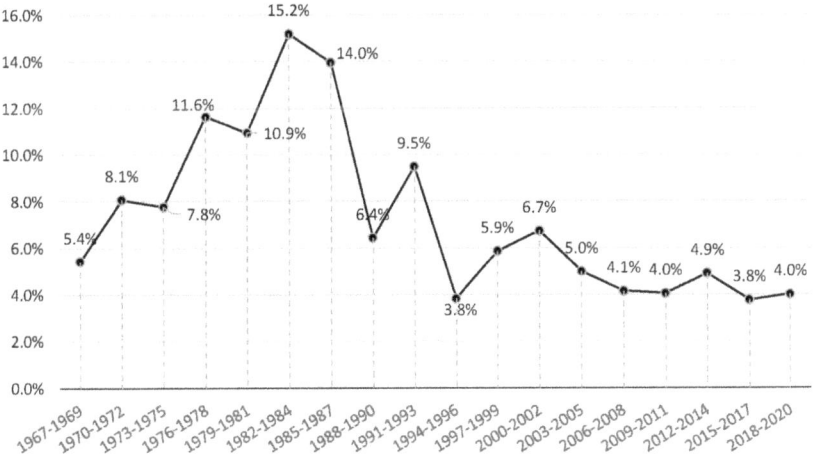

Figure 2.2 Percentage of articles supported by IEPs* for each of the three journals combined

* Includes all program designations that offered pre-matriculated academic English as understood through the content of the articles, e.g. ELI, ELP, IEP, American Language Institute (ALI), Center for English Language Training (CELT), Intensive English as a Second Language Program, 'intensive English coursework' and so forth.

provided the highest contribution (11.1%), followed by *Language Learning* (8.3%) and *Modern Language Journal* (1.9%). The amount of IEP representation in the journals naturally varies from one three-year interval to the next. During the 1982–1984 interval, both *TESOL Quarterly* (22.6%) and *Language Learning* (18.2%) experienced their highest percentages of IEP representation, while during the same time period *Modern Language Journal* experienced one of four intervals with 0%. Figure 2.2 demonstrates that the 1970s-1980s was a period of critical influence for IEPs in applied linguistics research, primarily driven by both *TESOL Quarterly* and *Language Learning*. Since an editorial goal of *Modern Language Journal* is to publish 'high quality work in non-English languages' the lack of IEP representation within the journal's pages is perhaps unsurprising. The overall influence of IEPs began to wane around the 2003–2005 interval and has remained relatively stable since that time at around roughly 4%. Curiously, around the same time period as *TESOL Quarterly* and *Language Learning* began publishing fewer articles supported by IEPs, the percentage of IEP-supported articles in *MLJ* increased a couple of percentage points. However, rather than an increase in the amount of IEP-based research represented in *Modern Language Journal*, the change primarily seems to arise because of an increase in contributions from authors affiliated with IEPs as well as from an increase in direct mentions of IEPs in footnotes and in-text references. While authorship and mentions in *Language Learning* and *TESOL Quarterly* remained relatively stable during this period, articles in these journals utilizing IEPs as a site of research decreased. The increase of authorship, footnotes and citations affiliated with IEPs in *Modern Language Journal* reflects, perhaps, a certain maturity of the field as IEP practitioners became more established in their careers and previous research conducted in IEPs became more ensconced in academic discussion.

While, on the one hand, 7.3% of the published research over a 54-year period (levelling out around approximately 4% influence over the past 15 years) may not seem overly significant, these percentages nevertheless demonstrate an enduring influence of IEPs within the wider field. To wit, from the 1970s to early 1990s, roughly 10% of the research in these key journals was supported by IEPs. This influence is particularly relevant when one considers trends in the field that were occurring during the periods of greater influence, such as the founding of professional organizations (e.g. University and College Intensive English Programs (UCIEP) and American Association of Intensive English Programs (AAIEP)) as well as a sort of 'coming of age' of applied linguistics as a field (e.g. the founding of new departments and shifts in the focus and context of study). These influences are discussed in more detail in the next section.

The above results combine the term 'IEP' to represent the range of programs offering pre-matriculated tertiary English, yet programs naturally employ a range of names to identify themselves. The five most common terms among the data were American Language Institute (ALI), Center for English Language Studies (CESL), English Language Institute, English Language Program and Intensive English Program. Figure 2.3 shows the frequency of these five nomenclatures; other, less frequent terms that also signified IEPs (e.g. Center for English Language Training, Intensive English Institute, etc.) were not included in this set. Figure 2.4 uses the same data set to identify the institutions most frequently associated with each term, so articles with author affiliations at more than one institute were excluded, as the actual location of the data collection was not always identifiable. Terms are categorized by the same three-year intervals applied previously. From the 1967 to 1969 period up through the 1985 to 1987 period, the most common term was ELI; this was then replaced by IEP in the years thereafter. In other words, following the 1985 to 1987 interval, IEP seems to have become the preferred or default term for referring to pre-matriculated academic English language programming. ALI was most prominent during the 1970s and has primarily dropped out of usage, with only a single publication since 2000. CESL occurred most frequently in the 1980s, then similarly declined. ELP was the most infrequent of the four terms, the majority of which were identified during the decades of 1970 and 1980 with four instances each, then with roughly only one mention per subsequent decade. Figure 2.3 (below) shows the distribution of these terms within three-year intervals from 1967 to 2020.

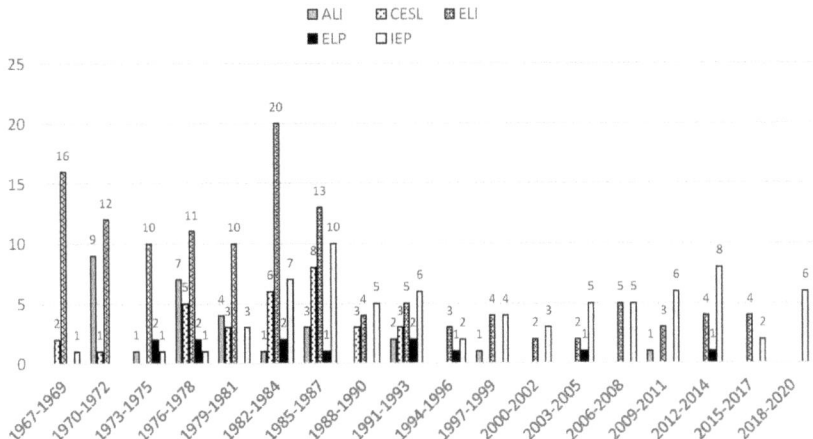

Figure 2.3 Combined frequency of terms American Language Institute, American Language Institute (ALI), Center for English Language Studies (CESL), English Language Institute, English Language Program and Intensive English Program

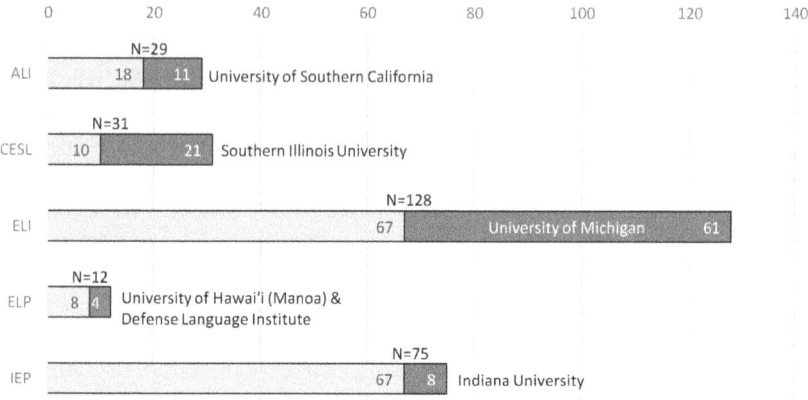

Figure 2.4 Language program designation (American Language Institute, Center for English as a Second Language (CESL), English Language Institute (ELI), English Language Program (ELP), Intensive English Program (IEP)) and primary institution represented for each designation

Institutional representation among the articles varied widely. Figure 2.4 shows the institution(s) most frequently represented for each of the four main program nomenclatures. Under the category for ALI, the most frequently represented institution was the University of Southern California (N=11); for CESL, the most frequently represented institution was Southern Illinois University (N=21); for ELI, the most frequently represented institution was University of Michigan (N=61); for IEP, the most frequently represented institution was Indiana University Bloomington (N=8); and for ELP, the Hawai'i (Manoa) and the Defense Language Institute were each represented twice. Figure 2.4 does not indicate authors' names, but data indicate that some authors were more prolific than others. For instance, articles referencing CESL were composed by 28 different authors, the most of which were from Patricia Dunkel and Kyle Perkins, who each had eight publications (six of which were single authored). ELI involved a total of 65 different authors, the most prolific of whom were Diane Larsen-Freeman (N=5), Douglas H. Brown (N=4), Susan Gass (N=4) and John A. Upshur (N=3). IEP involved a total of 111 different authors, the most prolific of whom was Kathleen Bardovi-Harlig (N=6).

As Figure 2.4 suggests, the dominance of the ELI nomenclature until that period seems to have been largely driven by the outsized role of University of Michigan. Removing the 61 instances of ELI from University of Michigan from the data, for instance, IEP then becomes the preferred term, with 75 total mentions. Removing the most frequently cited institution for ELI (University of Michigan) and IEP (Indiana University), both terms occur 67 times in the data. Nevertheless, as Figure 2.3 indicates, IEP seems to have become the preferred term for referring to pre-matriculated academic English around the mid to

Table 2.2 Chi-square contingency table of standardized residuals for intensive English nomenclatures

		ALI	CESL	ELI	ELP	IEP
1967–1984	Observed	11	4	39	3	13
	Expected	7.412	4.118	27.588	3.294	27.588
	R	1.817	−0.078	**3.639**	−0.216	**−4.652**
1985–2020	Observed	7	6	28	5	54
	Expected	10.588	5.882	39.412	4.706	39.412
	R	−1.817	0.078	**−3.639**	0.216	**4.652**

x^2 (2) = 24.142, $p < 0.001$, Cramer's $V = 0.377$.

late 1980s. This observation is supported by the fact that US-based professional organizations in the field (e.g. TESOL, American Council on Education (ACE), Institute for International Education (IIE), etc.) also use IEP when referring to these types of tertiary language services.

Table 2.2 demonstrates that these observations are supported by a chi-square test of independence using R programming (RStudio Team, 2021). The test was conducted to see if there was a significant association between specific periods and the use of the different intensive program nomenclatures. A subsequent residual post hoc analysis was also conducted in order to identify the largest contributor to the association. When the absolute value of a standardized residual is greater than 2.00, the cell is considered to significantly contribute to the association, with a negative value indicating fewer counts than expected and a positive value more counts (MacDonald & Gardner, 2000). The counts of the most frequently cited institutions were excluded from the analysis. The terms were divided into two periods (i.e. before and after the year of 1985) and were found to be significant (x^2 (2) = 24.142, $p < 0.001$) with a large effect size (Cramer's $V = 0.377$, 95% CI [0.266, 0.532]). In other words, there was a significant difference of the five nomenclatures between the two time periods. The two major contributors to the association were the frequency of the terms, IEP and ELI with the standardized residuals larger than 2.00. Before the year of 1985, the term ELI was used more than expected ($R = 3.639$) and IEP less than expected ($R = -4.652$). As of 1985, the trend reversed as IEP was used more than expected ($R = 4.652$) and ELI less ($R = -3.639$).

Discussion

Results indicate that, from 1967 to 2020, the average number of articles in which IEPs were represented in the three journals under review was approximately 7.1% – or, for each journal, *Language Learning* (7.9%), *Modern Language Journal* (1.9%) and *TESOL Quarterly* (11.0%). After a peak of 15.2% during the 1982–1984 period, the overall influence of tertiary pre-matriculated academic English programs waned throughout the 1990s and subsequently has remained relatively stable since the early 2000s at around roughly 4%. These numbers align with other trends in the field. For instance, Canagarajah (2016) observes that around 1995, articles in *TESOL Quarterly* – the journal with the greatest representation of tertiary English language programs (11.0%) – began featuring fewer inner circle contexts, likely a result of US-based authors moving to conduct research at locations outside the country 'in order to understand pedagogical concerns in more diverse settings' (2016: 28). Since the tertiary programs considered in this volume are exclusively those located in the United States, it is logical that the research these programs supported declined alongside articles taking place in inner circle contexts. Correspondingly, the surge in the 1980s of publications supported by pre-matriculated English programs follows the expansion of tertiary ESL in the 1970s (Eaton, 2013). In other words, as the opportunities to conduct research within the context of IEPs increased, the number of articles supported by such programs also grew. IEP representation in the journals waxes and wanes in accordance with the contexts of research in the journals.

Of the five main nomenclatures for pre-matriculated academic English programming identified in the data (ALI, CESL, ELI, ELP, and IEP), the latter seems to have become the preferred term around the late 1980s. This switch from ELI to IEP as a default for tertiary English programs accompanied other changes within domestic higher education. According to Heller and McElhinny (2017), in 1965 there were 30 linguistics departments in the US; five years later in 1970 there were 135. Indeed, during the early years of the time periods covered by this project (1967–2020), there was extensive growth in higher education of departments that were focused on language. And, language programs, an almost natural extension of these new departments, accompanied their growth. At the same time, 'the traditional view of [higher] education as a public good' was shifting 'to one that sees education more in business terms' (Winkle, 2013: 10). In the 1970s ESL programs shifted from being 'purely scholarly pursuits' to 'cash cows' for the institutions that housed them (Eaton, 2013). The period of late capitalism had arrived. This era ushered in an assemblage of neoliberal readjustments requiring flexibilization of labor and products that were focused on 'niche markets' with 'transnational implications' (Heller & McElhinny, 2017: 232). It was also during this time that the term IEP displaced ELI. Even during these early years, tertiary English programs were associated with the neoliberal constructs of innovation and flexibility (Litzenberg, 2021) in curricula design, scheduling, and financial procedures (Barret, 1982; Stoller, 1992, 1994). The niche product of IEPs, in other words, arose concomitantly as part of an increasingly neoliberal zeitgeist.

The transition from ELI to IEP may also arise from a change in the focus and function of tertiary English programming. During the

1980s–1990s, tertiary pre-matriculated English (which, by that time, more or less fell under the default term of IEP) transitioned into a modern 'industry' (Walker, 2010). Pat Byrd (personal communication) recalls the reorganization of her own ESL program in the 1980s but suggests that '[t]he big change for ESL in the late 1990s was the shift away from credit-bearing ESL courses to a true IEP model'. While the distinctions in usage between ELI, ELP and IEP lack categorical cleanliness, the shift may represent an evolutionary development. That is, programs assuming the IEP moniker became synonymous with a business orientation while programs assuming the ELI and ELP monikers maintained a broader, more service-inclusive orientation – yet at the same time, IEP also became the default term for referring to all such programs.

This period was also a time of increasing specialization. Larsen-Freemen (Chapter 1, this volume) relates an incident that characterizes the shifting foundation of tertiary English language programming during this era. Around 1985–1986, the dean requested that the ELI at the University of Michigan provide greater support to matriculated students rather than 'strangers', i.e. non-matriculated international students. In response, the ELI began offering more credit-bearing English for Academic Purposes (EAP) programming designed to meet the communicative demands that international students encounter during their time in US higher education. EAP (in the form of ongoing support for matriculated international students) was becoming distinct from traditional non-credit IEP services that were designed for pre-matriculated academic English (see Grosik, this volume, for discussion of other non-traditional IEP models). Understanding historical trends of the IEP industry such as these can facilitate program innovation and evolution. An increasing number of programs, for instance, are incorporating credit-bearing work into their course offerings, and professional organizations are opening up membership to non-traditional IEP models. The evolution of the IEP at the University of Michigan also highlights how these programs are often part of larger language service units.

The motions that eventually provided IEP a type of default status were perhaps also cultivated by other developments in the fledgling industry. For instance, in 1967, UCIEP, a consortium of 13 IEP directors 'who met to discuss challenges and provide leadership in their growing field' (UCIEP, 2022), was founded. Then, in 1990, another organization, AAIEP (now EnglishUSA) was formed; it offered IEPs 'a robust agenda [of] standards of quality for English language education, liaison with overseas advisors, and interaction with other professional organizations' (English USA, n.d.). The explicit use of 'Intensive English Program' or 'IEP' as part of these organizations' names lent the term a professional significance not available to the other terms (ELI or ELP). Moreover, in between the founding of UCIEP and EnglishUSA, the short NAFSA publication, *The Administration of Intensive English Language*

Programs (Barret, 1982) became one of the earliest formal publications to use IEP as a 'catch all' term, further solidifying the parameters of the types of programs included under the concept. Programs offering English language instruction for 'non-native speakers', providing at least 18-hours of weekly instruction, and operating at least nine months of the year were now 'IEP's. By the time the Commission on English Language Program Accreditation (CEA) began accrediting its first IEPs in 1999, IEP had already become the default term of reference in the field for pre-matriculated academic English. Modern usage of IEP by professional organizations such as TESOL and IIE demonstrate the term's solidified default status.

Within the wider field of applied linguistics, there were other shifts occurring that affected the supporting role of IEPs as sites of research, and these shifts impacted the representation of IEPs in the three journals considered. In his review of *TESOL Quarterly*'s first 50 years, (Canagarajah, 2016) observed as early as the mid-1970s a shift in the journal's articles from the cognitive to more social aspects of language learning. Larsen-Freeman's 1997 *Applied Linguistics* article on Complex Dynamic Systems Theory (CDST) 'profoundly shifted' the field's understanding of the social aspects of second language development (de Bot, 2015); around the turn of the century, this social turn culminated with the publication of (Firth & Wagner, 1997) in the *Modern Language Journal*. Thus, as the focus of applied linguistics shifted from formal theoretical linguistics to more socially oriented, usage-based approaches in more diverse contexts, the representation of IEPs in *Language Learning, Modern Language Journal*, and *TESOL Quarterly* became less influential, stabilizing at around 4% of published research in these journals over the past 20 years. In other words, IEPs became less relevant as sites of research and research support as the focus in the field began to shift from looking at formal instruction at formal institutions to including more social and cultural issues of language use and acquisition. Thus, the change in the representation of IEPs in these three journals is a reflection of wider theoretical and contextual foci of the field.

The journal data presented in this study trace the evolution of the terms ELI, ELP and IEP as a reference for tertiary pre-matriculated English language instruction in three major journals and demonstrate how the latter term – IEP – became the default reference for these types of programs. The representation of these programs has varied over the 53-year period reviewed here, ranging from peaks in the 1980s of over 15% representation to the more recent 4% of the last 20 years. IEPs, it seems, may have arrived at a position of relative stability in their role as a source of support for applied linguistics research. Programs continue to offer a unique site for ESL research on language development and teacher preparation, as ongoing projects demonstrate, although they are perhaps a context of limited global applicability. While IEPs may occupy a reduced role in their support of research endeavors, they continue to support their institutions and home units in other important, innovative and imaginative ways (see Anderson & Godfrey, this volume; Grosik, this volume). Indeed, research is only one way that IEPs contribute to their host institutions. The history of IEPs shows how programs have innovated in lockstep with changes within the wider field: As the relationship of IEPs to applied linguistics research waned, an industry backed by professional organizations and an accreditation system recognized by the US government evolved into its modern form. Knowledge of the historical trends of these programs accompanied by their innovative potential suggests that IEPs of the future may look considerably different than they do today.

References

Anthony, L. (2020) AntConc 3.5.9 (Windows) (Build 3590).
Barret, P. (1982) *The Administration of Intensive English Language Programs*. Washington, DC: NAFSA.
Byrnes, H. (2016) Notes from the editor: Celebrating 100 years of the modern language. *Modern Language Journal* 100 (S1), 3–18. https://doi.org/10.1111/modl.12321.
Canagarajah, S. (2016) TESOL as a professional community: A half-century of pedagogy, research, and theory. *TESOL Quarterly* 50 (1), 7–41. https://doi.org/10.1002/tesq.275.
Catford, J.C. (1998) Language learning and applied linguistics: A historical sketch. *Language Learning* 48 (4), 465–496. https://doi.org/10.1111/0023-8333.00054.
de Bot, K. (2015) *A History of Applied Linguistics: From 1980 to Present*. New York, NY: Routledge.
Eaton, S.E. (2013) The administrator of English as a second language (ESL) program in higher education. In Y. Hébert and A.A. Abdi (eds) *Critical Perspectives on International Education* (pp. 165–180). Leiden: Brill.
Ellis, R. (2016) *Becoming and Being an Applied Linguist: The Life Histories of Some Applied Linguists*. Amsterdam: John Benjamins.
English USA (n.d.) https://www.englishusa.org/ (accessed February 2022).
Firth, A. and Wagner, J. (1997) On discourse, communication, and (some) fundamental concepts in SLA research. *Modern Language Journal* 81 (3), 285–300.
Heller, M. and McElhinny, B. (2017) *Language, Capitalism, Colonialism: Toward a Critical History*. North York, ON: University of Toronto Press.
Jensen, C. and Soppelsa, E.F. (1996) Strategies for research in intensive English programs. *Journal of Intensive English Studies* 10 (Spring/Fall), 1–17.
Kayser, C.F. (1916) The federation and the proposed modern language journal. *Modern Language Journal* 1 (1), 1–9.
Language Learning (2022) https://www.wiley.com/en-us/Language+Learning-p-9780JRNL65027 (accessed February 2022).
Litzenberg, J. (2021) Innovation, resiliency, and genius in intensive English programs: Decolonializing recruitment and contradictory advocacy. *Applied Linguistics* 42 (5), 905–923. https://doi.org/10.1093/applin/amab015.
Liu, J. and Berger, C.M. (2015) *TESOL: A Guide*. New York, NY: Bloomsbury.
MacDonald, P.L. and Gardner, R.C. (2000) Type I error rate comparisons of post hoc procedures for I j chi-square tables. *Educational and Psychology Measurement* 60 (5), 735–754. https://doi.org/doi.org/10.1177/00131640021970871.
Mitchell, R. (1997) BAAL history 1967-1997. *BAAL Newsletter* (Special Issue), 57.

Modern Language Journal (2022) https://onlinelibrary.wiley.com/journal/15404781 (accessed February 2022).
Pennycook, A. (1998) *English and the Discourses of Colonialism*. New York, NY: Routledge.
Phillipson, R. (1992) *Linguistic Imperialism*. Oxford: Oxford University Press.
Reed, D.W. (1948) Editorial. *Language Learning* 1 (1), 1–2.
Robinett, B.W. (1967) Editorial. *TESOL Quarterly* 1 (1), 2.
RStudio Team (2021) RStudio: Integrated development environment for R. RStudio. See https://www.r-project.org/ (accessed February 2022).
Smith, R. (2016) Building 'applied linguistic historiography': Rationale, scope, and methods. *Applied Linguistics* 37 (1), 71–87.
Stoller, F.L. (1992) Taxonomy of intensive English innovations. *Journal of Intensive English Studies* 6, 1–25.
Stoller, F.L. (1994) The diffusion of innovations in intensive ESL programs. *Applied Linguistics* 15 (3), 300–327. https://doi.org/10.1093/applin/15.3.300.
TESOL Quarterly (2022) About this journal. https://onlinelibrary.wiley.com/journal/15457249 (accessed February 2022).
UCIEP (2022) University and college intensive English programs. See www.uciep.org (accessed February 2022).
Walker, J. (2010) *Service, Satisfaction and Climate: Perspectives on Management in English Language Teaching*. Bingley: Emerald Group Publishing Limited.
Winkle, C. (2013) *University Partnerships with the Corporate Sector: Faculty Experiences With For-Profit Matriculation Pathway Programs*. Leiden: Brill.

3 Founding the Modern Era: A Conversation Among Former IEP Directors

Sharon Cavusgil, Martyn J. Miller,
Rebecca Smith-Murdock and Betty Soppelsa

Introduction

This chapter presents a conversation among the four contributors, all former Directors of different Intensive English Programs (IEPs) at institutions based in the United States during various times throughout the years 1980–2003. All Directors were active during the 1990s, a period of exponential growth in the IEP industry. The conversation was moderated, and the Directors were provided with the questions in advance. The discussion has been edited for clarity and coherence, and the moderator, who played a minimal role in the discussion, has been removed as a contributor in the conversation. There are five subsections, separated according to the discussion questions that facilitated the conversation. Current IEP practitioners can most certainly relate to the insights and experiences of the Directors in this chapter, providing justification for their own actions and decisions. At the same time, the chapter offers insight to a specific historical period of an ever-evolving industry: the changes, challenges, concerns, motivations and humanity of the field.

Please contextualize your program: The size, the mission, the administrative unit and the number of teachers, students and levels. Would you describe your program as having an 'outsider' status at its host institution?

Martyn: When I started in 1990, the program was housed in the Georgia Center for Continuing Education. It was the proverbial 'redheaded stepchild' within a 'redheaded stepchild' itself. At the time we didn't have too many very good connections with the rest of the university. We were averaging about 60–62 students a quarter (it was on a quarter system). When I left in '99, we were at about 225 students a semester (by that time, we had moved to semesters). But over the years, we were able to establish more ties with the university. We became responsible for the International Teaching Assistant Program, working with the graduate school and the Center for Teaching Excellence (or whatever it was called at the time).

The mission of the program was 'To provide English language instruction to individuals who were seeking admission to a university but whose language skills were not yet sufficient' – pretty much the same thing as everyone here. We did have the ITA[1] part, which made us a little bit different. We also became the English language proficiency evaluators for graduate admissions, and occasionally for undergraduates. We did insinuate ourselves into the university a little bit more than the one would normally do sitting in a Continuing Education center.

Were we outsiders? Not within the Georgia Center, because we were that proverbial 'cash cow'. They all loved us, as long as we continued to give money. For the rest of the university, at the beginning the program was an outsider. By the time I got out of there, I would have to say that we were no longer an outsider.

How many levels did we have? Five levels: beginning, lower-intermediate, intermediate, upper-intermediate, advanced.

Sharon: Georgia State's IEP was – and continues to be – fortunate to be housed in the Department of Applied Linguistics and ESL. The department included, at the time, research faculty who were interested in second language acquisition, assessment, and pedagogy. We also had a core group of non-tenure track faculty who were hired primarily to teach ESL. The IEP faculty were and continue to be considered part of the Department's faculty. We attended the same meetings, worked together on the department's mission statement, and things like that. This is one of the reasons I believe we were fortunate to be housed in an academic unit. The IEP also serves as an English language teacher training lab for Master's students. The department has since expanded to include a doctoral program and an undergraduate program. We have those different dynamics happening in the IEP, as far as teacher training.

The IEP officially opened in fall of 1998. Around 1996 or 1997, the university dissolved the Department of Developmental Studies, which was the Department that had been responsible for remedial math, reading and English. The higher-up administration decided that admitted and enrolled students should not need any remedial support, so that affected non-native and native speakers. Prior to the IEP, we had a credit-based ESL program; students in that program were mainly residents, not international students. When we were no longer able to offer students those credit courses, we needed to quickly begin to create the self-supporting IEP.

In our 'heyday' we employed – I don't have the exact numbers, but my recollection is – between 12 and 18 full-time faculty, ranging between five and 10 GTAs,[2] and two to three staff. We were serving approximately 240 students a semester, and almost all of them were full-time. In the early years we expanded quite rapidly – more so than expected.

Our curriculum included 25 courses, five different courses for each of the five levels: Beginning, low-intermediate, intermediate, high-intermediate and advanced. We focused on EAP,[3] but at the lower two levels, it was a mixture of basic skills with some EAP focus. I don't believe that the IEP was considered an outsider because we were an integral part of the department and the teacher training that was key to the Applied Linguistics graduate programs. We had a lot of support from our chair, who praised our services to the college and other departments.

Martyn: I would add that the 'destruction' of Developmental Studies was not just at Georgia State, but it was a University System of Georgia thing. A lot of the programs in the State suddenly had similar needs. I think ours was one of the programs that had already existed at the time. Other universities in Georgia created IEPs because of the reduction of Developmental Studies, if I'm not mistaken.

Betty: Our program had many facets. We were an Intensive English Program with full-time students, but we also had part-time students who were already admitted to the university and who were required to take English studies until they reached a certain level of proficiency. The university had conditional admission, which many other universities did not have. It meant you could be admitted into your field of study or to the undergraduate school, but still need English language work.

In general, we were English for Academic Purposes, but as time went on, we branched out into short-term programs with very specific groups of individuals from certain academic backgrounds. There was then more flexibility in what the curriculum would cover. We did Graduate Teaching Assistant training for the university – students from all disciplines. We did some community English Language Programs. In those programs it was often spouses of university students who needed to learn English. At our highest, we had 500 students – for a while, we were bigger than the School of Business at the University of Kansas! We had about 50 faculty and graduate students – full-time and part-time teaching – plus administrative staff and counselors. We had our own cross-cultural counselors and academic advisors. We had four levels of intensive English courses, plus the additional programs that I've talked about.

Initially, we were housed in the College of Liberal Arts and Sciences, which worked fine. But later – I think in part because of personalities within the faculty – graduate studies and international programs were merged into a new unit. We were merged into the new unit, and, actually, it was very effective because the Dean was a professor of Spanish literature, and really understood language teaching and was a real advocate for us.

We did a lot of advocacy for international students on our campus; it was something that both I and the rest of the faculty were involved in. I would say we had 'insider' status at the university. The physical location of our center was sometimes an issue in my time. When I got there, we were in a small house at the edge of campus, but with the connection to a graduate school and international programs, we moved to a center campus building where we had a lot of space.

Rebecca: The first program I ever got started with was at the University of Arkansas, Little Rock, because – honest to God – an administrator there had signed a contract with the Saudi Mission in 1978 to receive one of the first bunches – I think there were seven bunches of students – who came to the States. But there was no program, and nobody in town to develop the program! When I got there, they had a retired pharmacist, a librarian ... we were a hodgepodge. That's how the program started. I walked in – I was taking a bit of a leave of absence from my job teaching Literature – to the office of the Chairman of the Foreign Language Department at the university and said, 'I just got back from a training program in TEFL. Does anybody here do English as a foreign language?'. Within 30 minutes, I was signing the contract as the Director of the Intensive English Language Program, which was to be created within the next three weeks because the Saudi young men would be arriving!

I started in '79. We went from about those 10 young men, who were then joined by some Jordanians. Then we got in the influx of Malaysians, Venezuelans, Iranians, Nigerians ... back in the interesting old days! Some very different clientele from currently.

When we started, there were three teachers and a very tiny staff. We were all the time affiliated with Continuing Ed. We were never 'outsiders' – everybody worked with us. They just thought it was weird and interesting. Everybody was just fascinated, because there were not very many international students in Little Rock.

We grew to about 150 – which is not huge – over 10 years. The guy from Idaho and I used to exchange notes about trying to sell a program in those states!

We had seven levels: A truly beginner basic level with people who didn't know the alphabet, all the way up to college admission. It was an academic preparatory program, which is why we got those students – they were there for academic prep.

We had the graduate Dean on our side, we had the admissions office on our side ... it was really a very interesting situation because it was a very small university – and the IELP was something totally weird and wonderful.

I was there 10 years and then moved to the University of North Texas, where they had had a program since 1977. In '89, I was coming after three predecessors. When I got there in the fall, we had 75 students. When I left in '01, we had about 300 students. Then, with everybody else through the time after that, we went up to 500. A huge mix of students!

How did you become an IEP Director?

Sharon: I've been in education my entire career, although I wasn't initially teaching ESL – I was involved in business education. In my first years of teaching, I taught at the community college level, where I had a lot of after-class conversations about language and culture with international students. I started to realize – *Oh, talking about language can be fun!* I also volunteered for several years with the Literacy Volunteers of America. For whatever reason, I was always assigned to work with non-native English speakers. I later met someone who was working with non-native English speakers at the university-level, and she influenced me to earn a Master's in TESOL. Also, my husband is a second language speaker, and I always had hopes that we would eventually move to his home country of Turkey, where a degree in TESOL would serve me well.

That's how I fell into the field. When I accepted my position at Georgia State, my role included teaching and serving in an administrative role in special programs. The department offered special programs, where we offered community-based ESL courses. We also designed courses for businesses in metro Atlanta, and I believe because of those experiences, when the department needed to quickly design an IEP, I was brought in.

Betty: I got started by graduating from college during the Vietnam War – and having a husband who wanted to serve in a peaceful way.

We went into the Peace Corps, and we were trained to teach English in French speaking West Africa. I had no plans to do that. In college, I had majored in sociology and anthropology, but Peace Corps changed our lives in many ways. I was delighted with teaching English as a foreign language in the Peace Corps.

When I got back, we went to Columbus – my husband is an Ohio native – and we went back to Ohio State University. The English Department had a composition-based kind of program for international students, not an Intensive English Program. I walked in with my bachelor's degree and Peace Corps experience to meet the Director of this program, and she said, 'What are you doing next week?'. And so, I started teaching.

The next Director of the program encouraged me to get a graduate degree while I was there, so I got a Master's degree and at the same time I was Assistant Director of this program in the English Department. I was there for about five years and then I got hired by Kansas and became the Director of the Applied English Center.

In sum, 'Peace Corps' is my ultimate answer to the question.

Rebecca: Peace Corps was where I was headed, but my husband at the time … the draft board in Texas would not let him go into the Peace Corps, so instead we went to Canada.

I entered a PhD program in English Literature. I'd have the international students in my classes. I would say to people how cool that was, so they started loading the international students into my freshmen comp classes. As you know, PhD students in English literature taught composition! Of course, the logical place to get English-as-a-Foreign-Language teachers for any program is to raid a PhD Literature Department. So, that's how I got drafted into my first EFL job: the public school system was looking for English-as-a-Foreign-Language teachers for community programs ... and I loved it!

During a sabbatical, I went to England and took – back in the olden days! – a Royal Society for the Advancement of the Arts teacher training program in TEFL. When I came back – I had another semester before I went back to my job teaching literature – I went into the chairman's department, signed the contract ... and I fell in love with it. I had a three-month very intensive teacher training course, but no other preparatory backgrounds. This was '78, '79. And that's when NAFSA[4] was very involved, because a lot of people like me (and Betty, who I met through NAFSA) were entering the field inadequately prepared. In NAFSA, there was a lot of new administrator training, or 'what does an EFL administrator need to know' type stuff. We did lots of those – we in the field knew we were inadequately prepared.

Well, I became a Director because they were desperate ... and I was interested – my family was all entrepreneurial, good at business. That was the biggest challenge for most of my colleagues who had way more applied linguistics training – nobody knew how to run a business. We were just all small businesses. As long as we were – as Martyn said – the 'cash cow', we were very valued. Because I was pretty good at business management, I loved it.

Also, I got in at a time when if you really didn't screw it up, you got to be okay as an IEP Director because there was just such a demand and so many students coming. I say that now while people lament, 'Oh, what do we do? You were there in "the golden days"'. And I say, 'Yeah, but we didn't create it. We just showed up at the right time'. A very different environment.

Sharon: Something Rebecca said made me think of this ... I had a business background, I had been teaching management and such, but honestly (I've given this a lot of thought, too, because I was very young in the field and new in the department) I think that one skill I have is that I'm a good organizer.

And, I was kind of naïve – I didn't realize how much work it was going to be! But I do think that my organizational skills were one reason why I was asked to take over the management of the IEP.

Martyn: I had a very different trajectory than the others. I was literally born into it. I was raised in Lebanon, and I was and am in a bilingual family. Teaching English-as-a-Second Language has been part of everything I've ever known. My father was a university administrator.

As far as getting into it formally, my goals were to take degrees in English Literature – primarily, T.S. Eliot and J.R.R. Tolkien. In 1982,

I was back in Beirut, and the Israelis came to Lebanon and decided they wanted to stay for a little bit. My brother was a language teacher at the time, and he decided to get out of Lebanon. He said, 'Do you want my job?', and I said, 'Hell, why not?'. That's how I started teaching. The 'Israeli invasion of Lebanon' is my ultimate answer.

After that, I went to The University of Georgia to do a Master's in Tolkien and a PhD in Eliot. I ended up with my Master's in Tolkien (before anybody knew who Tolkien was, let alone how to pronounce his name!), but instead of doing a PhD in Eliot, I did a PhD in William Langland. I finished my oral exams, and I was walking around the hallway when I saw the Director of the language program. I had taught at the language program a few years before, because of my Lebanese background ... some of you might remember the Hariri[5] group of students?

Betty: We had them!

Martyn: Well, 42 of the Hariri group landed at The University of Georgia. Somebody saw my resume, and they had the crazy idea that I could control 42 Lebanese students, so they asked me to teach for the summer.

Then, later, I saw the language program Director in the hallway, told him that I had just finished my oral comprehensives, and asked if he had a job. Two weeks later, he called me and said he had a full-time faculty position if I wanted it. I had a daughter, and I had another daughter on the way; I decided I might as well start feeding them, so I took the job. Later, when the Director was leaving, nobody else on the faculty was naïve enough – to use Sharon's expression – so, I took the position. Again, the Israeli invasion is my ultimate answer. I 'thank' them for the job and my wife – I met my wife because of them.

Rebecca: Early IEP Directors ... We were really not thinking that this would be our life profession. I mean, we just kind of blundered and lucked into it. It sounds like all of us.

Martyn: Do any of you remember Martha Pennington's book that we all looked to?[6] That was 'the Bible', wasn't it? For those of us who didn't know what to do. And – excuse me, Betty – but I would always say to myself, 'What would Betty do?'.

Rebecca: We were always jealous in Texas, because you guys [in Kansas] had conditional admission. It took us almost five years to get conditional admission at North Texas. You were always a role model at Kansas.

Betty: I think the Kansas program was different from other programs. It was founded in 1964; it was the University of Michigan generation – the very beginning group of University of Michigan faculty – who founded it. When I got there in 1980, it was a well-established program. It was the quality of program that I was interested in. We didn't have the sort of growing pains, or the 'fall-into-it' because something else isn't available. It was an established program. When I went there, it was very intentional on my part. I redesigned basically everything, but had it not been for what went before me, we wouldn't have been what we became.

Martyn: In my case, the program had started in 1979. It had been there almost 12 years before I got there. The person who started it was a faculty member in the TESOL program in the College of Education. It was an 'outsider' position for that program, but at least [the faculty who started it] was relatively well-known on campus. He was the only thing that kept the program going until I got there.

Frankly, the only reason I was able to succeed was because I had the PhD. I mean, that was the only way at the time.

Rebecca: You've got to have the credentials if you want to be at the table – even if it was in the wrong field, like yours and mine in literature or whatever.

Martyn: Yeah, we had that PhD – they could not deny us a seat at the table. That is what it took in a lot of cases: we forced our way to the right tables because we were able to say we have that same piece of paper that you all have.

Sharon: I do not have a PhD, and I was not invited to the table at the college level. The Chair of the Department would meet with higher ups, then bring information back to me. We would talk and then she would go back, if necessary, to talk again with members in the Dean's office. I was not allowed to interact directly with the Dean's office.

Betty: I have just an MA – not a PhD – but the committee that hired me were PhD linguists who wanted a practitioner. Not a literature person. They wanted someone who knew how to teach and who had some sense of administrative ability. I think they believed it was an asset for the program that I didn't have a PhD in some other field, or even in theoretical linguistics. It's just the circumstances of the places where we were, and who there was making decisions about staffing these programs.

Martyn: In my case, Georgia was still an unranked school at the time. They were looking for people with big degrees.

Would you describe the program where you were Director as 'flexible' and 'innovative'?

Rebecca: I think we were making it up as we went along. At the University of Arkansas, there were few models – Kansas, and we always looked to Oklahoma because they had a lot of schools for a long time, because of Don Meeks. There were some other models around, but we weren't an academic unit. There was a kind of freedom … a lot of flexibility. There was no chain of command. If the Director of Continuing Ed said we could do it, we could do it. There were very limited book resources at that point ... the University of Michigan books and Azar[7] – God bless Azar! Certainly, from the mid-70s on Azar was available, but there weren't very many books. An IEP like ours, which was not located in a university department that had the resource of linguists and so on, we innovated all the time.

At that point, unfortunately, you got hired if you wanted to do it – as long as you had a bachelor's degree. Early on, if you had a bachelor's degree, and some teaching experience and would cooperate – you know, go to the TESOL meetings and watch the videos and do what you were supposed to – people were taken in as teachers. The teachers were innovating all the time with the limited materials and their limited training.

Regarding flexibility ... there was nobody who knew anything about anything. Because I had taken my 400 hours of TEFL training, I got to be the Director. I looked to the resources in the region, the people who I met at NAFSA, mostly, who were IEP Directors.

We needed lots of 'intakes'. We changed from semesters to putting our program on an eight-week instructional period. We went to five sessions a year, and you could pretty well join any time. We had to be flexible because our clientele kept changing. You certainly don't teach young Japanese students the same way you do young Saudi men.

I would say that in our particular program we innovated because there was no structure. At University of North Texas, that program had been there since 1977, but we went in and changed everything because they were in the old semester model. One time I participated in a panel convened by Frederika Stoller[8] about change and innovation. She said to list everything we had changed – it was everything from the carpets to the filing cabinets. Everything in that system got into the changes because it wasn't working in that environment in the '90s, which was very vibrant. Like I said, if you had a real program, you had good teachers, and you ran your business, then you could have students. Yeah, I have been in situations where it was all innovation.

Martyn: I would say 'ditto' to everything Rebecca said.

We were a small program. We were in the Center for Continuing Education, and the Directors of the Center had no idea whatsoever about ESL. It was 'Do-whatever-you-want, as long as you don't upset the university administration and as long as you don't upset the cash flow'. I hate to say it, but that is what we were there for: the cash flow. The students, of course, didn't see themselves as 'the cows' who were feeding the university, the state's coffers. But that's exactly what they were. We did everything we could to ensure that the students didn't feel that, but we knew that at the Center that is what we were doing, or that is what the language program does. We continued to amend the program or the curriculum in order to meet the students' needs so that they would continue coming.

Rebecca: Martyn, can I ask a question? Were you doing academic prep for your university, so that you were also feeding fully resourced undergraduates into your university?

Martyn: Absolutely. This is one of the examples of our creativity, or innovation: our primary mission was EAP. Our students were getting prepared for admission to the university; we had a TOEFL course like everybody else, and it was the biggest class in the program. But the better classes were the upper-level writing classes and things like that.

However, about '96 or '97, we started seeing a new kind of student and this was not the one who wanted a full-time program. As Betty described – the spouses, for example, who were there for non-academic purposes, and also other people coming into the state. We had a growing number of international businesses moving into the state, and they needed to train their folks, but not on a full-time basis. We, therefore, created a parallel curriculum. We had an EAP curriculum, and then we just had pure communication skills. The faculty kept telling me that it wasn't going to work, we're not going to have enough students. In the end, of course, we had just as many students in EAP as in communication skills; they were both successful.

Innovation and flexibility? Yes, because the students demanded it. And because we were required to continue to provide students to the university and dollars to the Center for Continuing Education.

More than that, though, I think the flexibility and innovation was administrative, in addition to curricular, innovation. When I first began, we had only part-time teachers teaching all of the classes and three administrative/full-time faculty, but the bulk of the faculty was part-time – no benefits, no nothing. Some of them had Master's degrees in the field, but not all of them; the majority of them did not. They were more like me, people who just sort of got in by accident. As the program matured, we started arguing for more permanent positions. From a program that had only three full-time faculty who were also administrators, and 12 part-timers ... when I left, we had 12 full-time faculty positions and about 12 other part-timers who would fill in when needed. These jobs were called 'Academic Year Teaching Associates'. It was a position that had never existed and took us about four years of fighting with the administration, but we finally got the University System of Georgia – which is not small! – to allow us to create completely new, non-tenure full-time tracks in order to reflect the professionalism and the contributions of the program to the university.

That's flexibility and innovation that I was very happy with. The administration allowed us – albeit, through many painful battles – to move the program, and, ultimately, the University System of Georgia in a more professional direction when it came to ESL.

Rebecca: Have you noticed at Georgia that they have stepped back from that? Because at the University of North Texas, people had faculty-like staff positions. They got all the benefits, they got everything like full-time faculty positions, but since about 2016, those started going away ...

Martyn: At Georgia it was worse. Three, four years after I left, they closed the program!

I was replaced by a gentleman who got into a fight with the graduate school Dean. His contract was not renewed, and then after him somebody else came in who also did not last very long. Then they gave it to a young man who didn't have the skills or the degrees or the training. He was a really great, great guy, but he just couldn't keep it going. They closed the program down, fired all of the faculty. I wrote a letter to the editor of the school newspaper saying: 'You're going to regret this'. And, five years later, they reopened the program in what used to be called Developmental Studies, not in the Georgia Center – not even in an academic program.

Yes, innovation was in the administration as much as in the curriculum.

Sharon: Our program was newer. We started talking about the curriculum in 1997. At the time, our curriculum was considered extremely innovative. We had a department of both tenure and non-tenure track faculty working together on the curriculum. Those were some of the most joyful memories I have of working with my colleagues. We would work together on a weekly basis, talking about how to design the IEP curriculum plan. We had the leadership of the department chair, Joan Carson,[9] who was doing research on the academic literacy demands of undergraduates. Our IEP was going to focus primarily on EAP for students who planned to pursue undergraduate degrees at Georgia State or another higher ed institution. We chose to focus on task-based and content-based courses, and we had current research to inform our decisions. Actually, Joan had published a study with others on – I think it was in '92 – on literacy demands. It focused on how academic prep programs need to have a curriculum that actually prepares students for the demands of the university. We made sure that our curriculum was research-based, and we designed our courses from scratch. We didn't have textbooks; we, both the tenure and non-tenure track faculty, created the materials, built around authentic academic texts, which I think was quite unusual and innovative at the time. Many of those courses have been revamped, but the foundation still exists today. We went on to be awarded the university's Instructional Innovation Award in 2002, for the IEP curriculum.

It was very rewarding, very fulfilling to have a group of people with different perspectives – from the perspective of research and from a love of teaching ESL – just meeting to create a well-prescribed and effective curriculum together.

Betty: Like Martyn, one of my goals was to create faculty-like positions at the university. We found a track called 'Specialists'. They were mostly researchers, so you could get tenure at the University of Kansas as a researcher if you met the criteria outlined for the Specialists. We used that as our model for how to create permanent positions for our teaching faculty.

When I first got to the university, there were three faculty and almost 50 graduate teaching assistants. I wanted to turn that on its head. It took a little doing to get the university to approve these Language Specialist jobs, but once they did, we had people who could get through the faculty tenure process, etc. It was a really important step, and mostly it was because I wanted to professionalize. It was hard work to keep graduate students on the right track, trying to keep a uniform quality across all of these courses and levels. I wanted the program to grow and to become a really first-rate program.

The other thing ... we developed short term programs. Some of them came about to cement relationships with other units on campus. For example, there was a program for Japanese language held in Japan by the university. They were interested in a reciprocal exchange, so we developed a program for Japanese students who came short-term, who weren't going to matriculate at the university. They were interested in studying in the United States in general, so it had to be academic-based. We did other things – we had normal IEP classes, but then students were allowed to audit classes in fields that they were interested in.

Some of those short-term programs were to build relationships with other departments and other units on campus, which worked very well. Also, it was a new revenue stream for us. It gave new opportunities to the faculty to develop a different kind of curriculum, much more content-based and ... just responding to whatever the group was, whatever their future plans were.

The other thing that was important ... for most of my years, our money was our money. We didn't have to pay a fee to the university for our space, for the use of the language laboratory or any of that stuff. We built up enough cash that we could pay faculty to do research. We developed, for example, an oral proficiency test. That was incredibly good, and it was because we had money. We had the flexibility to deploy faculty the way we wanted to and to give them time to do really serious research.

Those are some of the things that were significant in terms of innovation. I think all of us feel you have to be flexible in Intensive English Programs. There are so many audiences to please, so many administrative challenges. There are just a lot of reasons to remain flexible, to be able to change, and to deploy resources in new ways if the need arises.

Rebecca: There are so many facets to the job. It's the business part, the curricular part, the liaison-on-campus part, the recruitment-off-campus part. So many areas...

Betty: I had great support from the university administration, which is key. And from faculty. One of the things I did was move so that I could appoint faculty to be on the advisory committee to the Applied English Center. I could hand pick people who I knew would champion us and who had some intellectual reason to contribute to what we were doing.

I felt like I figured out [the job] by the end, but it took 20 years! One of the things I was the least prepared for were emotional, personnel issues. When I got there, I felt that I was just like these people who were teaching. But the minute I had the Director title, they didn't see me as being just like them. And I had to figure out: How do you lead without offending or without taking away people's creativity and their desire to innovate? That was that was part of the learning curve.

Martyn: I was the youngest kid on the block. I didn't have degrees in ESL. I had taught for the same program maybe two months prior to becoming Director. They couldn't understand why I was there. By the time I left, though, there were tears, and people were saying, 'Please don't go'.

I guess I didn't do too bad a job ... it took 10 years. As Betty said, it's not something you figure out right away.

And the personnel. The hardest part of the job is keeping people motivated.

Betty: One of the anomalies of my position was that I was 32 years old when I became Director, and my three faculty colleagues were 60-year-old men. To be 'a girl', in their eyes, and to be the boss was pretty challenging.

Sharon: I felt that I very quickly had to learn things. I also was surrounded by a group of people who were excellent mentors. I was fortunate to have other colleagues who took on IEP administrative roles. One colleague taught in the IEP and also focused on teacher training and working with GTAs, and another colleague taught and focused on student services, which allowed me to manage the budget and personnel.

Betty talked about the personnel being the most difficult. I was the IEP Director during 9/11[10]. The IEP was quite successful leading up to that tragic event, but then we saw a dramatic drop in enrollment, like most IEPs around the country. This decrease in enrollment impacted our revenue. The most difficult thing for me was letting people go, good people who were full-time, long-term faculty. I wasn't taught how to do that, how to have those difficult conversations.

Rebecca: In my time, the best resource that was available as a developing Director was NAFSA. They had the best, most relevant and helpful training programs. There was so much involvement from the field; things got tailored to really help people with personnel and budgeting. It was invaluable.

The past 40 to 50 years have experienced increased professionalization and oversight in the field of English language teaching. How did these changes impact your programs?

Rebecca: I always saw my role as managing the institutional structure of the program. I was fortunate enough to have people who were eager to be the specialists in the skill areas, assessment areas, and so on. They are the ones who went to TESOL,[11] which was invaluable. They went to those kinds of specialized workshops. But NAFSA was always the place where I would find other Directors. I started in '79; I'm a million years old! Back then, everybody was kind of making it up as we went along. I would *long* to go to NAFSA. Just getting the information, the camaraderie, the reassurance ... because you mostly were making it up as you went along. There weren't prototypes.

In regards to increased professionalism ... I couldn't hire myself now. I'm a big fan of CEA[12] – and if you want to be respected by faculty as a specialist in an area, then you probably need to have a degree in that particular area because that's 'the creds' on the campus. The push towards that has been difficult because lots of people got in as faculty before a degree was a requirement, and it was difficult in lots of older programs. I think now people are hiring MA-TEFLs and so on, but back in the day, that was a real professional-growth issue.

Betty: I want to share an anecdote. I did a session at NAFSA while I was at the University of Kansas on how to raise the quality of a program. One of the things I suggested was that faculty must have graduate training in applied linguistics or related fields. A member of the audience took umbrage with my statement. It was kind of an unpleasant exchange because this guy across the room was saying, 'No, we have nice, sweet old ladies who are teaching and we want to keep them'. It was a new idea in 1980 to have credentials. It used to be the idea of 'anyone who speaks English can teach English'. It took a while for [a degree] to become the norm. Of course, it raced ahead, eventually to PhD for Directors and faculty and so on. That was an important change.

Martyn: As I said, we were able to create 12 academic year teaching associate positions, but with the university's understanding of, 'We'll give you these positions, but you have to give us something in return'. That something was professionalizing.

I couldn't hire myself now either; even though I've been in the field 35 years. I'm not qualified anymore.

We had these teachers with degrees in one or another field, but not in TESOL. We had a guy who had a PhD in Comparative Literature and had been teaching for years. I said, 'Okay, we will convert all of you to academic year teaching associates, but you need to get this the certificate that they're asking for'. It was just three classes (it's an add-on to whatever you already had). If you have a Master's in English Literature, you could do a three-class add-on and you're qualified to be an ESL teacher.

Rebecca: Still kind of embarrassing, isn't it?

Martyn: Yes, it was. It's a little different now.

The faculty member with the PhD in Comparative Literature would argue, 'I have a PhD in literature'. I would say, 'I understand that, but we've all agreed as a team to move forward with this requirement'. We gave them four years to get this coursework under the belt, and for four years I encouraged this gentleman. Every semester: 'Are you going to go?', 'Yes, I'll do it'. 'Are you going to go?', 'Yes, I'll do it'. Then, in the fourth year, I said, 'You know, your time's up. And, he said, 'Sorry, I didn't do it'. I had to terminate the gentleman. You know, the hardest part of the job is terminating.

Professionalism was extremely important at the time; it had to be done. I think in the end, the profession benefited by forcing people to get these degrees. I don't think there's anybody – at least very few administrators that I know of – who would say we should not have professionalized the field of ESL teachers.

Rebecca: There are individual people who were gifted, and it's regrettable if they couldn't buy into the price you had to pay to stay on the payroll. Spend the time and money to get a TESOL Certificate ... some people just couldn't do that.

Martyn: I think a lot of it was ego, really: 'Teaching for 20 years, I'm a great teacher, look at my teaching evaluations. Why do I have to get another piece of paper that says I can do what I know I can do?'. I sympathize completely. Again, I could not hire myself right now.

Betty: I think CEA was one of the huge milestones for the field in terms of professionalization. It placed requirements on programs that they had never had to meet before. It helped everyone across the field come to consensus about what it meant to have a professional-type English language program. I think that was a huge advance for the field.

Sharon: Because of where we were housed – in an academic department that offered a graduate degree in Applied Linguistics – I can't really relate to the conversation about professionalism or advanced degrees. That was just something that was always a 'given' from 'day one' because we had this pool of Master's-level students who, because of our connection to the department, were employed through the IEP.

Betty: In part, I think it's because we were older. We were from programs where that was not the case. A little bit of a shift in generation.

Rebecca: Betty, you started in '80, but your program started in '64. Sharon's program started in 1998, so it's a pretty new program in the big scheme of things. And it was started within an academic department of the university, so maybe it's not the age – it's the location administratively of a program within an institution that influences the initial professionalism of the program.

You know, there are plenty of top-notch proprietary programs out there nowadays because they have to be accredited. I've worked for CEA for a really long time, and when the law came down that sites had to be accredited if they weren't part of a university or college …. The growth within the field outside of colleges and universities has just been wonderful, really something to be proud of as a profession.

During your time as Director of an IEP, how did you view the relationship between your program and the wider field of ELT – in particular, TESOL and Applied Linguistics?

Betty: You have campus departments in those areas [TESOL and Applied Linguistics] who can contribute to the IEP, who learned from the IEP and who sometimes get jobs through the IEP.

You have opportunity for faculty to participate in educational organizations. They have to have a chance to be in touch with other professionals, to hear what the new research is in either TESOL or applied linguistics, and to bring that back to the program and also to contribute to those fields. I think that both the faculty and the administrators have a role to play in advancing knowledge in whichever discipline makes sense for them. It flows all through the organization; everybody should be connected to those areas, and everybody should be participating as much as they can in the work of those areas – both on campus and in the wider field.

Martyn: We were very close to Georgia TESOL. They looked to The University of Georgia and Georgia State – their language programs, TESOL programs, applied linguistics programs – for guidance. You know, most of us were at one time or another President of our state organization. There was very active participation in Southeast TESOL, and even big TESOL. I used to go there; there was some good interaction, good conversations with the professional associations. We would have conversations for hours and hours at TESOL about CEA, and there were fights and all the rest of it until CEA finally became a reality. I think that the language programs at the time guided the conversations for the professional associations.

NAFSA was a little different. We'd look to NAFSA much more as help to us, but I think TESOL, we went to them and said, 'Let us help you'. Maybe I'm misremembering.

Of course, we were also the labs for the Master's candidates. We were where the Master's candidates learned how to teach. That was essential. It was a great relationship; the TAs[13] were a good relationship between us and the wider field.

Sharon: Our curriculum was developed as a result of research in the fields of Applied Linguistics and TESOL. We had faculty like Joan Carson, Pat Byrd, Gayle Nelson and John Murphy.[14] They published in collaboration with faculty in the IEP. And we had the Master's students, who would bring ideas and research that they were studying in their applied linguistics classes into the IEP; it would seep into the courses and the curriculum. We would not have been the kind of program that we were if we weren't deeply connected to those fields.

Martyn: Those names all bring up decent memories.

I would go to Georgia State to get ideas. In Georgia, we were constantly going to each other for help. We were sending students back and forth. It was a good relationship. This is when we had lots and lots of students that we could send back-and-forth: 'Hey, I've got this trouble, child. You want to deal with him for semester?'. That really happened.

It was all by phone in those days; we didn't have email. We'd actually call people and talk to people.

Rebecca: Or write letters.

Martyn: Handwritten letters, even!

Rebecca: Back in the really olden days ....

Before we finish up, I'd like to hear everyone take about a minute to say their advice to people interested in going into the field as a Director.

Martyn: My first answer: don't.

But then, strap in and get ready for a wonderful ride.

Sharon: Three things I would advise someone interested in getting into IEP/ESL administration: I would tell them to work on their communication skills because you need to talk up the program, you need to be able to market it to students. You need to be able to market it to the institution, and communicate goals to the faculty. I would also tell them to absolutely be sure to surround themselves with a great team because I truly don't think one person can make a program successful. Then, get ready to work like crazy, but don't let the job take over your life or impact your health – it can easily take over your life.

Betty: Sharon's right on. The other thing I would add is to decide what the mission is from the outset, and to set up objectives for what they want the program to do. And a measurement strategy: How are they going to provide evidence for what they do? In our day, that was not the first thing that occurred to you. I would definitely say they should start at the top and say, 'Who are we? What are we trying to do and how? What are our means?'.

And, certainly in a campus-based program – probably any program – work on building alliances. Find the people who can understand what it is you're trying to do and who will support you one way or another. Working in a vacuum as an English program without connections to the surrounding territory is a recipe for disaster. Alliances are critical.

Rebecca: And have a product before you go out marketing; the product would be: a mission, faculty, a program that's not trying to be everything to everybody. Like Betty was saying: know what your intention is.

Oh, and know about how to handle money ... don't spend all the money!

Notes

(1) International Teaching Assistant (ITA).
(2) Graduate Teaching Assistants (GTA).
(3) English for Academic Purposes (EAP).
(4) NAFSA: Association of International Educators, formerly known as the National Association for Foreign Student Affairs.
(5) Reference to students sponsored by the Hariri Foundation, a Lebanese NGO established in 1979.
(6) Pennington (1991).
(7) Reference to series of books Betty Schrampfer Azar that began with *Understanding and Using English Grammar* 1981.
(8) Frederika Stoller is referenced throughout the Introduction and Chapter 2 of this volume. Her earliest published work on innovation in IEPs is: Stoller (1994).
(9) Professor Emerita, Department of Applied Linguistics and ESL; Georgia State University, Atlanta, Georgia, US.
(10) A reference to the events in New York City on 11 September 2001.
(11) A reference to the annual conference held by TESOL International Association.
(12) Commission on English Language Program Accreditation (https://cea-accredit.org/).
(13) TAs – Teaching Assistants.
(14) *Joan Carson*, Professor Emerita, Department of Applied Linguistics and ESL; *Patricia Byrd*, Professor Emerita, Department of Applied Linguistics and ESL; *Gayle Nelson*, Professor Emerita; *John Murphy*, Professor Emeritus; Georgia State University, Atlanta, Georgia, US.

References

Pennington, M.C. (1991) *Building Better English Language Programs: Perspectives on Evaluation in ESL*. Washington, DC: NAFSA.
Stoller, F.L. (1994) The diffusion of innovations in intensive ESL programs. *Applied Linguistics* 15 (3), 300–327.

4 Employment Trends in English Language Programs

Jeremy D. Slagoski

Tracking Employment Trends

Since September of 2009, when I started my first year as a doctoral student, I have been tracking full-time jobs for English language teachers. At that time, the job market was quite bad, not just for education but all sectors because of the 2008 economic crisis. My motivation for tracking jobs was to help future graduates in English language teaching and applied linguistics understand the market.

I started tracking job announcements with the 'TESOL' label from HigherEdJobs.com and the TESOL Career Center for tenure and non-tenure professorships in universities and community colleges. In 2010, I expanded my tracking to include instructor positions at universities (mainly Intensive English Programs, or IEPs) and *Other* jobs, which were previously primarily governmental, non-profit and publishing jobs. Since around 2017 and up until the beginning of the pandemic, *Other* was predominantly in the for-profit higher education English language teaching (ELT) industry, including corporations like Shorelight and INTO, which offered jobs within universities. In 2011, I again expanded to include administrative TESOL positions. While most of those were director or assistant director positions at IEPs, a smaller proportion were curriculum and assessment coordinators.

I did not track K-12 jobs or part-time/adjunct positions. For a few years, I tracked TESOL jobs overseas, but I stopped because HigherEdJobs.com's job board was inconsistent with job boards more specialized on overseas jobs. I also did not track jobs that required or strongly preferred applicants to have a specific religious affiliation or background, as I considered the religious requirement an additional qualification beyond one's education. Figure 4.1 highlights the findings of my data collection from 2010 through 2021. Data from 2009 were excluded because tracking started in September was therefore not

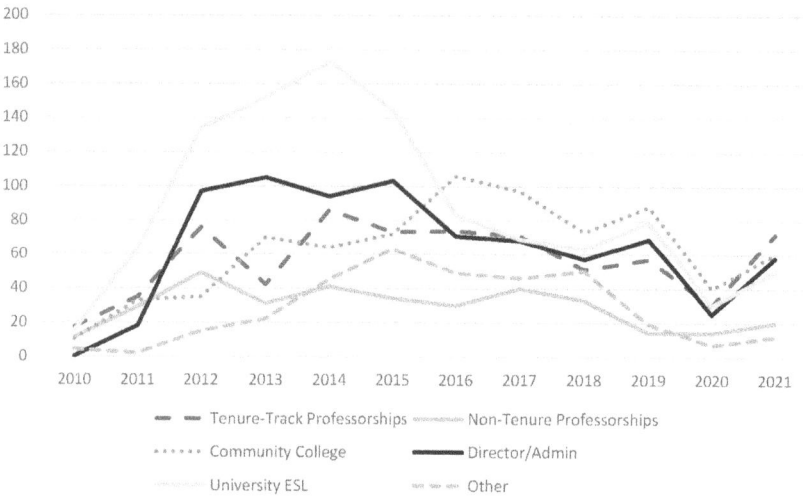

Figure 4.1 TESOL Jobs in the United States, 2010–2021

representative of the whole year. In addition, data collection for *Director/Administrative* job announcements began in August 2010, making 2010 the most logical place to start the analysis.

Since I began tracking jobs after the 2008 financial crisis, the English language teachers' job market seemed to have nowhere to go except up. From 2010 to 2014, prospects were promising, especially for *University ESL* jobs. While this upward trend dropped noticeably in 2016, there continued to be increases in positions labelled as *Other*; these were mainly with third-party organizations like Shorelight and INTO that administer some IEPs (see Winkle, this volume, for a discussion of proprietary IEPs). Nearly all of the job positions tracked by these third-party organizations were for teaching positions at host universities. One could speculate that these organizations were beginning to succeed at outcompeting IEPs administered by a university or college. Another explanation, but one not represented in the data, is the reduction in Saudi scholarships. According to NAFSA (n.d.), there was a noticeable increase in scholarships from Saudi Arabia in 2012, which correlates with the *University ESL* jobs data. Those numbers dropped four years later as the Saudi government enacted tighter restrictions on the King Abdullah Scholarship Program (see Redden, 2016; Walcutt, 2016), a change that also correlates with these data.

The data from 2021 indicate a recovery for most sectors of the profession, with the exception of *Non-tenure-track Professorships* and *Other* jobs. For the first time, *Tenure-track Professorship* job openings outnumber all other sectors. There could be many reasons for this dramatic increase, the most likely is making up for the inability to hire professors during the initial stages of the pandemic in 2020. *Community*

College teaching jobs and *Director/Administrative* positions also increased from 2020 to approximately the same number of openings as the tenure/non-tenure positions, but also not a return to their peak. Finally, in 2021 *University ESL* jobs saw their first increase in job openings since 2013, signifying a recovery from the initial impacts of the pandemic. These recent trends may help inspire some cautious optimism for the profession, yet this historical volatility of IEP enrollments and the dependency on external, global factors make predictions of stability – and much less claims of a 'recovery' – difficult.

Perhaps unsurprisingly, the data in Figure 4.1 track similar to the IEP student enrollment data from IIE's Open Doors report (2021) (see Figure 4.2). Student enrollment at IEPs peaked in 2015, one year after university ESL job openings peaked. Open Doors data are released one year after having been collected, so the 2021 data for IEP student enrollment were not available at the time of writing. If they are correlated with the number of job openings posted, then we should see an increase in IEP student enrollment for 2021. Regardless, 2020 had the lowest quantities for both sets of data since 2010.

There are numerous anecdotes of how the employment and student enrollment trends of the past decade have impacted opportunities within the field, and my own career path is no exception. The sudden increase and decrease in Saudi English language learner enrollment affected my first post-dissertation employment. In 2015, I was hired as an administrator to coordinate the curriculum and assessment for an IEP that had over 20 instructors. Over 80% of the students in this program were from Saudi Arabia. When the Saudi funding began to decrease the following year, so did the program's student enrollments

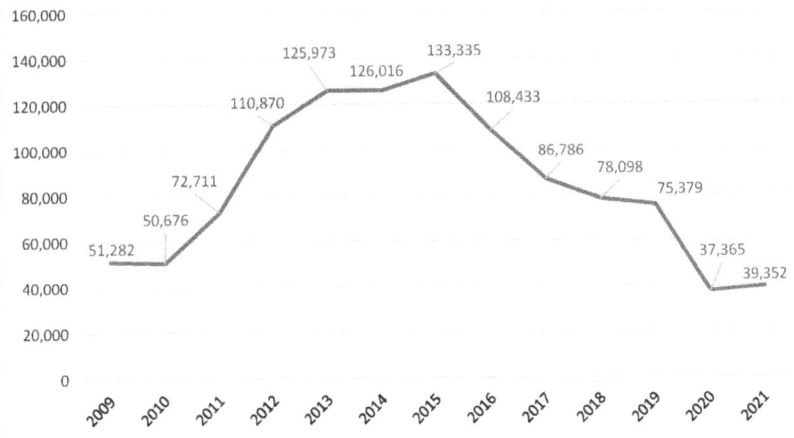

Figure 4.2 Annual IEP student enrollment numbers, adapted from the *Open Doors* report (Institute for International Education, 2021)

and their need to hire and maintain a high number of faculty. The following year the program employed only 12 instructors, and by the end of my third year, half of those instructors (including myself) did not have their contracts renewed. In 2017, I speculated that, if there were fewer university jobs due to this drop in enrollment, it might also impact the demand for new English language teacher educators.

Returning to Figure 4.2 for a closer analysis of tenure/non-tenure positions, the job market seems to have been relatively robust from 2010 to about 2017, with the exception of 2013, which demonstrates a steep, almost pandemic-level decline. From 2017 to just prior to the onset of Covid in 2020, the tenure/non-tenure job market was trending downwards. Since 2021, the data indicate a recovery for tenure-line positions, although less so for non-tenure positions. While the employment data prior to 2009 were not collected, anecdotal evidence from colleagues describe a wonderfully vibrant job market prior to the 2008 economic crisis. Indeed, the job market for tenure and non-tenure professorships in nearly every field has experienced stagnation since 2008 (MLA Office of Research, n.d., 2017; Monaghan, 2019; Patel, 2018).

Highlighting the dynamic nature of the English language teaching field, Figure 4.1 also shows that in 2016 English language teaching jobs in community colleges increased and surpassed university ESL jobs, and these opportunities have more or less remained higher since that time. An important point to consider, however, is that more than 30% of the community college job announcements have been in the state of California (see Table 4.1). In fact, as Table 4.1 demonstrates, the job openings in California (N=223) during the 2009–2021 period were over three times more than the next highest state, Texas (N=69). My experiences with community college jobs in Maryland and Iowa are that full-time positions often go to adjunct instructors who are already part of an institution or program and that many of these openings are therefore not be truly competitive at a national level. This may also be the case with the job openings in California, creating a somewhat skewed image of the opportunities available.

Table 4.1 Number of community college ESL job openings by state, 2009–2021 (top 16 states)

California	223	Pennsylvania	23
Texas	69	Arizona	19
Washington	54	New Jersey	19
New York	45	Oregon	14
Florida	43	Iowa	13
Illinois	27	North Carolina	12
Massachusetts	27	Ohio	12
Maryland	26	Wisconsin	10

Since California accounts for over 30% of the community college English language teaching jobs in the United States, closer consideration of the California community college job openings seems worthwhile. Fifty-eight community colleges in California have posted job openings since February 2010, with the Bay Area institutions of Contra Costa Community College and San Mateo Community College both tied at 11 job postings. The job openings at each of these colleges is more than those in Oregon, Iowa, North Carolina, Ohio and Wisconsin combined. Contra Costa Community College and San Mateo Community College account for 10% of the total job openings during roughly this one-decade period and, arguably, deserve their own place among the states in Table 4.1. However, one should keep in mind that often times jobs are posted for a community college *district* rather than a specific college within the district, so these numbers should be considered with some caution.

Since 2016, there have been more community college jobs posted than university jobs for English language teachers. One reason may be because many English language learners have found that community colleges are a more affordable pathway for matriculating in higher education, regardless of whether the degree they seek is from that specific community college or a university with a transfer agreement with that college (Loo, 2016). For example, the University of California Los Angeles (UCLA) gives preference to students, including international students, transferring from California community colleges, and recent reports show that community colleges have become more dependent on revenue from international students (West, 2018; Wheeler, 2021).

For individuals looking for administrative rather than teaching work, the administrative positions follow a similar trajectory as the university ESL instructor positions, but at a lower rate until recently. Since 2015 postings for administrator positions have declined. Similar to the teaching positions, many non-executive administrative positions naturally depend on student enrollment numbers. Anecdotally, there have been many vacancies at the Director level because of the retirement of professionals from the so-called 'Baby Boomer' generation, but chatter among Directors within professional organizations suggest some vacancies may not always be filled as programs re-evaluate their administrative needs in light of the increasing difficulty in predicting student enrollments. There is, however, no clear way to track correlations between administrative changes and new job openings.

For English language professionals looking for alternative options, the *Other* sector showed promising growth until 2019, the year before the pandemic began. However, universities partnered with these for-profit English language organizations have posted few (if any) full-time teaching positions since 2019, and nearly all the *Other* job openings since that time have been for online language proficiency assessment companies, publishers, or consulting/research firms and do not include any administrative or teaching duties.

The trends observed in Figure 4.1 suggest a dynamic and somewhat unpredictable set of employment opportunities for ELT professionals. There are no publicly available data indicating the numbers of MA-TESL graduates, but it is likely that there is also some interplay in the number of graduates and the number of job openings. Grawe (2019) predicts a dramatic drop in international student enrollment in the United States in the mid-2020s. Grawe's prediction in conjunction with the ELT employment trends portends a crisis in the field as MA-TESL programs continue to flood the job market with new professionals who are competing for an ever-decreasing number of positions. Part of this crisis could perhaps be averted if state and federal governments make their public universities more accessible to international students. It is certainly within the best interest of the TESOL profession to resist isolationist or nationalist ideologies.

The Future for TESOL Graduates

IEPs are clearly past the high-demand bubble of 2014/2015 for English language teachers, a time when Saudi-sponsored scholarships gave the field an inflated sense of security. Yet just as many English language programs were coming to recognize that similar enrollment numbers may not return, the pandemic intervened, dramatically raising the challenges for entering the profession.

MA-TESL graduates in the United States have at least two main routes to pursue after earning their degree. The first route is as an instructor or administrator in higher education. The second route is teaching abroad. Positions at universities outside of the United States often have a higher level of job security compared to the riskier entry-level positions at private English schools, most of which do not require graduate degrees. For some, a third route is available to those who possess state licensure for teaching in public or private PK-12[1] schools. The demand for English language teachers in elementary and secondary schools has been more reliable as the demographics of the United States continue to shift towards more multilingual students (NCES, 2022).

Unfortunately, those with a Master's degree in TESOL without state licensure for PK-12 teaching have seen job opportunities become increasingly rare over the past several years. The pandemic placed an obvious pause on hiring in higher education, and international travel stopped or was dramatically reduced. These changes created a 'bubble' for online English language teaching jobs, with the highest demand in China (and many of those jobs did not require a Master's degree). One of the biggest online ESL employers was VIPKid, which required a bachelor's degree and two years teaching or tutoring experience (VIPKid, n.d.).

While I did not track most of these jobs because a graduate degree was not necessary, I nevertheless observed many of my colleagues taking these positions during the pandemic. This bubble, however, burst faster than the Saudi bubble due to changes in the Chinese government's regulations for online tutoring for elementary and secondary students (Koenig, 2021).

With the return to in-person courses in higher education, employment trends seem to have returned to pre-pandemic levels. While, on the one hand, this may be positive news for TESOL graduates in the coming years, there are still large numbers of unemployed or underemployed TESOL graduates from roughly 2019–2021 who have been waiting for the job openings to return, and the formally employed TESOL professionals who lost their jobs as governments began reducing scholarships for English language study should also not be forgotten. At a minimum, the past two decades (and the initial years of the pandemic) demonstrate that the instability of the TESOL profession, as the number of job openings is difficult to predict from one semester to the next. IEPs are impacted by global political and economic trends. The backlash to globalization in the form of isolationism and nationalism as evidenced in the US-China trade war that began under the Trump administration highlights this trend. It is not a coincidence that the 'golden days' of the TESOL profession was during the period of post-Cold War globalization from the 1990s through the 2010s (see Cauvisgil *et al.*, this volume, for a discussion of IEPs during the 1980s through the early 2000s). The terrorist attacks of 11 September, 2001 demonstrate how xenophobia and travel restrictions can impact the field. Isolationism and nationalism continue to be a threat to IEP well-being, as these tendencies continue to transform the TESOL profession and global demand for English language learning.

Another factor that may transform the global demand for English language learning faster than nationalist policies is technology. Recent previews of this technological transformation is evidenced in the rise of online language learning programs like VIPKid and language learning apps like Duolingo. The pandemic exposed the potential of both innovations. Teachers, teacher educators and administrators in IEPs must learn how to adapt their teaching, curriculum and programming to compete with, work with or work around these high-demand English language learning services. Although the lifespan of certain technologies may be limited, technology-integrated learning and teaching will continue to evolve in the long term. It is therefore likely that English language teaching jobs will increasingly require knowledge or skill of technology integration.

Isolationism, nationalism, technology and global pandemics can rapidly change the demands on and for the TESOL profession, and IEPs are particularly vulnerable. In addition, the state IEPs in the

United States has been changing due to increased competition within and beyond national borders. Prior to the pandemic, the number of college and university governed IEPs as well as those administered by proprietary agencies partnering with universities (e.g. Shorelight and INTO) was growing around the country (Winkle, 2014). Shorelight's model specifically capitalized on the Pathway program model, which allows upper-level IEP students to concurrently enroll in one or two academic courses at the partner university. This model met the need for students to begin their degree studies sooner while also providing them with opportunities for continued skills development they needed for matriculation and for enrolling in courses that required students to speak or write at a higher English proficiency level.

While many IEPs and agencies were capitalizing on this Pathway model, (also sometimes referred to as 'Bridge Programs'), the US government agency responsible for managing non-immigrant student visas, Student and Exchange Visitor Program (SEVP) redesigned one of its primary documents for entering the country, the I-20 form. Previous regulations allowed international students to enroll in English language learning courses and academic courses concurrently. The new form, however, required students to be fully enrolled in either one or the other type of courses (i.e. non-credit language courses or credit-bearing academic courses), thus making it difficult for many Pathway programs to legally exist. Since the change in 2016, English language programs and their host institutions have been required to re-certify with SEVP (Study in the States, n.d., 2021) in order to continue offering Pathway programming. This re-certification process has been slow for many IEPs, thus giving the advantage to IEPs and agencies that were able to rapidly move through the process. A popular pre-pandemic model, often used by Shorelight and their university partners, was to begin the Pathway model at the highest or next-to-highest levels of the IEP; program participants could then take one or two academic courses that did not demand too much of their language skills while simultaneously being enrolled in language classes through the IEP. Students could then fully matriculate into the university after one or two semesters of such programming. Another similar model implemented at some institutions provided fully matriculated international students language and cultural foundational courses during their first year.

By offering Pathway programs, some IEPs have been able to fortify themselves against dynamic changes in expansion, stagnation and losses in the traditional IEP model. While the pandemic paused this transformation for a short time, there seems to be a continued trend toward Pathway programs and away from the traditional IEPs, which may eventually make IEPs outmoded. Directors and program administrators must ensure that their program design is one that best meets the needs of near future international student populations while adhering to all university rules, regulations and guidelines to maintain and increase funding, fulfill institutional goals and leadership values, and earn or maintain accreditation. In addition, one semester in a Pathway program can be more cost effective than one semester at a community college IEP and other university English programs because students can earn university credit via the Pathway program, and some of those credits may count towards graduation. IEPs attached to prestigious universities may be able to enroll students while maintaining tuition rates, but many programs may not have such advantages. Add to this challenge the increasing offerings for English language instruction in students' home countries as well as via technology, it seems possible that university IEPs may be priced out of competition. Directors and administrators often have only limited capacity for reducing tuition and fees or for offering larger scholarships. Indeed, to maintain affordability, they will likely need to use (or develop) the rhetorical skills for influencing university leaders, stakeholders and state legislators.

Innovating Intensive English Programs

With the future of US university and college IEPs looking unstable at best, we need to consider how they can maintain viability through the eyes of their host institutions, their current and prospective students and their teachers. A core component of ensuring viability is for IEP professionals to ask the fundamental, existential question of: Who needs an IEP at this institution? Why? IEPs primarily have been founded upon the need to provide English language classes to international students who wanted to matriculate fully into college and university degree programs, and for many IEPs this mission is still primary. However, nowadays international students have a wider range of options to improve their English language skills before matriculating into the institution of their choice. For instance, they can learn at English language programs in their home country, in other countries with more affordable classes, at US community colleges with pathways into partner universities, and online. IEPs are the luxury or premium option but not necessarily most efficient and convenient for matriculating into the academic program of the students' choice.

Programs, in other words, must find ways to stand out. Accreditation through the Commission on English Language Program Accreditation (CEA) is one method that many programs use to increase their attractiveness to potential students, as accreditation can lend an impression of quality and assurance to stakeholders. While accredited programs generally claim to have a higher trustworthy standard, accreditation is also open to community college and stand-alone programs. Job announcements for most university and community colleges require a minimum of a Master's degree and 2–3 years of experience. Table 4.2 compares minimum

Table 4.2 Minimum employment qualifications for two TESOL jobs

English as a Second Language Instructor (Tenure Track); Lower Colombia College, Longview, WA	Assistant Professor – LIEOC (Long Island Educational Opportunity Center); Farmingdale State College, Farmingdale, NY
• Master's degree (MA) in English as a Second Language, or related discipline • Two (2) years of experience teaching ESL in a higher education environment • Experience teaching High School Diploma/GED content areas • Experience using Microsoft, Google Suite, learning management systems and/or similar programs/technology • Strong communication skills	• Master's degree in TESL/TEFL, Applied Linguistics with ESL focus, or related field • At least three years of experience teaching ESL/EFL in adult-education, higher-education, and/or IEP settings • Strong oral and written communication skills • Experience using remote instructional technologies, such as Google Meet and Classroom • Willingness to teach mornings and evenings • Ability to teach in person and virtually

job requirements for an English teacher at a community college in the state of Washington and a state college in New York (excerpted from HigherEdJobs, June 2022). Both positions require a minimum of an ELT-related Master's degree, although the postings also state that a related field is also acceptable. Additional requirements include familiarity with technology, strong communication skills, and a minimum of two years (Lower Colombia College) or three years (Farmingdale State College) of professional experience. This latter requirement is not uncommon among positions of this nature and it highlights a hurdle encountered by many recent MA-TESL graduates who will generally have less experience than professionals who have been engaged in the field for a longer time. Although not shown in Table 4.2, Farmingdale's position announcement listed a 'Doctoral degree in TESL, Applied Linguistics, or a related field' as a preferred qualification, an addition that seems to be increasingly common. Pennington (1992: 18) warned that if the field was not moving toward a PhD as a minimal qualification, professionals would most likely need to 'settle in to being second-class citizens in a society of PhDs'. Even though the PhD is not a required qualification, the trend toward more PhDs in ELT seems to nevertheless be continuing. A PhD may benefit professionals in the ever-changing context of IEPs.

Pathway programs are a popular way that numerous programs have sought to diversify their offerings. A benefit to both homegrown and corporate-partnered Pathway programs is that they give students more immediate experiences in academic courses with less time segregated from the wider student population. A disadvantage for both types, however, is that as programs focus on Pathway programming, course offerings for lower proficiency students are often reduced. For corporate-partnered Pathway programs, a disadvantage is that universities must share the revenue with the corporate partner. And in my own IEP, for instance, we have not shifted entirely to a homegrown Pathway program because a majority of our students are in lower proficiency levels. Moving to a Pathway-only model would lose roughly half of our student population. Despite reductions in international government sponsorships for their students, our program still has numerous new students who arrive through connections from friends and family; international spouses and family members of our students continue to request admission. Our IEP has also experienced growth in less proficient students because of interest from the local community as well as new populations of students arriving from countries in eastern Asia.

Yet there are other ways to innovate beyond adopting a Pathway model. The rapid shift to online learning at the onset of Covid provided IEPs with new avenues for making their services accessible on and off campus. The most readily available tool that made IEPs accessible online was using internet video conferencing (IVC), with Zoom being the favorite across many campuses worldwide. IVC enabled online learning to become more engaging through synchronous interactive language practice. Many Directors, however, may have viewed IVC as a temporary option until international travel restrictions eased, and in-person learning returned. While this has happened, some international students have preferred to remain online a bit longer or even permanently. At my institution, some international university partners saw online IEP classes as a safer and more affordable way to continue the partnership. In-person learning is still highly valued, but now students have the option of learning online at home for a longer period of time, thus reducing the duration of their in-person experience. Many programs continue to experiment with remote and hybrid options, and it is too early to tell whether such options dramatic impact IEP enrollment numbers and their ability to hire new professionals.

Online learning also offered another opportunity for IEPs to engage in open education through virtual exchanges. Virtual exchanges are simply a method that use technology to connect people for the purposes of teaching and learning about a subject and about one's co-participants – clearly an important element within the concept of 'exchange'. Virtual exchanges can be both open and closed, but open virtual exchanges are usually agreed upon by two or more partner institutions. According to Stracke (2019), there are three beliefs that underscore the ideology behind open education, namely:

(1) Learners cannot be forced to learn but can only learn by themselves.
(2) Learners have to explore and create their own knowledge, skills and competences.
(3) Educators should not be teachers but facilitators of these self-directed learning processes. (Stracke, 2019: 184).

Although open education may not be as profitable as the traditional IEP or online learning model, virtual exchanges enable learners from partner institutions to interact and engage with IEP students and instructors, thus making their learning more meaningful.

At my IEP, we have set up virtual exchanges with several institutions across the world where students, scholars, and faculty meet freely and openly to exchange ideas and collaborate on projects or course assignments. While our university is open to most any partnership for virtual exchanges, the only requirement is that the parties involved have a signed a Memorandum of Understanding, or for more complex virtual exchanges, an additional Memorandum of Agreement that lays out the guidelines, expectations and points of contact. Since IEP faculty and staff are familiar with working with students from diverse cultures and backgrounds, they are already equipped with the skillset to navigate cross-cultural and intercultural challenges that may arise when two groups of students or faculty work together, and they are perhaps the most suited for engagement in such initiatives compared to other faculty at the institution. In this sense, the IEP can serve as advisors and consultants for the virtual exchanges across all academic units of the university.

Furthermore, an IEP can host its own virtual exchanges around language learning, which I refer to as Teletandem English Language Learning, or TELL. The primary purpose of TELL is to help grow and strengthen international partnerships. A secondary purpose is to offer opportunities to international partnerships who have English language learners who lack the resources to learn English in person. These exchanges also help IEP teachers and their counterparts abroad to learn from each other's teaching approaches and practices. Like many virtual exchange programs, TELL does not need to last an entire semester. Shorter TELL models last one to two weeks, whereas longer models last between four and six weeks. TELL works best when developed by participating teachers at the IEP and counterpart English language programs. Moreover, Teletandem language learning does not need to be restricted to English. A university's foreign language department can also offer similar programs; my current institution offers something similar to this for its Spanish language courses with university partnerships in Spain. My department has partnerships in Chile, Colombia and Mexico that are also interested in these courses plus other bilingual projects.

Bilingualism and biliteracy run adjacent to multiliteracies pedagogy. Conceived in 1996 by the New London Group,[2] a multiliteracies pedagogy is framed around three concepts: cultural diversity of the learners, the impact of technology on learning and multimodal communication (Holloway & Gouthro, 2019, 2020). Examples modes of communication are text, speech, body language, videos and memes. While more traditional definitions of literacy focus mainly on text, newer interpretations broaden the concept of literacy to address the ways people express themselves across cultures and technologies. In higher education contexts, multiliteracies pedagogy has been a central component in designing and facilitating courses that integrate English learning outcomes with academic disciplines (McPhee & Pickren, 2017). These initiatives support Zhang and Zou's (2020) conclusions that teachers' role as designer and facilitator are essential to the students' success in a blended learning course that uses multiliteracies as the pedagogical approach. Zhang and Zou report that a multiliteracies approach promoted intellectual engagement and challenges for students.

In order to develop a course or curriculum with a multiliteracies pedagogy, teachers should have a clear understanding of literacy and the nature of multiliteracies pedagogy. In Rowsell *et al.*'s (2008) study on pre-service teachers, a weak grasp of literacy and multiliteracies pedagogy coupled with the pressures of churning through content in the public school system made it challenging to pay attention to the individual cultures represented in the class. Fortunately, most higher education courses do not suffer from the same time pressures as secondary and elementary school classes. In collaboration with other departments, IEPs can play key roles in supporting a multiliteracies approach to open education. IEP professionals can assist instructors from other departments and their students gain background knowledge in languages, communication and sociology to navigate through the linguistic and cultural differences in an open learning environment, providing ample opportunities for research within and across these disciplines. For example, theories in intercultural communication, media literacy and translanguaging can be explored and tested, and in turn, this research can be immediately applied to the development of better-informed teaching practices.

A challenge with all this collaboration is compensating faculty and staff for their time and effort in making successful and innovative programs. The profit motive in US universities exerts an outsized influence upon the decision-making processes in higher education and in IEPs (Litzenberg, 2020), but I believe it is possible to run free and open projects while at the same time developing adjacent courses for credit and certificates. Funding these programs depends on the individual universities and departments involved, the scope of which is beyond this paper.

Conclusion

This chapter has shown the tenuous nature of the job market for English language professionals in the United States, specifically for those who wish to teach in or administer programs for adult, pre-university language learners. The data presented in this chapter are based on job announcements in HigherEdJobs.com and *The Chronicle of Higher Education* from 2010 to 2021 for full-time tenure and non-tenure professorships, community college teaching and administrative positions, university teaching and administrative positions and *Other* (i.e. jobs in publishing, test development and teaching in proprietary English schools for adult and higher education students). The number of job openings fluctuates from year to year, with some sectors having more than 160 openings in one year and others fewer than 10. A majority of the teaching positions were in IEPs throughout the 2010–2015 period, but were eclipsed by community college positions around 2016. This shift in IEP employment opportunities is likely a result of reduced government funding for English language studies, improved primary and secondary English language education in students' home countries, the high cost of a US education, increasing international competition and other factors external to the programs themselves. Indeed, the job market data correlate strongly with global trends in education and health (i.e. the Covid pandemic). IEPs do not seem to be the best option for stable employment. Additionally, a Master's degree is in many cases no longer the preferred qualification, with programs nowadays expressing a preference for professionals with a PhD. ELT positions in adult higher education are scarce, offer unpredictable long-term security, and are increasingly requiring more advanced qualifications.

Nevertheless, IEPs continue to innovate, searching for ways outside of traditional models that allow them to better address the needs of their current and future student populations. This chapter provided several suggestions, such as Pathway programming or an open bilingual multiliteracies program. Many English language teachers may be daunted by such innovations, moving into areas such applied linguistics or K-12. And, IEP professionals may find that many of their skills are transferrable (e.g. knowledge of pedagogical technologies) to other lines of work, such as instructional designer, where high demand exists for developing curricula for learners struggling with specific content knowledge and intercultural competencies. It is at the heart of English language teaching to make input comprehensible and to develop intercultural communication skills. These career paths, which some may find to be more financially secure, rewarding and even more culturally enriching, run parallel to English language teaching, and, of course, there is always opportunity to return to the field as markets shift. Professionals, however, should be prepared for changes, be willing to adapt the focus of their career trajectories, and maintain a flexible, open mind regarding the options before them.

Notes

(1) K-12 refers to Kindergarten through 12th Grade of the United States primary and secondary educational system.
(2) A group of 10 academics who met September 1994 in New London, New Hampshire, United States with the goal of developing a literacy pedagogy for educators.

References

Grawe, N. (2019) International student and U.S. higher education. *Econofact*. See https://econofact.org/international-students-and-u-s-higher-education (accessed November 2021).
Holloway, S.M. and Guthro, P.A. (2019) Mapping a multiliteracies pedagogical approach in adult education and higher education. *CASAE: Canadian Association for the Study of Adult Education* 38, 148–148. https://scholar.uwindsor.ca/educationpub/33.

Holloway, S.M. and Guthro, P.A. (2020) Using a multiliteracies approach to foster critical and creative pedagogies for adult learners. *Journal of Adult and Continuing Education* 26 (2), 203–220. https://doi.org/10.1177/1477971420913912.

Institute of International Education (2021) IEP enrollment by total students and total-student weeks, 2009–2020. Open Doors Report on International Educational Exchange. See https://www.opendoorsdata.org (accessed December 2021).

Koenig, R. (2021) Online tutoring in China was booming. Then came a dramatic shift in regulations. *EdSurge*, 26 July. See https://www.edsurge.com/news/2021-07-26-online-tutoring-in-china-was-booming-then-came-a-dramatic-shift-in-regulations (accessed January 2022).

Litzenberg, J. (2020) 'If I don't do it, somebody else will': Covert neoliberal policy discourses in the decision-making processes of an intensive English program. *TESOL Quarterly* 54 (4), 823–845.

Loo, B.K. (2016) Community colleges: An unexpected on-ramp for international students. *World Education News + Reviews*, 8 November. See https://wenr.wes.org/2016/11/international-students-u-s-community-colleges (accessed September 2021).

McPhee, S. and Pickren, G. (2017) Blended learning with international students: A multiliteracies approach. *Journal of Geography in Higher Education* 41 (3), 418–433. https://doi.org/10.1080/03098265.2017.1331208.

MLA Office of Research (n.d.) Reports on the MLA job list. *The Modern Language Association of America*. See https://www.mla.org/Resources/Career/Job-List/Reports-on-the-MLA-Job-List (accessed January 2022).

MLA Office of Research (2017) Report on the MLA job information list, 2016–17. *The Modern Language Association of America*, December. See https://www.mla.org/content/download/78816/2172744/Report-MLA-JIL-2016-17.pdf (accessed January 2022).

Monaghan, P. (2019) Academe as the dystopian workplace. *The Chronicle of Higher Education*, 24 November. See https://www.chronicle.com/article/academe-as-the-dystopian-workplace/ (accessed February 2022).

NAFSA (n.d.) Scholarships bring record number of Saudi students to United States. See https://www.nafsa.org/about/about-international-education/scholarships-bring-record-number-saudi-students-united-states (accessed February 2022).

National Center for Educational Statistics (2022) English learners in public schools. See https://nces.ed.gov/programs/coe/indicator/cgf/english-learners (accessed May 2022).

Patel, V. (2018) How a famous academic job-market study got it all wrong – and why it still matters. *The Chronicle of Higher Education*, 9 September. See https://www.chronicle.com/article/how-a-famous-academic-job-market-study-got-it-all-wrong-and-why-it-still-matters/ (accessed February 2022).

Pennington, M.C. (1992) Second class or economy? The status of the English language profession in tertiary education. *Prospect: An Australian journal of TESOL* 7 (3), 7–19.

Redden, E. (2016) Saudi enrollment declines. *Inside Higher Ed*, 18 July. See https://www.insidehighered.com/news/2016/07/18/saudi-student-numbers-fall-many-campuses (accessed September 2021).

Rowsell, J., Kosnick, C. and Beck, C. (2008) Fostering multiliteracies pedagogy through preservice teacher education. *Teaching Education* 19 (2), 109–122.

Stracke, C.M. (2019) Quality frameworks and learning design for open education. *The International Review of Research in Open and Distributed Learning* 20 (2), 180–203.

Study in the States (n.d.) Reminder: All F and M students must have the redesigned form I-20 by July 1, 2016. U.S. Department of Homeland Security. See https://studyinthestates.dhs.gov/2016/05/reminder-all-f-and-m-students-must-have-redesigned-form-i-20-july-1-2016 (accessed December 2021).

Study in the States (2021) Form I-17 – initial Certification. U.S. Department of Homeland Security, 5 October. See https://studyinthestates.dhs.gov/sevis-help-hub/school-records/school-certification/form-i-17-initial-certification (accessed December 2021).

VIPKid (n.d.) Teacher requirements. See https://www.vipkid.com/teach/teacher-requirements (accessed January 2022).

Walcutt, L. (2016) The scholarship struggle Saudi Arabian students are facing. *Forbes*, 28 September. See https://www.forbes.com/sites/leifwalcutt/2016/09/28/the-scholarship-struggle-saudi-arabian-students-are-facing/?sh=3b6dd761cd9b (accessed September 2021).

West, C. (2018) International students are keeping community colleges afloat. *Pacific Standard*, 12 March. See https://psmag.com/education/international-students-are-keeping-community-colleges-afloat (accessed September 2021).

Wheeler, W. (2021) Global connections: Why international students remain important for community colleges. *Community College Daily*, 11 March. See https://www.ccdaily.com/2021/03/global-connections-why-international-students-remain-important-for-community-colleges/ (accessed January 2022).

Winkle, C.A. (2014) *University Partnerships with the Corporate Sector: Faculty Experiences With For-Profit Matriculation Pathway Programs*. Leiden: Brill.

Zhang, D. and Zou, Y. (2020) Fostering multiliteracies through blended EFL learning. *International Journal of Linguistics, Literature and Translation* 3 (2), 40–48. https://doi.org/10.32996/ijllt.2020.3.2.5.

5 Beyond Revenue: IEP Service to the University and Community

Sarah Arva Grosik

Introduction

The first university-based English language programs in the United States began in the 1940s as service-oriented programs. In their inception, these programs were created by universities in an effort to provide English language instruction as a support for their international student populations. However, by the 1970s, universities had already realized the economic potential of such English language programs. Around that time, universities stopped seeing their IEPs solely as service programs for the international students on their campuses and, instead, began viewing their IEPs as revenue streams (Eaton, 2013; Eskey, 1997). In the decades since, many university-based IEPs have expanded and have become an important source for recruitment of pre- or non-matriculated international students. These IEPs now serve as an intermediary step for the many international students who cannot obtain direct admission to the degree program of their choice. Some of these IEPs function as a direct pipeline to matriculation in undergraduate and graduate degree programs at their host institution. While other IEPs, especially those situated in highly selective universities, provide admissions support and English language instruction for international students who are striving to gain acceptance into degree programs at their own and/or other selective and highly selective institutions. Students in this latter category of IEPs often work to complete numerous university applications while simultaneously endeavoring to improve their English proficiency and standardized test scores through their IEP studies. In either case, such university-based IEPs play an important role in preparing international students for their subsequent academic studies with a rigorous program of English language instruction and academic skills preparation. Nevertheless, these IEPs generally function as self-sustaining units within the university structure that are designed (and required) to generate a profit for their host institutions (Eaton, 2013; Litzenberg, 2021).

In addition to, or perhaps as a consequence of, the fact that IEPs function in a pay-for-service model, it is important to also consider the fact that IEPs have long held a marginalized status within their host institutions (Carkin, 1997; Grosik & Kanno, 2021; Litzenberg, 2021; Thompson, 2013; Williams, 1992). This marginalization manifests itself in a multitude of ways: program administrators and instructors who teach in these university-based ESL programs often hold non-tenure track positions without the affordances or academic privileges that come with full faculty appointments (Carkin, 1997; Eaton, 2013; Thompson, 2013); international students enrolled in IEPs are accorded unequal status within their host institutions as pre- or non-matriculated students who are not (yet) full-fledged members of the university community and generally receive no (or very little) credit for their IEP coursework (Grosik & Kanno, 2021; Williams, 1995); and IEPs, as programs, are often ill situated within the university structure and may be housed anywhere from the continuing education unit to the English department or even the international affairs office (Grosik & Kanno, 2021; Litzenberg, 2021; Thompson, 2013).

Despite their marginalized and monetized status, IEPs support their host institutions in various ways. IEPs play an important role in helping to diversify university campuses and therefore serve as a crucial element in the attainment of institutions' internationalization priorities. Furthermore, many universities across the United States rely on IEPs as a means of increasing their international student enrollments and improving access to underrepresented student groups. Moreover, these programs function as gatekeepers for access to higher education by offering international students the linguistic resource of academic English (Grosik & Kanno, 2021; Litzenberg, 2021). It is, thus, important to consider how the pay-for-service model impacts the access that IEPs are (and are not) able to provide: IEPs largely serve members of the global elite who are able to pay often hefty tuition rates of the IEP and (eventually) the host institution, while remaining unreachable for the majority of international students around the world. Those who do have the resources necessary to attend these programs believe that IEP enrollment and the subsequent degree program admissions will improve the human capital of themselves and/or their children (Litzenberg, 2021).

If internationalization, equity and access are, in fact, priorities of the academy, then the role that IEPs play in these initiatives cannot be ignored. Thus, we should argue for a reconceptualization of the nature and status of the university-based IEP as more than simply sources of revenue. This is not to suggest that IEPs should no longer generate revenue. Rather, the ways in which universities have marginalized their IEPs should be considered in relation to the non-monetary worth that these programs possess. In this way, IEPs should be re-envisioned for the value they (also) bring to their host institutions as service units. Building off the idea of reimagining IEPs as English Language Programs (ELPs) in a broader sense (Anderson & Godfrey, this volume), this chapter provides an overview of the variety of service-based programs that one IEP has created for both matriculated students within its host university and for a variety of groups outside of the university community. These service programs allow this IEP to not only demonstrate its diverse and dynamic value, but also its resilience and innovation in instructional design and delivery.

A Case Study

The IEP described in this chapter is contained within the English language programs at an elite, private university located within a large city in the northeast United States. This university enrolls 10,000 undergraduate students and nearly another 13,000 graduate students, while its yearly undergraduate tuition rate of almost US$62,000 makes it one of the most expensive universities in the nation. As is the case with many prestigious American universities, this university has made global engagement, inclusion and diversity strategic priorities with international students making up 13% of the most recent undergraduate class and 56% of that class being identified as racially and/or ethnically diverse. The IEP in question is situated within the College of Liberal and Professional Studies, the lifelong learning division of the university's School of Arts and Sciences. Despite its situation in this peripheral university unit, this IEP still enjoys many privileges associated with being housed at such a prestigious university, including the university's status and reputation, the diverse climate and the numerous student resources available on campus. Nevertheless, it is also important to note that this IEP's high tuition cost ($5600 for one seven-week session) limits access and leads to a certain exclusivity in this program. Consequently, the students who are able to afford to attend this IEP as a precursor to their degree studies tend to come from the type of affluent and privileged backgrounds described earlier.

IEP practitioners, such as myself, must acknowledge and contend with the inherent exclusivity and controlled access to the linguistic resources they provide through these programs. One way in which administrators and instructors can challenge the commodification of their instructional expertise is by engaging in service programs in tandem with their in-person intensive language programs.

Service within the university

University-based IEPs have long provided language support to the matriculated international students on their campuses and this IEP is no exception. Though the students enrolled in the IEP itself are largely non-matriculated international students, the administrators and instructors at this IEP have an extensive history of also providing English language support to matriculated graduate students from across the university. Here we see the limiting nature of the term IEP (Anderson & Godfrey, this volume) as the support provided by this English language program comes in a wide array of formats: we provide training and testing for international doctoral students seeking teaching assistantships; we offer credit-bearing courses on academic discourse skills and research paper writing for international doctoral students; we have developed and delivered targeted language programs for international students enrolled in graduate programs across the university (e.g. the business school, law school, nursing school, design school, etc.); we administer oral proficiency interviews for visiting scholars to demonstrate their English proficiency as a requirement of their J-1 visa[1]. This approach – serving as a resource connector across campus for international students – is not unique to this IEP but is often an (un)written mission of many IEPs across the country. In universities throughout the United States, academic departments repeatedly seek the perspective and linguistic expertise of IEP practitioners because they have a unique understanding of the language challenges inherent to academic study. The following sections offer an overview of the internal service programs that this IEP provides for matriculated students on its campus.

International teaching assistant training and testing

Every summer, this IEP is home to a seven-week intensive English program for matriculated international graduate students who will hold Teaching Assistant duties in the coming academic year. This institutional service program is not only free for all doctoral students in the School of Arts and Sciences who want to participate, but the graduate division at the school also pays them a robust stipend to participate. The IEP does not generate revenue from this program, but conducts it as a service to the students, the school, and the Provost's Office of the larger university. Historically, this program has enrolled 20–40 students each summer. These international teaching assistants (ITAs) hail from a variety of academic departments, with the majority enrolled in PhD programs in the Chemistry, Economics, Mathematics and Biology departments. These students represent a variety of L1 backgrounds, with Mandarin and Korean being the most frequent. This distribution of departments and languages is similar to other east coast institutions of comparable size who also run ITA development programs (Harklau & Coda, 2019). Because these students are entering doctoral programs, most of the participants are in their 20s, though there are usually a few more mature students who are making a career pivot. Over half arrive to campus for the first time in the summer in order to participate in the training program, whereas the remainder are generally rising second year doctoral students who have been encouraged to participate by their departments before assuming teaching responsibilities. During this training program, students attend two daily core courses and receive one-on-one tutoring sessions. In these courses, students focus on instructional language development and on improving their overall delivery in English, including segmental pronunciation, word stress and intonation. There is a programmatic emphasis on supporting students in honing their self-monitoring skills so that they may continue to develop after they exit the program. Further, program participants have the opportunity to review recordings of their practice teaching with an experienced TESOL professional who helps them attend to particular linguistic features.

Importantly, neither the IEP nor the Graduate Arts and Sciences division mandates that any particular student participate in the program. This is advantageous, as it means many of the students who enroll have self-identified into the program and are serious about improving their language. However, there is a state law that states that '…each institution of higher education operating in this commonwealth must file with the department a certification stating that the instructional faculty members…are fluent in the English language' (English Fluency in Higher Education Act, 1990, Sec. 4). To abide by this mandate, the university maintains a Standard of Fluency in the Faculty Handbook and assesses any nonnative speaking teaching assistants according to that standard prior to conferring any instructional appointments. Students can demonstrate their fluency to meet this mandate through one of two means: they may submit an adequate score report from an internationally recognized standardized test (e.g. TOEFL iBT, IELTS, etc.), or they must successfully pass an in-house language assessment administered by the IEP called the Interactive Performance Test (IPT). Successful completion of the Summer ITA Training Program does not exempt students from demonstrating their fluency with a test score, but it does help to prepare these students for passing the IPT.

In supporting the host university to meet this English fluency requirement, our IEP is responsible for administering, scoring and reporting IPT results once every semester. On average we assess the language skills of 200 students per year, which is no small feat. While we do assign a small charge to departments for any student that takes the IPT, it is simply to cover the administrative costs of space, raters and equipment. At the conclusion of each testing cycle, we produce fluency certificates that are approved by and filed with the Provost's Office in support of the yearly attestation with the state government. The IEP and university at large levy no penalty against students who do not pass the IPT, nor do we limit the number of times any student may attempt the test. However, students who fail the IPT will not receive teaching assistantship appointments from their departments, and if their programs do not have a proper Plan B in place, this can have implications for their living stipend (e.g. some students who have to delay serving as a teaching assistant must instead accept work as lab assistants, which is compensated at a lower rate).

As many readers are probably aware, the training and testing of ITAs is not without controversy (Subtirelu, 2017; Williams, 1992). However, at this IEP we assume a resource perspective in valuing the diversity these international students bring to their departments and the university at large. Further, we believe that the talents and skills of our international teaching assistants are vital in maintaining the university's intellectual excellence and standard of instructional quality. Frankly put, this university, like most around the country, relies on the time and talents of international TAs to educate the vast number of undergraduates it enrolls. Thus, ensuring that these individuals are provided with adequate support and training is crucial to serving not only the best interests of the ITAs themselves and their host departments, but those of the entire university community.

Academic speaking and writing courses

In addition to the non-credit summer training program, two semester-long courses are also offered by this IEP to address the language needs of international matriculated graduate students: one focused on oral English language skills and the other on academic writing development. Through these courses, the IEP team serves approximately an additional 30 international graduate students each year. The speaking course is a partial continuation of the ITA summer training program and serves to support instructional discourse development via practice teaching presentations, self-monitoring recorded speech samples, listening logs and group discussion of teaching strategies. Some students enroll in this course because they did not achieve fluency certification on the IPT upon completion of the summer training program, while others enroll because they were unavailable to join the summer program, but nonetheless recognize the need to improve their instructional discourse in English. Graduate study is a challenging academic endeavor for all students, and it is without question that the linguistic challenges that most international graduate students face throughout their academic study in the United States make this endeavor even more difficult for these students. In particular, many international students struggle with speaking production and listening comprehension in academic discourse throughout their graduate studies (Kuo, 2011; Ranta & Meckelborg, 2013). This course, then, is one small means of support to address this international student need.

The academic writing course, on the other hand, focuses exclusively on graduate level writing in English for students to apply in their coursework, dissertations and publications. This course is offered each fall and spring semester by the IEP staff, and frequently has a waiting list for participation. The course follows a typical structure for the first half – meeting twice a week, reviewing assigned readings and conducting writing exercises in pairs or small groups – but for the second half it transitions to a one-on-one writing consultation structure. Students send their instructor written work in advance of a recurring appointment and then they workshop that writing together, focusing on voice, flow, concision and appropriate academic citations. As with oral and listening support, international graduate students likewise have a need for academic English writing skill development and support throughout the duration of their graduate programs (Ravichandran *et al.*, 2017). Through both of these courses, this IEP is able to provide a critical service by offering linguistic support to the population of international graduate students they serve.

Tailored support for departments

In addition to the more general academic English support courses that this IEP offers, we have also designed and delivered courses, workshops and programs for specific academic departments and schools across our campus. Many of these supports have arisen out of an identified need from individual departments who request help from our IEP. These support programs and services have taken a variety of forms in order to support departments across campus including a series of communication workshops for international Dental students, admissions interview support for doctoral applicants in the Nursing school, a legal English elective for Master of Laws students, a series of workshops to provide targeted writing support for master's students in the School of Design and a professional writing course for cohorts in the Master of Business Administration program. Additionally, this IEP has also responded to expressed interdepartmental needs by offering evening workshops on pronunciation and writing, which are open to master's, doctoral and post-doctoral students from across the university community. Through these extensive programs, the IEP continually functions as an important lifeline that academic departments rely on to support their international graduate students.

Fluency testing for J-1 scholars

Another important support service that this IEP provides is the English language testing for J-1 scholars on its campus. In 2015, the US Department of State released new regulations for the J-1 Exchange Visitor Program that specified an English language proficiency requirement for its non-native English-speaking participants. In response to this regulatory change, the IEP collaborated with International Student and

Scholar Services (ISSS) and numerous university departments to create a plan of action to meet this requirement. This IEP has been an integral component of its host institution's verification of applicants' English language proficiency, through its expertise in establishing minimum score requirements on standardized English language tests and by creating an internal assessment for those individuals who do not have up-to-date standardized test scores. In order to assess scholars' English proficiency, the IEP modified an existing assessment tool to create an adapted advisory oral proficiency interview using the American Council on the Teaching of Foreign Languages (ACTFL) framework. This has involved extensive and continued in-house training in order to better support the university-wide needs by increasing the number of trained interviewers on staff at the IEP. Individuals coming to the university on J-1 visas include post-doctoral students, professors, research scholars and world-renowned experts who possess specialized knowledge in a specific field. To date, this IEP has conducted over 1000 interviews of such J-1 scholars. Coordinating the assessment and verifying English language proficiency of such a large number of individuals has required considerable interdepartmental and university stakeholder communications and management. With this important service, this IEP maintains an important role in supporting the larger university community by helping both the individual scholars and the departments in meeting this federal regulation.

All told, this IEP continues to provide considerable support to the matriculated international students and academic departments on its campus. These supports demonstrate value beyond that of an exclusively revenue-generating unit.

Linguistic service beyond

IEPs have long been sites of innovation and resilience; often forced to shift and reconceptualize program delivery models in response to sudden drops or increases in international student populations (Litzenberg, 2021). In the wake of the Covid pandemic, IEPs saw their in-person enrollments plummet as universities around the world had to make the sudden shift to online learning. While this change was challenging, to say the least, for the educational community at large, it was particularly problematic for IEPs who promote themselves as providing immersive language learning experiences. The ability to offer intensive in-person language instruction on US university campuses has long been the primary 'selling point' that these programs have used to distinguish themselves from English language programs available in students' home countries and has helped IEPs to justify their high tuition rates. Consequently, IEPs were once again forced to demonstrate their resilience and innovation when the Covid pandemic obliged them to embrace, or at least live with, online learning.

At the IEP in question, online learning platforms have allowed this program to expand both its reach and access to much wider global audiences. Online learning was already in place at this IEP when the pandemic hit; however, the majority of our focus had been on maintaining in-person programs prior to the spring of 2020. Indeed, a positive outcome of the pandemic has been that it has forced us to divert our attention away from in-person instruction so that we could instead focus on the creation of new programs and the re-envisioning of some of our existing program models. By offering online language courses to diverse learner populations outside of the university, IEPs can provide value to their host university through outward facing service programs. Such service programs can have a much greater reach than IEPs may otherwise be able to provide through in-person programs on their campuses. These external programs can take the form of grant-funded projects, partnerships with outside funders and community service programs. This section outlines the ways in which our IEP has engaged in external service programs in these three areas.

Grant-funded programs

Within higher education, grants provide an important avenue of financial support for a wide variety of research and educational initiatives. IEPs can do important work and bring value to their universities through grant-funded programs: grant funding can allow IEPs to create innovative instructional content and delivery models outside of the scope of their typical courses; grants can give IEPs an opportunity to provide instruction for learners who would otherwise be unable to access their language courses and programs; and when in-person student enrollments decline, as a result of global health or geopolitical issues, grant funding can provide a vital safety net for IEPs.

This IEP has engaged in numerous large-scale online language learning projects that have been funded primarily through grants from a variety of US federal agencies and diplomatic entities. In 2015, this IEP received a grant to create and administer five Massive Open Online Courses (MOOCs) from the US Department of State Bureau of Educational and Cultural Affairs, Office of English Language Programs. These MOOCs were designed for pre-intermediate and intermediate English learners worldwide with the goal of improving learners' English language skills, broadening their opportunities for professional growth and enhancing global understanding of the United States. Each MOOC was originally developed on the Coursera platform with the intent of providing content-based English language instruction in one of the following topic areas: Career Development, Business and Entrepreneurship, Journalism, Media Literacy and Science, Technology, Engineering and Mathematics.

Since these five MOOCs launched in 2016, they have reached nearly 2.5 million learners on the Coursera platform where they are still enrolling thousands of new learners each week. As the design and delivery for all of these courses was funded entirely through the grant, this project gave our program the opportunity to create five robust courses from scratch, while at the same time enabling us to innovate many of our instructional approaches to both online language learning and content-based instruction. Although the grant stipulated that we would administer each MOOC on Coursera for two years, we have continued to support and facilitate these courses in the years since the conclusion of the grant.

A significant aspect of the grant for the MOOC creation was that it stipulated that we create these courses as Open Educational Resources (OERs) under Creative Commons (CC) licensing. As a result, these courses and all of their individual components (i.e. video lectures, readings, quizzes, assignments, etc.) are able to be reused and repurposed for free distribution. This has provided an outlet for the courses and their content to reach even wider audiences. Although the number of OERs is ever growing, there still remains a dearth of OER courses that are linguistically accessible for learners with lower levels of English proficiency (Rets et al., 2020). Importantly, the MOOCs we created as part of this grant were designed for learners with pre-intermediate to intermediate levels of English language proficiency and thus, can be accessed by broader populations of English learners. Much of the reuse of these courses has been by outsiders unaffiliated with our program; however, we have also repurposed these materials for additional use internally as well. After the original grant for the MOOC creation and administration ended, we have continued to work with the Office of English Language programs at the US Department of State and US embassies on several other grant projects. These projects have allowed us to repurpose, expand on, and tailor some of the MOOC content and courses for specific learner populations.

In 2018, 2019 and 2021, the IEP received grants from the Office of English Language programs to design and deliver a version of the English for Journalism course for three separate cohorts of journalists in Kazakhstan. In delivering this tailored version of the MOOC, we moved the course content to Canvas and once again, had the opportunity to innovate the instructional model to meet the specific needs of these learners. These innovations to the program model included an in-person component and direct instructor feedback in order to provide a more robust learning experience. These grant projects were much smaller in scope than the original MOOCs, with each cohort containing between 82 to 295 learners. Nevertheless, the impact of providing over 500 journalists in Kazakhstan with a course that allowed them to gain confidence in their English language abilities and in their capacity to use English in journalistic contexts should not be underestimated. Most recently, this IEP has received a grant from the US Embassy in Seoul to provide a version of English for Career Development to six cohorts of embassy contacts during 2022 and 2023. In this model, students attend a weekly live class meeting with their instructor and receive instructor feedback on all major assignments. Throughout this two-year grant, we will be able to teach 300 learners about the job search, application, and interview process while helping them to improve their language skills to achieve their professional goals.

Certainly, these grant-funded projects have enabled this IEP to innovate its approaches to instructional design and delivery by engaging with new platforms, approaches, and technologies. But what is perhaps even more valuable to this IEP, and those of us who have worked on these projects, is that these grants have enabled us to democratize our instruction and reach millions of learners around the globe who we would have otherwise never have had the privilege of teaching.

Partnership scholarship programs

Another important way for university-based IEPs to be able to provide service beyond the bounds of its host institution is by partnering with outside organizations who can fund scholarships. Undoubtedly, many IEPs have partnerships with agencies and sponsors who pay for part or all of certain students' tuition to attend their in-person intensive program courses (Friedenberg, 2002; Grosik, 2017). Because the tuition for most university-based IEPs is so costly, these partnerships are incredibly important in diversifying student enrollment and increasing access to these in-person programs. However, there are many students who do not have the resources or capital to leave their home countries and attend an in-person IEP, even when a scholarship to cover tuition is given. For these such students, alternative opportunities for scholarships to participate in online programs can be particularly impactful.

At this IEP, one such scholarship opportunity has been developed by partnering with the philanthropic division of a multinational financial services company. Notably, it was the English for Career Development MOOC that led to this partnership. The philanthropic organization learned about our popular MOOC when looking for a partner to collaborate with in offering scholarships for an online English language course focused on advancing non-native English speakers' careers, but with more personalized attention than students would receive in a MOOC. Once more, we were able to repurpose the OER materials that we had created for the aforementioned MOOCs. In order to meet the needs of this population of students, we innovated once again to offer instructor-guided versions of English for Professional Development, English for Business and Entrepreneurship and English for Science,

Technology, Engineering and Mathematics. Our experience with the programs we ran for the journalists in Kazakhstan was able to inform our approach for this program as we shifted the instructional model to one that included a weekly live class meeting with an instructor as well as instructor feedback on all major assignments.

In 2021 and 2022 alone, we have been able to offer these instructor-guided online courses to 1500 students, all of whom received full scholarships to attend the program. These scholarships were aimed at non-native English speakers in South and Central America, along with Europe. These learners applied to participate in this program with the goal of improving their English language in hopes of advancing their career prospects in the global marketplace. There has been enormous interest in the opportunity to take these courses at no cost, which was demonstrated by the more than 36,000 applications we received for the 1000 scholarships that were offered by this program in 2022. Unquestionably, the massive number of applications we received is a testament for the need for more online English language courses offered to learners at no cost through scholarship programs.

Community service programs

There has long been a disconnect between university-based IEPs and their ability to provide English language instruction to the local immigrant communities in which they are situated. The high tuition costs and availability to attend full-time English language study causes IEP enrollment to be simply out of reach for most immigrant English learners. Instead, students attending these IEPs are almost always international students on F-1 visas who are able to participate in intensive English instruction as a steppingstone for furthering their ultimate academic and/or professional goals (Blanco et al., 2020; Hamrick, 2015). Since IEPs are largely unattainable for the majority of adult immigrants in their communities, these programs should look for alternative means to provide support to the English learners living in their communities.

This IEP recently had the opportunity to participate in such a community service program through a provost's office initiative to provide academic skill development, university preparation and career exploration to rising high school seniors living in the city where the university is situated. While this university-wide service program was not targeted specifically at English learners, it did provide a diverse population of high school students with a virtual summer program designed to improve post-secondary access. Not only is this program free of cost, but participating students also obtained a high school credit and some received a stipend of up to US$1000 for their completion of the program. In 2021, this IEP partnered with members of the foreign language and Middle East studies centers on campus to design and deliver a weeklong module on languages for global careers, which was repeated the following year. Through this collaboration, the IEP was able to participate in a university-wide service initiative aimed at increasing educational access and equity. While doing so, the IEP was also able to highlight the work that we do as language educators and give participating students the opportunity to consider international and language-based career pathways. Teaching in this program has allowed IEP administrators and instructors to engage directly with community members, such as the student who made the following anonymous comment on the program evaluation:

> I liked the global language one the most because I have always thought about studying abroad and then being a bilingual myself, I would like to probably learn more language and then take that elsewhere to benefit myself and others.

Although the long-term impacts of this program are yet to be seen, direct community service programs, such as this one, are a vital aspect of university outreach efforts in which IEPs should be involved.

Discussion and Implications

When considering the types of programs and services that are offered within a university-based IEP, it is important to consider the practitioners who are creating, administrating and teaching in these programs. IEP practitioners are educators and applied linguists. Many of these individuals entered the field of language education after living, studying and/or working abroad. These practitioners tend to be passionate about using language instruction as a vehicle for expanding educational access and opportunity to populations worldwide. Herein lies a fundamental contradiction between the motivations of IEP practitioners and the commodification of the language instruction that they are tasked to provide (Duchêne, 2020; Litzenberg, 2021). These IEP practitioners are largely unconcerned with the amount of revenue generated by the programs in which they teach and are instead motivated by teaching opportunities that allow them to work with a wide range of learners, beyond the privileged subset who are able to afford in-person IEP tuition, in developing their English proficiency. One way to address this incongruity is through English language service programs that IEPs can offer both internally to the matriculated international students in need of linguistic support on their campus and externally to global audiences beyond the bounds of their campuses (see Table 5.1). By reconceiving our programs in broader terms as ELPs, our roles in internationalization and multilingual learner support can become more visible within the university structure (Anderson & Godfrey, this volume).

Table 5.1 ELP service-based programs

Service within the university	Service beyond the university
• Training and testing for international teaching assistants • Courses for matriculated students • Tailored support for departments • Fluency testing for J-1 scholars	• Grant-funded programs • Partner-funded scholarship programs • Community service programs

The value of the institutional services that ELPs provide to their host universities across the country is often recognized and appreciated on individual student or faculty levels, but wider university appreciation is frequently missing. ELPs should seek to raise awareness of the inherent value that they provide to matriculated international students at the university level, perhaps through interactions with the graduate college(s) of the university and/or the Provost's office. This outreach and awareness raising will look a little different at each institution. However, one way to foster increased awareness is by establishing and maintaining networks of relationships with existing campus voices that advocate for their university's international learners. Yet this responsibility should not be left to the ELP administrators alone. Instead, university administration at higher levels must appreciate the value of their ELPs and accordingly, work to better integrate these programs into university-wide inclusion and diversity efforts. With increased support from central academic offices, ELPs can remain resilient and innovative. University administration will hopefully realize that even when intensive program enrollments decline, ELPs can still provide essential service to the university.

Internationalization has been a strategic priority for universities across the United States for more than three decades. However, it is now time to rethink how and what we are pursuing with this internationalization in higher education. Indeed, universities and those of us who work in higher education must be more intentional about our internationalization strategies and work in pursuit of a more 'inclusive international and intercultural learning for all' (de Wit, 2020: 33). ELPs must be seen as an important stakeholder in this reconceptualization of the global engagement initiatives on their campuses. One avenue to pursue a more intentional approach to internationalization is through the development of OERs. ELPs can play a particularly strong role in this endeavor by democratizing and increasing access to language education. When ELPs develop language learning courses and content that are openly accessible to learners worldwide, we can play a pivotal role in making global learning more inclusive for all.

Acknowledgements

I would like to extend my sincere thanks to Elizabeth Gillstrom for her expertise on these programs and her contribution to this chapter, Eve Nora Litt for her insight on J-1 scholar testing, and the students, instructors and administrators who I have the pleasure of working with at our ELP.

Note

(1) The U.S. Department of State website (Department of State, n.d) describes J-1 as: 'The Exchange Visitor (J) non-immigrant visa category is for individuals approved to participate in work-and study-based exchange visitor programs'.

References

Blanco, K., Tanner, M.W., Hartshorn, K.J. and Eggington, W.G. (2020) Factors influencing ESL students' selection of intensive English programs in the Western United States. *TESOL Journal* 11 (3), e00510. https://doi.org/10.1002/tesj.510.

Carkin, S. (1997) Language program leadership as intercultural management. In M.A. Christison and F.L. Stoller (eds) *A Handbook for Language Program Administrators* (pp. 49–60). Burlingame, CA: Alta Book Center Publishers.

de Wit, H. (2020) Internationalization of higher education. *Journal of International Students* 10 (1), 31–37. https://doi.org/10.32674/jis.v10i1.1893.

Department of State (n.d.) J-1 visa basics. See https://j1visa.state.gov/basics/ (accessed July 2023).

Duchêne, A. (2020) Multilingualism: An insufficient answer to sociolinguistic inequalities. *International Journal of the Sociology of Language* 2020 (263), 91–97. https://doi.org/10.1515/ijsl-2020-2087.

Eaton, S.E. (2013) The administration of English as a second language (ESL) program in higher education: Striking the balance between generating revenue and serving students. In Y. Hébert and A.A. Abdi (eds) *Critical Perspectives on International Education* (pp. 165–180). Rotterdam: Sense.

English Fluency in Higher Education Act of 1990. See https://www.legis.state.pa.us/WU01/LI/LI/US/PDF/1990/0/0076..PDF (accessed March 2022).

Eskey, D.E. (1997) The IEP as a nontraditional entity. In M.A. Christison and F.L. Stoller (eds) *A Handbook for Language Program Administrators* (pp. 21–30). Burlingame, CA: Alta Book Center Publishers.

Friedenberg, J.E. (2002) The linguistic inaccessibility of US higher education and the inherent inequity of US IEPs: An argument for multilingual higher education. *Bilingual Research Journal* 26 (2), 309–326. https://doi.org/10.1080/15235882.2002.10668713.

Grosik, S.A. (2017) The path to university admission in the United States through intensive English programs. (Publication No. 10604241). Unpublished doctoral dissertation, Temple University. ProQuest Dissertations & Theses Global.

Grosik, S.A. and Kanno, Y. (2021) Peripheral or marginal participation? University-based intensive English programs as an entryway to US academia. *Journal of International Students* 11 (4), 914–931. https://doi.org/10.32674/jis.v11i4.1828.

Hamrick, J. (2015) Intensive English programs. In M. Christison and F.L. Stoller (eds) *A Handbook for Language Program Administrators* (2nd edn, pp. 321–328). Palm Springs, CA: Alta English.

Harklau, L. and Coda, J. (2019) Situating ITAs in higher education and immigration policy studies. In S.D. Looney and S. Bhalla (eds) *A Transdisciplinary Approach to International Teaching Assistants: Perspectives from Applied Linguistics* (pp. 136–153). Bristol: Multilingual Matters.

Kuo, Y.H. (2011) Language challenges faced by international graduate students in the United States. *Journal of International Students* 1 (2), 38–42.

Litzenberg, J. (2021) Innovation, resiliency, and genius in intensive English programs: Decolonializing recruitment and contradictory advocacy. *Applied Linguistics* 42 (5), 905–923. https://doi.org/10.1093/applin/amab015.

Ranta, L. and Meckelborg, A. (2013) How much exposure to English do international graduate students really get? Measuring language use in a naturalistic setting. *The Canadian Modern Language Review* 69 (1), 1–33. https://doi.org/10.3138/cmlr.987.

Ravichandran, S., Kretovics, M., Kirby, K. and Ghosh, A. (2017) Strategies to address English language writing challenges faced by international graduate students in the US. *Journal of International Students* 7 (3), 3–7. https://doi.org/10.5281/zenodo.570033.

Rets, I., Coughlan, T., Stickler, U. and Astruc, L. (2020) Accessibility of open educational resources: How well are they suited for English learners? *Open Learning: The Journal of Open, Distance and e-Learning* 38 (1), 38–57. https://doi.org/10.1080/02680513.2020.1769585.

Subtirelu, N.C. (2017) Students' orientations to communication across linguistic difference with international teaching assistants at an internationalizing university in the United States. *Multilingua* 36 (3), 247–280. https://doi.org/10.1515/multi-2016-0061.

Thompson, A.S. (2013) Intensive English programs in the United States: An overview of structure and mentoring. *TESOL Journal* 4 (2), 211–232. https://doi.org/10.1002/tesj.55.

Williams, J. (1992) Planning, discourse marking, and the comprehensibility of international teaching assistants. *TESOL Quarterly* 26 (4), 693–711.

6 Multilingualism, Multiculturalism and Advocacy: How Intensive English Language Programs can Impact Campus Culture

Michael E. Anderson and LeeAnne Berger Godfrey

Introduction

As previously described in this volume, intensive English programs (IEPs) have often been situated on the periphery of university functions, sometimes seen as just revenue generators that bring more international students to degree programs at an institution, and places where students study to achieve the minimum proficiency to get into the university. However, there are other roles that IEPs can play within universities, including being a place where students prepare culturally, linguistically and socially for participating in university life and also as units that support multilingual students[1] throughout their careers at university as well as support the people who work with them.

One of the reasons colleges and universities recruit international students is to advance campus internationalization goals. The American Council of Education (ACE) defines internationalization as 'a strategic, coordinated framework that integrates policies, programs, initiatives, and individuals to make colleges and universities more globally oriented and internationally connected' (American Council on Education, n.d.: para. 1). One way of accomplishing internationalization goals is by bringing a broad group of international students to campus. International students bring linguistic and cultural diversity to university campuses and, with that, new perspectives and ways of knowing. These varied backgrounds are seen as particularly beneficial for infusing the campus with global perspectives and providing all students with opportunities to develop intercultural competence and appreciation for diversity (Hoekje & Stevens, 2018; Mikk & Steglitz, 2017).

IEPs have and continue to play a role in campus internationalization goals because they attract students from various parts of the world who want to learn and develop English in an immersive academic setting. They support students in their linguistic and academic transition. Eventually, many IEP students go on to enroll in degree programs at the university.

While IEPs have been important to the recruitment of international students, they have not always been recognized as being part of university-wide efforts in internationalization. Campus internationalization strives to ensure that domestic students, along with international students on campus, develop global competencies and are prepared to work in diverse global environments. IEPs have not always been perceived as integral to this work. Instead, they have been thought of as the place where students initially study when arriving at the university until their English language skills are adequate to join the university community. This deficit approach separates newly arrived multilingual learners of English from the broader university community and misses an opportunity to have an integrated approach to language learning that recognizes the continuous nature of language development and the benefits of an approach to internationalization that is inclusive of all students on campus.

IEPs, Internationalization and Diversity, Equity and Inclusion

In recent years, institutions of higher education have increased attention to diversity, equity and inclusion (DEI) across campus activities. Campus internationalization efforts are no exception. In fact, ACE's most recent framework of comprehensive internationalization now includes an overarching DEI lens and calls for internationalization efforts to be 'anti-colonial, anti-racist, and globally and locally inclusive' and that in doing so, institutions need to 'actively consider who is part of planning and decision-making' (American Council on Education, n.d.: para. 4). Given IEPs' connection to internationalization, this is a call to be part of these efforts and to work to bridge a common international (global) and multicultural (local) divide. Especially relevant to IEPs is that this updated internationalization framework also names linguistic diversity as something that needs to be accounted for. This is important because DEI initiatives often don't explicitly name the role of language or linguistic diversity in their work despite the deep connections between language and identity, language and power and language and access to learning – issues that international and multicultural students may share. How these issues and experiences are addressed on campuses can impact the success of campus internationalization efforts, making IEPs more central to campus-wide DEI work.

Students who come to IEPs to study English often do so to gain access to education at US institutions or increased social capital and economic power often afforded to those with English language skills. This language learning endeavor and the ensuing commodification of English has greatly benefited IEPs and their hosting institutions, financially and by increasing campus diversity. However, the teaching of English, and the field of TESOL as a whole, is deeply rooted in colonialism, linguistic imperialism, racism and Whiteness (e.g. Canagarajah, 1999; Flores, 2020; Gerald, 2020; Kubota & Lin, 2006; Motha, 2014; Phillipson, 1997; Rosa & Flores, 2017). In addition, the global dominance of English has contributed to creating and maintaining social inequalities related to who has access to English and which variety of English is taught or used. This, in turn, can impact who is able to participate in US higher education and whose linguistic skills are valued. While on the one hand IEPs serve a market for English language instruction, they, along with their hosting institutions, have also been complicit in maintaining the dominance of English and upholding colonial ideologies (for further discussion see Litzenberg, 2021).

Shifting course in terms of these ideologies and practices necessitates coordinated and sustained efforts. IEPs need to work with other units on campus such as campus internationalization offices, equity and diversity offices, multicultural centers and centers of teaching and learning to ensure that English language learning is not remedial work and that 'non-standard' varieties and accents of English are not considered deficient or lesser in any way. As campuses attempt to fulfill DEI initiatives, it is essential to consider (English) language ideologies and ways that classroom instruction take up decolonizing, anti-racist and inclusive practices. In addition, it is important to collect data on the performance, engagement and satisfaction of multilingual students on campus. As Evans and Andrade (2015: 19) explain, 'Both national and global discussions on access and success must include those for whom English is not a first language. English language proficiency is not recognized as contributing to a lack of participation or completion, primarily because the ESL population is generally not identified or tracked at institutional or national levels'.

Scholars in TESOL, applied linguistics and sociolinguistics, and other related fields, have been highlighting ways English language teaching and the teaching of multilingual students in content classrooms can be more just and inclusive (e.g. Flores, 2020; Hsu, 2017; Kumaravadivelu, 2006a; Motha, 2014; Rosa & Flores, 2017). Rosa and Flores (2017), for example, challenge the idea of English language learning as simply expanding linguistic repertoires and developing 'appropriate' forms of language for specific contexts particularly with goals of social mobility because it doesn't address the underlying problem of racism. They explain that 'antiracist social transformation cannot be based solely on teaching Latinx students to engage in the linguistic practices of the White speaking subject, but must also work actively to dismantle the hierarchies that produce the White listening subject' (2017: 187). While focused on the Latinx population this is also true for other marginalized groups. As more attention is given to ways the field of TESOL can be more just, IEPs should serve as leaders and models on campus in ensuring English language students develop critical understanding of the role of English in their own lives as well as in broader society. And, more importantly, they can contribute to the campus community understanding of the importance of a linguistically inclusive campus where non-standard varieties of English are destigmatized, where multilingualism (and multi-dialectism, when people speak two or more different dialects of a language) is valued, and where language learning is recognized for being an ongoing developmental process.

This shift in the way (English) language use and acquisition is perceived can help foster a greater sense of belonging to the university community for linguistically diverse students, including multilingual users of English. However, in order for diverse, international, multilingual IEP students to truly contribute to and benefit from internationalization efforts and global competency goals, they need to be integrated into the host institution and brought into the fold of university activities, both socially and academically. Unfortunately, this is not always the case for international students, who often feel a sense of isolation and long for more connection with domestic students (Anderson *et al.*, 2012).

Focusing specifically on IEP students, Grosik and Kanno (2021) explored the role one IEP played in supporting international student participation and integration into the broader university. They found that, while IEP students felt integrated and fully part of the IEP program and ultimately prepared for their university studies, they did not feel fully part of the broader university community. Even students who were taking IEP courses along with mainstream disciplinary credit courses did not feel like they were socially integrated into the university and with domestic students. The students recognized the linguistic and academic benefits of the concurrent enrollment but expressed difficulty in connecting with domestic students, despite their efforts. This is a problem in terms of both internationalization and DEI efforts and points to a need for opportunities to foster interactions between IEP and domestic matriculated students and to combat perceived and real boundaries of being affiliated as an IEP student and being a multilingual user of English. This marginalization could be further exacerbated due to IEP programs often operating on the margins of campuses physically and/or administratively (see Litzenberg, 2021).

We propose, therefore, that IEPs must further continue innovating and making contributions to university internationalization and DEI goals. Likewise, universities must include IEPs in their strategic efforts in these areas. As called for by ACE, IEPs need to be more central to university internationalization planning (American Council on Education, n.d.).

IEPs are shifting their practices and approaches to improve and support the experiences of multilingual users of English throughout their careers on campus and supporting them in being more critical consumers of English. As we will discuss, IEPs are expanding and diversifying what they do on campus, offering more credit classes, providing faculty trainings about supporting multilingual students and developing pathway programs (Hoekje & Stevens, 2018). They are providing programming through asset-based models that promote student learning and intercultural development and working to shift campus ideologies. These innovations can be seen in a variety of approaches that recognize and value language learning as an on-going process, while still supporting multilingual learners of English in their English learning and intercultural development.

Innovations

IEPs are organizationally unique on university campuses and often function both as academic and service units. They provide academic programs, but also provide services to students and others throughout the institution. Being such, the term IEP might not accurately describe what many programs do. IEPS are often part of a larger set of services and programs that the language center or department offers. It is important to have a term that encompasses the full set of English language programming but still differentiates it from the English literature program. Because of this, English language program (ELP) might be a broader term to describe these centers, though some studies have shown that it is a term that has been less frequently used since the 1990s (see Litzenberg & Kim, this volume). IEPs (or ELPs) have faculty and staff who are trained professionals with degrees in language acquisition and intercultural communication. With this expertise, they have the capacity to empower students, shift campus ideologies and provide professional development to the broader university community as well as support DEI efforts. Universities with very focused IEPs should consider other ways the programs can play broader roles within the institution. In what follows, we highlight current innovations that IEPs are undertaking to lead change on university campuses.

Empowering students

An important innovation in IEPs is how some are taking up the liberatory, anti-colonial, anti-racist and linguistically inclusive practices researched and advocated for in the fields of TESOL and applied linguistics. In the past, instruction in IEPs often focused on the development of English proficiency, assuming that speaking 'standard' English was the goal of all students. Often programs did not examine why students were compelled to study English, nor did they overtly recognize the importance of all the languages a student speaks. However, there is reason to believe that is changing (e.g. Klco, 2022). Some innovations within IEPs include employing pedagogies that draw on critical language awareness, plurilingual instruction, translanguaging or culturally sustaining pedagogies, which encourage instructors and students to critically examine themselves, their work, and the societal systems that uphold linguistic power and move beyond the simple focus on 'standard' English language proficiency. These critical approaches, in both large and small ways, can help empower students to advocate for themselves while also developing the English language skills and academic cultural understanding to fully participate in the university system. Litzenberg (2021: 920) suggests that IEPs can work to decolonize their own practices and effect change in subtle and more bottom up ways, such as 'in the design of curricula and the selection of materials, the representation of languages and cultures beyond those of the Global North, and the extent to which IEP students are "acculturated"'. By starting their careers at the university in a program that embraces diverse forms and accents of English and values diverse ideas, students can feel empowered and supported as they move on to degree programs.

Some innovative examples of such curricula are found in Galante's (2020a, 2020b) work on implementing plurilingual pedagogies in academic English classes in Canada. Plurilingual instruction is rooted in theories that 'oppose the monolingual tradition in TESOL and reject the idealized native speaker of a language as benchmark for measuring proficiency levels' (Galante *et al.*, 2020: 982) and draws on students' full linguistic repertoires (e.g. diverse languages and dialects or varieties of English) versus employing 'standard' English-only instruction. A plurilingual approach can work to shift common notions of linguistic deficit and empower students to recognize their own linguistic skills and assets (Payant & Galante, 2022; Suraweera, 2022). Allowing, even encouraging, students to use language(s) other than academic English can feel counterintuitive, particularly when the programmatic goals have been to focus on the development of academic English and approaches are steeped in a monolingual tradition. However, the innovative practice of taking up a plurilingual approach led Galante (2020a, 2020b) to develop assignments and tasks that 'included metalinguistic and cross-cultural reflections, and critically examined language status, language varieties, behaviours, values, and relations of power' (2020a: 242) which in turn 'allowed students to use their plurilingual agency to make mindful decisions about their language use and academic needs' (2020a: 248). Galante (2020a) explained how students used this agency while developing an understanding of the linguistic and cultural norms of the Canadian university and ultimately contributed to their academic success. Galante was also able to show the impact of plurilingual instruction on student self-awareness, 'plurilingual instruction enhances EAP students' sense of their plurilingual identities, from the recognition of the multiple languages and cultures within their repertoires to their creative representations of their linguistic and cultural resources' (2020b: 574).

Another innovative curricular approach in IEPs that also helps further campus DEI goals is the intentional use of content that exposes students to critical social issues and aims to promote social justice while developing English language and critical thinking skills. A recent case study by Mortenson (2022) illustrates the benefits of integrating a social-justice oriented approach to an English for specific purposes class. Course content and readings were selected with the goal of de-silencing race and exploring themes of justice, liberation, marginalization and equity. Students engaged with the readings and themes through a mix of formal and informal writing that included process writing of essays, classroom discussions and debates. Analyses demonstrated that the students, international multilingual learners of English, gained better understandings of racial inequities in the United States, made comparisons of systems of oppression between home countries and the United States and developed activist stances (Mortenson, 2022). Similarly, Walsh Marr (2019) reports on academic English courses she teaches that center First Nations' issues and activism in Canada. Using a content-based approach to teaching language, Walsh Marr supports students in critical examination of language (e.g. morphology, tenses, voice, evaluative language) and how it is used to construct meaning. In their work, Mortenson (2022) and Walsh Marr (2019) highlight the ability of the students to engage with critical materials and important ways IEPs can chose to disrupt white supremacist and colonialist traditions. It is important to note that these critical and justice-orientated approaches still aim to support students in their English language development and include attention to language use, form and meaning. The intertwining of both is beneficial to IEP students and to campus internationalization and DEI efforts (for further discussion see Walsh Marr, 2021).

Finally, other ways IEPs can and are working to empower students and decolonize the curriculum is by being intentional about representation, both in terms of materials and instructors. Materials could include texts that use World Englishes or that depict stories of immigration/migration and study abroad. Hiring culturally and linguistically diverse instructors can also serve to disrupt ideas related to ownership of English and notions of 'standard' English (Kumaravadivelu, 2006b). This can also better prepare students for communicating across accents and varieties of English they will likely encounter in globally diverse environments. These are only a few, but important, examples of ways IEPs are effectively taking up innovative pedagogical approaches that align with internationalization and DEI efforts. These approaches support students in developing linguistic and academic skills while empowering them to effect change. IEPs have much to learn from these examples as do instructors across the curriculum.

With a heightened awareness of language and greater sense of agency, students can then more actively participate in and contribute to internationalization efforts. This makes the goals of developing global competence mutually beneficial and therefore more accessible and inclusive. It also moves IEPs away from assimilationist approaches, where native English speakers are the norm and blending in is the goal. Instead, it aligns with multicultural approaches that aim to 'preserve group identities and protect endangered identities' and seek 'empowerment of the oppressed or neglected' (Geller, 2017: 18). Beyond this, other innovations in IEPs include work being done to shift broader campus language ideologies including normalizing language development and acquisition and valuing and using multilingual language skills.

Normalizing and valuing language learning

Higher education in the United States often assumes a linguistic homogeneity (Matsuda, 2006) and tends to operate from a monolingual tradition where 'standard' academic English holds power; and use of other languages or varieties of English is often not valued, or worse, is the source of linguicism. This can cause large groups of linguistic minorities, including international multilingual English language users, to be viewed from a deficit perspective, with a focus placed on the linguistic skills students appear to be lacking versus the acknowledgement of the skills they have. Studies have shown that students who are developing English skills can be embarrassed by errors they make and be more reluctant to participate in classes with native speakers (Anderson *et al.*, 2012; Evans & Andrade, 2015). Likewise, faculty and staff who work with multilingual users of English may be reluctant to give feedback on ways to improve proficiency for fear of shaming the student (Peters & Anderson, 2021). This environment of shame around language learning can hinder development when learners avoid taking risks in using the target language or avoid taking advantage of supports that accelerate their language development. Institutions need to create an environment of inclusion where multilingualism is valued and continued language learning is normalized and recognized as an important part of skills development for all students.

A deficit approach fails to recognize that all language learning, including academic language learning, is a long-term developmental process (Evans & Andrade, 2015). All students, not just multilingual students, learn new genres of writing, new vocabulary and new rhetorical ways of speaking while in degree programs. Research in academic discourse socialization demonstrates that students, especially learners of English, often benefit from explicit attention to the often subtle, even hidden, ways language is used across disciplines (e.g. Duff, 2010). IEPs support multilingual English learners in this socialization process through a language-focused environment as a first step in studying at a university. This part of their journey, while focusing on language primarily, is no less important than the other stages of their education. As a student exits an IEP and moves on to work in a degree program, for example, their language development continues and can be supported by other classes and support that the English program offers. It is the responsibility of the institution to provide support for multilingual students so that they can fully access and achieve success in the programs in which they are enrolled (Andrade *et al.*, 2015). As experts in the field of language acquisition, IEP faculty can help shift away from a deficit model and support internationalization and DEI efforts in doing so (e.g. Walsh Marr, 2021). However, shifting perspectives on campus to normalize on-going language development can be a challenge. So how do we affect change?

Updating Terminology: 'Multilingual'

One basic – yet important and innovative – way to shift campus ideologies is by changing how we talk about language acquisition. Using more asset-focused and decolonized terminology when referring students can demonstrate a change in perspective to students and to faculty and staff. Rather than using the terms such as non-native English speaker (NNES), for example, which describes what the person is not, one can use a term such as *multilingual student* when referring to students who come to the university as international English language learners. Some people use other asset-focused terminology such *second language user* rather than *second language learner* to describe multilingual students (Cook, 2002). The intent here is to acknowledge the diversity of the linguistic skills when referring to these students, rather than leading with what the student is not, and create a more inclusive and welcoming environment where developing language is celebrated and supported and not shamed. We do realize that the unique needs and circumstances of international English language users can sometimes be lost in this terminology and the term multilingual could also describe domestic students who speak more than one language, however the benefits may outweigh the lack of specificity.

Using a term such as *multilingual* helps promote an equality of languages, not putting one language as more important than others, and leads with an asset mindset versus being focused on a language deficiency. In communications across campus about better serving multilingual students, this term helps highlight the language skills and accomplishments of these students and can serve to position them more positively. The discussions become less about how to 'fix a deficiency' and more about how language skills are assets to be built upon and expanded and afford learners unique perspectives that can be shared with all in the classroom. Inclusion means also including multilingual students as part of internationalizing the curriculum and campus efforts.

When engaging with colleagues across campus, we also highlight the importance of leveraging students' multilingual skills for the diverse perspectives they bring to the classroom. This means inviting students to share how their languages might inform their views on a topic or allowing students to translanguage. It does not mean asking students to be unpaid interpreters or translators or to do other things that could be exploitative. The former aligns with internationalization efforts in which many faculty and staff are invested. With language comes a cultural lens and a unique perspective on the world. Encouraging students to tap into existing linguistic resources or learn new languages opens the opportunity for them to see and understand ideas and problems and potential solutions in different ways. It is important to normalize the ongoing learning and development of all languages, native and additional. This works to combat notions of remedial work sometimes connected to taking English language classes and brings all students into the fold of language learning. We can talk about English language learning and development in the same vein as talking about learning other global languages. We can and should highlight the added communicative power enabled by each language and variety of language a person has access to.

While we recognize that changing the language we use does not necessarily change practices in classrooms, it can be a step in changing attitudes. In some cases, it might also be a tool for opening up a discussion. When presenting to colleagues across campus, for example, one might begin with explaining what group a term refers to and why you choose to use that terminology. Likewise, IEP instructors can incorporate discussion about terminology and identity into English classes and invite student input on terms used in university processes.

Connecting to world language teaching

This innovative way of talking about English language learning and development also aims to value language learning and multilingualism across campus. It de-emphasizes ideas of deficit and fosters shared goals of developing multilingual competence. This provides opportunities for interesting collaborations between IEPs with campus language centers, individual language departments, and cultures and language across the curriculum (CLAC) initiatives, which all seek to make language learning a more integrated experience and contribute to internationalization efforts (Anderson, 2017). For example, some colleges are offering sections of undergraduate classes in languages such as Chinese, Spanish and Arabic (Pappano, 2019), or offering courses in a bilingual format using English and another language to teach math, political science or art history. Learners in these classes have the opportunity to expand a home language or further develop a learned language by using the language in a new academic setting and discipline. This opens up the curriculum to new multicultural perspectives and encourages curriculum development that creates meaningful cross-cultural interactions. In addition, instructors with linguistic skills in a language other than English become valued in a new way. This kind of dual language learning experience also shifts the power dynamics and role of the expert/novice among the students in the room in terms of language and demonstrates how an institution values multilingualism.

Giving Credit

Another way universities can demonstrate that they value English language learning is to grant college credit for English language coursework. While institutions of higher learning are set up in different ways, granting credit is the system within higher education to recognize a skill or knowledge as valued. Some IEPs offer credit for the courses in their intensive programs, while others offer credit courses to degree-seeking students. At the University of Minnesota, we offer a selection of credit-bearing academic English classes to students who are already in degree programs. These courses contribute to the students' credit load. For undergraduates, these courses are offered as upper-division courses at the 3000 level, indicating advanced content knowledge, equivalent to other courses taken by juniors and seniors. This aligns these English courses with courses taught in the foreign language departments in terms of proficiency. It recognizes that students taking these English courses are at a high level of proficiency already, certainly higher than the first two years of study in a language. This sends a message to students that having a strong proficiency in English is valued as much as having a strong proficiency in any other language taught at the institution.

While granting credit for English language courses is one thing an English language program can do, institutions can further innovate by including on-going English learning into other institutional options. One option is to align academic English courses with the liberal or general education requirements of the college or university. Academic English courses can and should fulfill requirements in areas such as writing, global perspectives, and so forth. This, of course, means ensuring course content and assignments align with the stated university outcomes for each of these designations. Another option is to offer a minor in English language proficiency or applied English studies. The latter could include courses that address language and identity, language and power and second language acquisition. An advanced English proficiency minor could focus on general academic English or be customized to a particular area such as business English or English for science and engineering. By filling core university requirements, academic English classes become more valuable and attractive to students and overtly recognizes how the university values the ongoing development of English language skills.

Supporting Faculty and Staff

In addition to courses or programs that they offer, IEPs can play a role by extending their expertise in adult education, in second language acquisition (SLA), and in intercultural education to impact and support the entire university community. An innovation at the University of Minnesota has been the creation of a position called faculty and staff liaison that is housed in the Minnesota English Language Program (MELP) and aims to support faculty and staff across campus in better serving international and multilingual students. The role is one of several projects across campus funded through an international undergraduate student fee. The faculty and staff liaison position uplifts the expertise of the unit, English language and culture teaching and sociolinguistics. Again, this is a way that an ELP can extend its work beyond offering IEP classes and become more central to supporting multilingual students across the university. The liaison does various projects to support faculty and staff who work with multilingual users of English. Some of the work includes providing workshops to faculty in various departments on working with multilingual and multicultural students, providing one-on-one consultations with faculty on issues related to supporting multilingual students, and providing resources for faculty, staff, and students.

Over time, the liaison role has also engaged in research to help inform the initiatives they undertake. Research has included work on understanding faculty perceptions related to supporting multilingual students (Peters & Anderson, 2021), as well as how international students coped with the switch to online learning during the pandemic (Godfrey & Yu, 2021). The liaison role has developed a resource website that includes two parts, resources for faculty and staff about supporting multilingual users of English, and also resources for students related to English language and intercultural learning (Minnesota English Language Program [MELP], n.d.). The content of this website is based on research findings concerning the needs of faculty and staff as well as students. Some of the pages that receive the most traffic include the topics of accommodations for multilingual students in content courses and supporting multilingual students in online learning.

The faculty and staff liaison role has helped increase visibility of the IEP and its other English programs and provides advocacy for multilingual students. The liaison does this by developing and strengthening important collaborations and partnerships with various units across campus including: International Student and Scholar Services, Internationalization of the Campus & Curriculum, Center of

Educational Innovation (the campus center for teaching and learning) and individual degree programs and departments including advisors. This has meant that a voice with expertise in language and culture acquisition and awareness of linguistic (in)justice and role of English in society, has been at the table and part of numerous conversations and efforts related to supporting students and faculty/staff.

The faculty and staff liaison has also been able to educate people on campus about the importance of approaching multilingual users of English from a strengths perspective and remind people of how small adjustments can make courses more inclusive and open up a rich sharing of different cultural perspectives. This role has expanded the work of the IEP beyond its intensive English classes to provide support to the entire campus and foster a linguistically inclusive and equitable learning environment.

Conclusion

The traditional role of IEPs on university campuses is changing, and it is innovation that is pushing these changes. IEPs have widely been viewed from a deficit perspective in the past, as places where students went to prepare their English for future study in a degree program, and as places where students worked on remedial skills that were not valued until they were perfected. As universities strive to internationalize their curricula and be more inclusive of all students, it is clear that plans around internationalization and DEI efforts must include the multilingual students. IEPs, or perhaps better termed English language programs, at universities are diversifying what they do and playing a more central role in supporting multilingual users of English on campus and in turn are integral to campus internationalization and DEI work. Innovations they are undertaking include moving away from a deficit perspective though terminology and also discussions of inclusion on campus. IEPs are enriching their curriculums to include more diverse and critical perspectives and to overtly recognize the importance of multilingualism. In addition, the English skills of multilingual students need to be valued in the university systems, so programs are granting credit for English language coursework and minors that send a clear message to students that their on-going language development is valued. Experts from English language programs providing support and resources to faculty and staff across campus is another way to have a positive impact on how multilingual users of English are viewed and included in classes and other activities.

Note

(1) We recognize the importance of terminology as well as the related ideologies and practices. In this paper, we have chosen to use the term multilingual to refer to English language learners to highlight linguistic and cultural assets.

References

American Council on Education (n.d.) Comprehensive internationalization framework. See https://www.acenet.edu/Research-Insights/Pages/Internationalization/CIGE-Model-for-Comprehensive-Internationalization.aspx (accessed March 2022).

Anderson, M.E. (2017) An English-as-a-second-language response and invitation to 'Making change happen.' *Modern Language Journal* 101 (2), 440–442. https://doi-org.ezp1.lib.umn.edu/10.1111/modl.12425.

Anderson, M.E., Isensee, B., Martin, K., Godfrey, L.B. and O'Brien, M.K. (2012) Student voices: A survey of international undergraduate students' first-year challenges at the University of Minnesota - Twin Cities. See https://global.umn.edu/icc/student-voices/index.html (accessed March 2022).

Andrade, M.S., Evans, N.W. and Hartshorn, K.J. (2015) Perceptions and realities of ESL students in higher education. In N.W. Evans, N.J. Anderson and W.G. Eggington (eds) *ESL Readers and Writers in Higher Education: Understanding Challenges, Providing Support* (pp. 18–35). New York, NY: Routledge.

Canagarajah, A.S. (1999) *Resisting Linguistic Imperialism in English Teaching*. Oxford: Oxford University Press.

Cook, V. (2002) *Portraits of the L2 User*. Clevedon: Multilingual Matters.

Duff, P.A. (2010) Language socialization into academic discourse communities. *Annual Review of Applied Linguistics* 30, 169–192.

Evans, N.W. and Andrade, M.S. (2015) Understanding challenges, providing support: ESL readers and writers in higher education. In N.W. Evans, N.J. Anderson and W.G. Eggington (eds) *ESL Readers and Writers in Higher Education: Understanding Challenges, Providing Support* (pp. 3–17). New York, NY: Routledge.

Flores, N. (2020) From academic language to language architecture: Challenging raciolinguistic ideologies in research and practice. *Theory Into Practice* 59 (1), 22–31.

Galante, A. (2020a) Plurilingualism and TESOL in two Canadian post-secondary institutions: Towards context-specific perspectives. In S.M.C. Lau and S. Van Viegen (eds) *Plurilingual Pedagogies: Critical and Creative Endeavors for Equitable Language in Education* (pp. 237–252). Cham: Springer.

Galante, A. (2020b) "The moment I realized I am plurilingual" – Plurilingual tasks for creative representations in EAP at a Canadian university. *Applied Linguistics Review* 11 (4), 551–580.

Galante, A., Okubo, K., Cole, C., Elkader, N.A., Carozza, N., Wilkinson, C. and Vasic, J. (2020) "English-only is not the way to go": Teachers' perceptions of plurilingual Instruction in an English program at a Canadian university. *TESOL Quarterly* 54 (4), 980–1009.

Geller, J.R. (2017) Terminology and intersections. In B.K. Mikk and I. Steglitz (eds) *Learning Across Cultures: Locally and Globally* (3rd edn, pp. 13–38). Washington, DC: NAFSA.

Gerald, J.P.B. (2020) Worth the risk: Towards decentering whiteness in English language teaching. *BC Teal Journal* 5 (1), 44–54.

Godfrey, L.B. and Yu, X. (2021) International student experiences in online learning post Covid-19. See http://ccaps.umn.edu/documents/DCP/ISSS-Online-Experience-Survey-Executive-Summary.pdf (accessed March 2022).

Grosik, S. and Kanno, Y. (2021) Peripheral or marginal participation? University-based intensive English programs as an entryway to U.S. academia. *Journal of International Students* 11 (4), 914–931.

Hoekje, B.J. and Stevens, S.G. (2018) *Creating a Culturally Inclusive Campus: A Guide to Supporting International Students*. New York, NY: Routledge.

Hsu, F. (2017) Resisting the coloniality of English: A research review of strategies. *CATESOL Journal* 29 (1), 111–132.

Klco, A. (2022) Leveraging home languages for literacy: Bringing a translanguaging pedagogy to life. Minnesota English Learner Education (MELEd) Conference, 18–19 November, St. Paul, MN.

Kubota, R. and Lin, A. (2006) Race and TESOL: Introduction to concepts and theories. *TESOL Quarterly* 40 (3), 471–493.

Kumaravadivelu, B. (2006a) TESOL methods: Changing tracks, challenging trends. *TESOL Quarterly* 40 (1), 59–81.

Kumaravadivelu, B. (2006b) Dangerous liaison: Globalization, empire and TESOL. In J. Edge (ed.) *(Re)Locating TESOL in an Age of Empire* (pp. 1–26). New York, NY: Palgrave Macmillan.

Litzenberg, J. (2021) Innovation, resiliency, and genius in intensive English programs: Decolonializing recruitment and contradictory advocacy. *Applied Linguistics* 42 (5), 905–923.

Matsuda, P.K. (2006) The myth of linguistic homogeneity in U.S. college composition. *College English* 68 (6), 637–651.

Mikk, B.K. and Steglitz, I.E. (eds) (2017) *Learning Across Cultures: Locally and Globally* (3rd edn). Washington, DC: NAFSA.

Minnesota English Language Program (n.d.) ESL resources. See https://ccaps.umn.edu/esl-resources (accessed March 2022).

Mortenson, L. (2022) Integrating social justice-oriented content into English for academic purposes (EAP) instruction: A case study. *English for Specific Purposes* 65, 1–14.

Motha, S. (2014) *Race, Empire, and English Language Teaching: Creating Responsible and Ethical Anti-Racist Practice*. New York, NY: Teachers College Press.

Pappano, L. (2019) What happens when college students discuss lab work in Spanish, philosophy in Chinese or opera in Italian? *The Washington Post,* 19 November. See https://www.washingtonpost.com/national/education/what-happens-when-college-students-discuss-lab-work-in-spanish-philosophy-in-chinese-or-opera-in-italian/2019/11/18/0eef3f7a-0985-11ea-bd9d-c628fd48b3a0_story.html (accessed March 2022).

Payant, C. and Galante, A. (2022) Plurilingualism and translanguaging: Pedagogical approaches for empowerment and validation – An introduction. *TESL Canada Journal* 38 (2), i–xxii.

Peters, B.D. and Anderson, M.E. (2021) Supporting nonnative English speakers at the university: A survey of faculty and staff. *Journal of International Students* 11 (1), 103–121.

Phillipson, R. (1997) Realities and myths of linguistic imperialism. *Journal of Multilingual and Multicultural Development* 18 (3), 238–248.

Rosa, J. and Flores, N. (2017) Unsettling race and language: Toward a raciolinguistic perspective. *Language in Society* 46 (5), 621–647.

Suraweera, D. (2022) Plurilingualism in a constructively aligned and decolonized TESOL curriculum. *TESL Canada Journal* 38 (2), 186–198.

Walsh Marr, J. (2019) An English language teacher's pedagogical response to Canada's truth and reconciliation commission. *New Directions for Teaching and Learning* 2019 (157), 91–103.

Walsh Marr, J. (2021) The promise and precarity of critical pedagogy in English for academic purposes. *BC TEAL Journal* 6 (1), 132–141.

7 Behold-Remold: Navigating and Innovating Liminal Spaces as an IEP Practitioner-Administrator-Scholar (PAS)

Nikki Mattson and Jacqueline M. Gianico

Introduction

The professional activity of educators and scholars serving international populations in higher education exists in spaces of tension forged by relationships between local, national and international stakeholders, shifting geopolitical agendas and priorities, and the influence of an ever-changing and interconnected global economy. In short, it is a complex professional and academic endeavor, sensitive to shifting external factors. The work of intensive English program (IEP) practitioners is no exception; indeed, IEPs have been seen as the proverbial canary in the coal mine (Fischer, 2020) for trends in international education, as fluctuations often become visible in these smaller programs before becoming writ large across universities. IEPs are sites of threshold, or liminality (Purdy & Walker, 2012), within which programs and their students exist on the cusp of entry into the academy, and practitioners operate in volatile and contested spaces that are unique within the field of international higher education. Although IEPs are often 'clearly positioned within the physical and social spaces of the academy', they function as 'a kind of anteroom that precedes the establishment of disciplinarity and yet identifies the student as belonging in some way to academic culture' (Purdy & Walker, 2012: 13). However ambiguously this physical and social space of transition presents itself, we – the authors – do not accept the English for Academic Purposes (EAP) identity as 'dysfunctional, confused, and conflicted' (Ding & Bruce, 2017: 204). On the contrary, we frame our positionality and identities as liminal and fluid, claiming a third-space perspective (Soja, 1996), where we view the real and imagined spatial, historical and social spaces of IEPs as sites of continual renegotiation and revision, and thus, innovation. As such, the findings of this collaborative ethnography show that the professional activity of the EAP practitioner is a site rich with potential for academic inquiry and respect, rejecting the appearance of EAP professionals as 'intellectually vacuous ... campus hobos ... beneath notice in terms of serious academic study' (Hadley, 2015: 84).

Methodology

We chose collaborative ethnography (Chang *et al.*, 2013) to participate in a systematic reflection of our roles in an IEP, engaging with representations of EAP practitioners others have constructed. Our collaborative ethnography is both analytical and evocative, as it interfaces directly with theory and research findings (Canagarajah, 2012), but also contains a liberal amount of personal voice and expressive discourse (Mirhosseini, 2018). Moreover, we incorporate critical ethnography regarding our experiences with and perspectives toward inequity in our work and advocacy for social change (Starfield, 2020). This inequity exists against the academic backdrop of our craft – i.e. applied linguistics, a field which 'remains largely resistant to the use of more personal voice and alternative formats, with many leading journals committed to publishing "objective", impersonal, quantitatively oriented research reports' (Keles, 2022: 466). Nevertheless, the format of collaborative ethnography allows us to amplify 'unique stories which would otherwise remain in the periphery and unheard' (Keles, 2022: 466).

The process of this collaborative ethnography began when we were invited to co-author a chapter highlighting the 'challenges of innovation' in an IEP, emphasizing the 'importance of the theory-practice feedback loop' in order to provide 'researchers with a detailed synopsis of the real-world, practical obstacles encountered by practitioners when implementing theoretical suggestions' in IEPs (J. Litzenberg, personal communication, 29 January 2021). It is important to note that the Director of our IEP is also the editor of this volume, a relationship that likely impacts this ethnography in both conscious and unconscious ways. One obvious benefit of our connection is that we were invited to contribute to this volume. On the other hand, more ambiguous aspects include the washback of this non-contractual obligation upon our professional duties in the IEP as well as the restrictions this relationship may place upon our ability to reflect openly and critically about our context.

Accepting the invitation, we (who have been colleagues and friends for 10 years) met via Zoom for several hour-long discussion sessions about what our contribution to the volume should be and how to articulate it. We eventually agreed to address the following research question: *how have our professional activities involved negotiating the theoretical and the practical to develop and sustain the IEP in innovative ways?* Throughout the project, we located and reviewed artifacts (emails, meeting notes, curricular documents, internal reports, etc.) most related to the research question. To manage 10 years of documentation, we focused on several time periods of notable shift within the program, including transitions of leadership, changes in university-level systems, redesigns of curriculum and assessment, and adaptations of the IEP mission. The search resulted in 49 artifacts, which we (re)read to stimulate our recollection of the events and their causes and effects. We identified four recurring themes: (1) our multiple and changing roles in the IEP; (2) the IEP's and our positioning and status within the university ecology; (3) reactivity and innovation within our IEP; and (4) tension and ambiguity around theory and practice. In the following sections, we argue that these four themes have allowed us to construct important knowledge and claim agency in a unique space of the academy. When referring to ourselves as colleagues and co-authors, we use 'we' or 'us'; our individual experiences, however, are presented in third person.

From Accidental Practitioners to Accidental Administrators: Our Stories

Before identifying as 'accidental scholars' (Bond, 2020), we entered the field as accidental practitioners and then became accidental administrators. Like many EAP professionals, Jackie did not set out to become a teacher of English. Her path to English language teaching was tangentially sparked by international travel and graduate study abroad. When a Master's degree in Italian did not immediately result in a job teaching Italian, she decided to return to graduate school and pursue a second Master's degree in applied linguistics. Jackie later began doctoral study in the same field but eventually left the PhD program and joined the IEP as a full-time instructor. With a similar interest in language learning and cross-cultural experiences, Nikki studied French as an undergraduate and traveled internationally with various university initiatives. Realizing she did not want to teach French, Nikki added an English minor and applied to graduate school in linguistics, with a TESOL concentration. After graduation, Nikki returned to France to participate in the Teaching Assistant Program as an English as a foreign language instructor. Upon returning to the States, she was fortunate to secure a full-time ESL teaching position at her current IEP.

Once we found our way to teaching in EAP classrooms, it was clear that we had found our vocations. We were professionally and personally gratified to support international students at various stages of their personal and academic pursuits. We were invigorated by the university atmosphere and myriad opportunities for development and engagement on campus. Perhaps unsurprisingly, the longer we engaged in our roles as practitioners in the IEP, the more we caught the attention of institutional managers who saw our potential to support the organization administratively and, thus, we were eventually invited to join the ranks of Blended EAP Professionals, or BLEAPs (Hadley, 2015). As Hadley (2015: 48) notes, because of their 'skill as teachers, their popularity with students, or because of their seniority amongst the other educators', those who primarily teach are often 'noticed by someone in ... management, ... groomed for a period of time, and then ... "raised up" to become a BLEAP'. Hadley refers to professionals who primarily teach as TEAPs (Teaching EAP Professionals). The trajectory of TEAPs rising up to BLEAPs is not uncommon within IEPs.

Although moving from TEAP to BLEAP is an indication of upward mobility, it is also a tricky and nebulous space where it becomes necessary to manage various aspects of an EAP unit 'without any formal authority or positional power' (Ding & Bruce, 2017: 110). Additionally, as noted by Hadley (2015), BLEAPs often undertake a variety of roles to try to support the success of their IEP – teacher, researcher, administrator, politician, salesperson, entrepreneur, human resource manager, business strategist, student advisor and recruiter, among others. Further, the workload, emotional investment and professional marginalization that BLEAPs often face may lead to exhaustion, embitterment and ineffectiveness over time (Hadley, 2015).

While we enjoyed some of the work of the non-teaching roles we assumed, at other times there seemed to be no option other than to continuously take on additional responsibilities merely 'to keep our program afloat'. Jackie's first role in sustaining the program began just two years after her initial hire as a full-time instructor. At that time, the IEP had been without an official director for almost a year, and the program was in the process of transitioning from an outreach unit to an academic department. When the Academic Coordinator left the program during this administrative transition, Jackie was promoted with an administrative buy out. Despite a lack of administrative experience, Jackie was excited about the promotion. She also recognized, however, that this advancement was a response to a programmatic gap that needed to be filled quickly – her first experience as an 'accidental administrator'. A little over a year later, Jackie found herself once again filling a programmatic vacuum, effectively co-directing the IEP with another TEAP turned BLEAP. This time, however, she worked as a full-time administrator, taking a temporary pause from teaching. This period was a stressful one for Jackie, as she had to evaluate former peers and colleagues, make hiring decisions, and manage requests from not only students and faculty, but staff, administrators and other stakeholders. After a year and a half as a full-time administrator, a new Director was hired, and Jackie happily re-entered the classroom. By the time of Jackie's departure from the program in 2021, she had occupied the titles of Academic Coordinator,

Interim Director (unofficially), Associate Director of Academics and, finally, Associate Teaching Professor of Applied Linguistics.

Since Nikki joined the IEP as a full-time instructor in 2009, she has held seven job titles with various levels of administrative responsibility. She was hired as Instructor when the program was part of the host institution's outreach unit, but the position was retitled to Lecturer when the IEP joined the Department of Applied Linguistics. For several years, she served as the Chair of the IEP Assessment Committee, a quasi-administrative role where she led her colleagues in reviewing assessment-related policies, procedures and materials at the IEP and making formal recommendations to the Director regarding areas for improvement. In 2014, Nikki discovered that there was no clear path for promotion in her position. She subsequently submitted documentation related to her performance to the department head and explicitly requested to be considered for promotion (eventually resulting in a regular set of policies for IEP faculty promotion). Nikki was subsequently promoted to Senior Lecturer and renamed Assistant Teaching Professor shortly thereafter due to a university-wide initiative. In 2016, she was promoted to Associate Teaching Professor. In 2019, the Assistant Director of Special Programs vacated their position; Nikki assumed several of the responsibilities from that portfolio. Like Jackie, Nikki felt a mix of excitement and apprehension taking on the extra share of work as an 'accidental administrator'. Although remuneration remained unchanged, Nikki negotiated the professional title of Coordinator of Strategic Initiatives (CSI) to better reflect her additional administrative and entrepreneurial responsibilities.

While the TEAP/BLEAP distinction resonates with us, the core identities of our multi-layered, changing roles as IEP practitioners are more accurately envisioned as Practitioner-Administrator-Scholar, or PAS. The order of the PAS nomenclature explicitly prioritizes our practitioner identities, while also recognizing our administrative service and the value of our scholarly work. The following sections demonstrate the creative resilience and innovation of a PAS identity within an IEP ecology.

Positioning and Status of the IEP

Historically, the field of English language education has benefited from the commodification of linguistic resources to the very populations empowered through the work. This inherent irony is not lost on many in the field. Litzenberg (2020: 832) notes that 'all employees of an IEP are service providers, and they must, at least to some extent, occupy themselves with the commercial viability of the organization, even if they are not comfortable with this reality'. This commercialism positions IEP practitioners as service-providers and students as consumers, and for some people within university ecologies, the commercialism may situate IEPs as inherently less academic.

Ding and Bruce (2017: 196) discuss how the view of EAP as a peripheral support service rather than as an academic field of study molds the identity and agency of EAP professionals. In the support-service view, TEAPs may be viewed as providing a 'commodified language repair service' for international students in need of 'remedial' language support. As such, having some sort of pre-service TESOL certification is seen as sufficient training, and practitioners are typically on 'teach-only' contracts with a relatively high course load compared to those teaching university classes for matriculated students. The academic-field view, however, 'places emphasis on ongoing practitioner development ... that connects practice, scholarship and research' (2017: 196). Indeed, in this view, there is expectation that EAP professionals actively engage in discourse communities that are seeking to understand the 'forces, theories, practices and ideologies' (2017: 207) of their discipline; they should endeavor to make scholarly contributions to the field in order to elevate their agency and become accepted, valued members of the community of practice. Thus, there is inherent conflict between heavy teaching loads and the expectation of scholarly engagement in the field.

Because of the various historical and structural contexts elucidated above as well as the fact that IEP practitioners generally work with pre-matriculated, international, non-credit students, it is not surprising that these individuals and programs typically exist on the periphery of the academy. In fact, Ding and Bruce (2017: 2) describe 'the fundamental conundrum of EAP practitioners' as 'their requirement to induct students into the literate practices and processes of the academic world despite their own ambivalent status within the academy'. EAP practitioners, they claim, 'are often not employed as, or considered to be members of the same academy into which they are inducting aspirant or novice members' (2017: 7).

'The fundamental conundrum'

The implications of an 'ambivalent status' in the university ecology may be illustrated rather poignantly through our experiences adjusting to two university-level decisions that had a significant impact on our IEP. First, in response to the economic recession in 2008, our host institution initiated a campus-wide review of the programs and processes of all academic and administrative units to maintain academic excellence while weathering the recession. A result of that review was a directive regarding auxiliary units, like the IEP: find an academic home or be eliminated (Academic Core Council, departmental communication). The IEP was subsequently moved from a non-academic outreach unit to the Department of Applied Linguistics (2011, graduate student report, personal communication; 2013, IEP History Timeline). At the time, we had different experiences of the transition: Nikki had been a part of the IEP since 2009 and knew the program before the move, while Jackie was a doctoral student in the department that assumed administrative control of the IEP in the transition.

We both felt the loss of agency and voice that initially accompanied the relocation into the academic department. A new workflow became clear as IEP instructors were to follow directives from the new administration and were not invited to participate in decision-making. In addition, our incongruent understandings of the positioning of IEPs and IEP practitioners within the new department became apparent: we relied on time outside of contact hours to create our best pedagogical materials while the new Executive Director prioritized economic savings. As a result, our teaching load was increased from 16 to 23 contact hours, and instructors struggled. In a meeting of instructors with the new Executive Director, Nikki explained that the increase was negatively affecting her practice, stating, 'I can't do the quality teaching I expect to do'. The Executive Director's response was not reassuring, comparing us to 'K-12 schoolteachers' who should have a comparable number of contact hours. 'This is not a democracy', Nikki recalls being told, 'This is a hierarchy'. We were invited to look for other positions if we were not happy with our new roles in the *academic* department. Thus, the social order was thrown into sharp relief, and the irony or paradox (Annala *et al.*, 2021) was clear: we could enjoy the privilege of being part of an academic unit if we were willing to concede our professional agency and follow top-down directives.

'A rather serious crisis'

Another university-level decision that directly impacted our IEP was the adoption of a new university-wide system for classroom allocation and reservations. The new system reallocated the six classrooms that our IEP had been using for over five years (and whose renovations the IEP had financed!) to credit-bearing courses. Unfortunately, IEP administration and faculty only learned of the classroom reallocations on the first day of the semester, when, to our surprise and bewilderment, we discovered non-IEP faculty and students conducting class in 'our' rooms. All IEP classes had been displaced. What we initially assumed was a benign institutional-level scheduling error was eventually revealed to be the result of our program's status within the university ecology: as a non-credit program we no longer had a right to reserve rooms in the campus allocation system, an unfortunate fact in and of itself that was compounded by the reality that our program was not made aware of the update ahead of time.

This situation created an instant crisis for the IEP, positioning us as 'campus hobos ... beneath notice in terms of serious academic study' (Hadley, 2018: 84). In the role of Academic Coordinator at the time, Jackie first experienced incredulity, followed by the immediate and immense responsibility for finding solutions. She, along with the administrative assistant and our newly hired Director, scrambled to connect with someone at the university who could advocate for the program. In the meantime, IEP classes took place outside (if weather permitted), in the much-too-small spaces of instructors' offices, and in reservation-only, limited-use library spaces. An email to the Dean describes the situation as 'a rather serious crisis over space … [which] can't go on for very long, else the students' national sponsors (who pay the bills) will rather reasonably withdraw their support and their students'. For more on marginalization of English Language Teachers (ELT) and ELT programs, see Winkle (Chapter 11).

As was the case in the move from outreach, the university-level reallocation of classroom space impacted our program in dramatic ways, this time without any advance knowledge. This forced us to develop *ad hoc*, viable ways to move forward as quickly as possible. Negotiations eventually resulted in approval for a college-level administrator to manually assign the IEP four classrooms on the edge of campus – the actual, physical periphery – in an un-renovated classroom building used primarily for Reserve Officers' Training Corps (ROTC) activities.

Renegotiation and innovation in the IEP

The positioning and status of the IEP and our shifting responsibilities within the program have certainly limited our professional agency in some respects. However, our changing professional identities combined with the peripheral status of the IEP has also provided unique opportunities for us to renegotiate and innovate significant curricular and programmatic changes. In fact, this tumultuous third space (Soja, 1996) is crucial to the innovative work we do. Like BLEAPs, who occupy 'organizational "third spaces" … which are typically responsible for administrative services, student support, service-learning, innovation, and academic skills development' (Hadley, 2015: 8) as PAS, we have experienced frequent and substantial challenges in navigating and weathering uncertainty and change. Nevertheless, even though we did not set out to 'wear all of the hats' we have donned in the IEP, doing so has shaped us into professionals who are adept at navigating – and even thriving – in obscure, ever-changing, and contested spaces. Hadley (2015: 58) might view us as 'highly talented people' who 'make the most of ambiguous spaces'. Indeed, this talent is tied to navigating and challenging the boundaries of our liminal spaces, which is always an innovative response. The subsequent sections describe instances of transformation within our IEP and illustrate how the perpetually changing third space of IEPs can both affect and effect innovation.

From discrete to integrated skills

In 2010, the Director at the time charged five IEP Instructors with conducting a formal needs assessment of several aspects of the program including program mission, curriculum and academic preparedness of its students. Their work resulted in a 74-page report that included a recommendation to 'add/develop integrated skills promotion criteria throughout the curriculum' and to 'create one or more positions within the [IEP] for curriculum development' (Bragaw et al., 2010). While insufficient financial and human resources prevented implementation of most recommendations in the report, an opportunity presented itself during the period when the program was transitioning from outreach to the applied linguistics department. Taking advantage of the circumstances, Nikki used the opportunity to lead the IEP instructors in a curricular revision that entailed reviewing the recommendations from the needs analysis in 2010, conducting a benchmark analysis of comparable IEP programs, and interpreting over 40 relevant scholarly texts. The overall curricular revision featured four main action steps: (1) integrate skills, (2) emphasize academic English, (3) distinguish grammar for writing and for speaking and (4) introduce content-based courses.

The new curriculum was rolled out over the course of one year, from Fall 2014 to Fall 2015 (Table 7.1). A new nomenclature was adopted to capture the emphasis on *integration* of *academic* skills. Reading and writing, for instance, became *Academic Literacies (AL)*, and oral communication became *Academic Interactions (AI)*. These names are still in use in the program. Throughout the revision process, we considered how theoretical concepts and proposed applications could work in the specific context of IEP classrooms within our particular university ecology (Pennington & Hoekje, 2010). The process of curriculum revision was creative and

Table 7.1 Selected timeline of major curricular developments at the IEP

Until 2014	Fall 2014 – Summer 2015	Fall 2015 – Fall 2019	Spring 2020 – Summer 2022
Discrete skills	Transitioning to academic, integrated skills and content-based electives	Addition of skill-based grammar	Distinction of spontaneous and prepared production
Courses offered Reading Writing Listening and Speaking Grammar **Levels** 1–4 **Term** 15 weeks	**Courses piloted** Academic Interactions Academic Literacies Science elective Humanities elective **Levels renamed** 110–140 **Term** 15 weeks	**Courses piloted** Grammar for Writing Skills Grammar for Speaking Skills **Courses offered** Academic Interactions Academic Literacies Science elective Humanities elective **Levels** 110–140 **Term** 15 weeks	**Courses offered** Academic Interactions Academic Literacies Grammar for Writing Skills Grammar for Speaking Skills Science elective Humanities elective **Levels** 110–140 **Term** two 7.5-week terms; Term 1 focused on preparing students for spontaneous productive and receptive skills, and Term 2 emphasized prepared, edited production and previously studied discourses

Table 7.2 Sample curriculum for advanced Grammar for Literacies

Course Goal 1: Identify, comprehend and evaluate the form and functions of lexical and grammatical patterns in student-generated and published academic writing at an advanced level.	**Course Goal 2:** Produce and manipulate lexical and grammatical patterns in writing at an advanced level to convey, evaluate and challenge ideas and concepts for academic writing tasks.
Course Objectives for Course Goal 1:	Course Objectives for Course Goal 2:
a. Demonstrate an understanding of corpora usage for increased familiarity (e.g. synonyms, frequency by discipline and common collocations/chunks by discipline) with lexical items (i.e. words, phrases, collocations/chunks) b. Evaluate the utility of various revision tools for lexical and grammatical revision c. Identify and evaluate the form and functions of grammatical patterns in academic texts d. Compare and contrast the lexical and grammatical patterns used in original writing and accompanying paraphrases e. Identify and distinguish between lexical and grammatical patterns in writing in and across academic disciplines	a. Use and manipulate a variety of appropriate lexical items in revised academic writing tasks (i.e. problem solving writing or empirical inquiry, source-responsible writing that is tied to an academic field, source-responsible responses to content-based short-answer questions and timed source-responsible reactions and/or critiques) b. Use various revision tools for lexical and grammatical revision c. Use and manipulate grammatical patterns appropriately and accurately in revised academic writing tasks (i.e. problem solving writing or empirical inquiry, source-responsible writing that is tied to an academic field, source-responsible responses to content-based short-answer questions and timed source-responsible reactions and/or critiques) d. Manipulate lexical and grammatical patterns appropriately for paraphrasing tasks
Sample Learning Outcome: Produce a corpus-informed vocabulary analysis (*synonyms, common collocations and discipline appropriateness, etc.*) of 10 lexical items from texts from Academic Literacies (minimum of 2 lexical analyses of student-generated texts; minimum of 2 lexical analyses of published academic texts)	

rewarding, not only in terms of moving our program closer to the goals outlined in the needs assessment report, but also in how we grappled and engaged with the field throughout the iterative phases of development and implementation. This work created a stimulating and productive space for the scholarship of applying and adapting theory to context-specific practice. While developing a single grammar course into two – one for academic writing and one for academic speaking – we reached out to a prominent PAS for insight. We shared our advanced-level 'Grammar for Literacies' curriculum as reference (Table 7.2) and received an encouraging response: 'Your writing curriculum guidelines look tremendous! Actually, they are more thorough, thought-out, and research-based than most that I have seen … You are doing fantastic work over there, and I am very impressed'.

Placement assessment design and redesign (and redesign)

Prior to the curriculum revisions, the IEP had utilized two instruments to determine level placement of new students: the paper-based Michigan English Placement Test and a timed written composition designed by the assessment committee of the IEP. Those testing instruments entailed several limitations that impacted validity, but they were also the most feasible option during a period in which the IEP welcomed up to 60 new students at a time. Yet with the new curriculum and with lower enrollment numbers in 2014, we saw an exciting opportunity to design a more valid placement instrument that also included an oral interview and a read-to-write composition task.

There were three parts, or phases, of the first iteration of the oral placement interview. The first two phases of the interview – general conversation and topic response, respectively – were used to assess oral competency. These results were then used to pair new IEP students for the third phase of the placement process, partner conversation. The development and validation of the oral interview placement were reported by Nikki and colleagues in Kimora *et al.* (2018) and presented by Jackie at TESOL (Gianico, 2016). This exam was redesigned twice, first for validity (in 2015) and then for expediency (in 2017). As a result of the Covid pandemic, the in-house IEP exam was temporarily paused in lieu of TOEFL, IELTS and Duolingo scores, but has since been re-implemented in stages. It was disappointing to abandon years of dedicated and productive work on the development of a valid in-house placement exam due to a global pandemic, yet the experience demonstrates the flexibility required of PAS in IEPs. In fact, it seems that functioning in a context characterized by shifting landscapes and new realties is actually a central component of our PAS identities. It behooves language teachers, as Waller *et al.* (2017: 23) point out, to 'expect the unexpected and have the ability to go with the flow'.

From 'unable to accommodate' to 'very excited for their arrival'

Another instance of this sort of reactive transformation arose during Jackie's tenure as the *de facto* Director of the program. Guided by the IEP's academic mission, Jackie explained to an interested third-party provider that the program was 'simply unable to accommodate all of [the] requirements necessary for [the] group' (J.M. Gianico, personal communication, 5 February 2016). Indeed, the partnership would require several atypical accommodations – e.g. an office for their local coordinator, evening classes, the use of a proprietary curriculum, and weekly progress reporting using a third-party learning management system. Two months later, however, largely due to the financial strain and associated pressures of declining enrollment at the IEP, Jackie and the leadership team made the fraught decision to adapt the IEP mission statement and to try to accommodate the requests of the group. Programmatic adaptations and compromises ensued as we worked to meet the requirements of the sponsor. We began evening courses and required strict adherence to the third-party provider's propriety curriculum, both of which had previously been opposed by the IEP faculty and administration. Jackie recalls the surreal feeling upon reading a colleague's email to the coordinator of the partnership program, stating that the IEP was 'very excited' for the students to arrive. These experiences of innovation and reaction highlight the contested third space where demands '[twist] down from the administrative realm ... while [also swirling] upward from the expectations of students' (Hadley, 2015: 38). With the above instance, we show that significant pressure also enters this 'site of both innovative creation and cultural chaos' (Hadley, 2015: 39) from external third-party stakeholders.

In another example, a confluence of bottom-up and top-down pressures eventually necessitated curricular restructuring to accommodate students who requested to arrive mid-semester. The IEP historically had denied admission to students who could not arrive before the end of week two in a 15-week semester. However, starting in 2020, we were not in a financial position to turn late students away, and the program bisected the semester into two halves, conveniently named 'Term 1' and 'Term 2'. In order to maintain the staff and not disrupt curricular objectives, Jackie devised an innovative solution. The materials and student outcomes of Term 1 were focused on spontaneous production and newly encountered texts and discourse, while the focus of Term 2 was on planned, edited production and previously studied texts and discourse. This division enabled students to enroll at the start of the traditional semester (Term 1) or midway (Term 2) and complete the course in any order (see Table 7.1).

Behold-Remold the Theory-Practice Loop

Problematizing the theory-practice narrative for pre-service teachers is not new (see Schulte, 2013), but the tension exists for experienced practitioners as well. As IEP PAS who must react to the ever-changing context and demands of stakeholders, the relationship between theory and practice becomes more ambiguous. In the 2014–2015 academic year, an attempt was made to address this ambiguity by explicitly identifying the theoretical underpinnings of the IEP faculty's daily classroom practices. At the request of the then executive director, a new instrument for faculty evaluation was developed to directly tie the inclusion of theoretical rationales in practitioner lesson plans to contract renewal and merit-based salary increases. One new criterion of the evaluation rubric included 'Knowledge about the profession (research and the craft)' under the teaching effectiveness category. It required detailed theoretical rationales for each lesson plan which were then submitted by faculty to the IEP Executive Director. Jackie, who at the time served as Academic Coordinator received the following email from Nikki:

> showing evidence of teaching rationale on a lesson plan every day, ... seems like extra paperwork. I am very supportive of fostering reflective teaching and 'talking smart' about what we do, but I am not sure daily lesson plans are the place. (N. Mattson, personal communication, 5 September 2015)

While we agree that IEPs afford many opportunities to narrow the gap between theory and practice, we found that documenting the relationship between theory and practice on daily lesson plans with full-time class loads was an untenable solution to the theory-practice tension. Our work in creating and revising oral placement instruments, however, illustrates the potential of the theory-practice relationship as a dynamic, productive, bidirectional process contextualized in a pragmatic reality (Kimura *et al.*, 2018). Carr (2001: 100) describes such action research work as 'a systematic process of organized self-directed reflection on practice, with the specific aim of materially altering (and improving) that practice'. Experiencing fragmentation or disruptions in the theory-practice loop, then, is the status quo for PAS, as we regularly *assess internal and external realities* and *innovate to advance*. As such, PAS engage with a reality-adaptation loop in addition to interfacing with a fragmented theory-practice loop. This process, which we call *behold-remold*, is the actual, lived activity of enacting and adapting approaches to language teaching in real time and space with complex individuals and groups. It is the critical, contextualized activity of 'highly talented people' who 'make the most of ambiguous spaces' (Hadley, 2015: 58) by applying language-learner and language- teacher education, experience, and flexibility to real contexts in specific local and global ecologies.

Akin to agile thinking, behold-remold captures the cyclical and iterative work of observing, reflecting upon and reacting to any sort of input (or lack thereof) in order to (re)build something to benefit stakeholders. This type of work is similar to the affirmational philosophy of 'yes, and' (see McCloskey & Tanner, 2019; Tanner & McCloskey, 2022) in improvisational theatre where an actor must be keenly aware of what is emerging around them, accept that whatever emerges is the new reality, and decide how to move the scene forward by adding to it. Behold-remold goes beyond developing new and creative curricular and programmatic ideas; instead, it is a (re)formulation of professional self that commits to innovating and moving forward in an ever-changing context.

The discussion of teaching activity through the lens of improvisational competency is not new but compared to analysis done in the 'root traditions' of improv (i.e. theatre, dance, jazz), it is not nearly as developed (Holdhus *et al.*, 2016). Nevertheless, inspired by the ethos of improvisation, we find that behold-remold is an essential philosophy for PAS professionals, extending beyond improvisation merely as a pedagogical skill for the classroom. Improvisation, according to Holdhus *et al.* (2016: 9) results when an individual 'is compelled to react or to resolve "uninvited" complexity … [and] one can develop expert knowledge and the ability to take chances in the risk society'.

The skill of behold-remold is an essential competency of PAS because we operate within the unplanned or 'uninvited' complexity of the IEP context where the traditional theory-practice loop is not an appropriate (or even realistic!) goal, as the loop is regularly fragmented and interrupted. The above examples of innovation in our IEP are a result of our ability to behold-remold. Indeed, behold-remold is essential to any form of innovation. It is an improvisational competency, or skill, which should be a regular feature of PAS education and training, so that pre-service practitioners and administrators learn to expect the unexpected in a post-method era (Waller *et al.*, 2017). The behold-remold skill goes beyond the related concepts of molding and shaping (Hadley, 2017) or even teaching as design (Laurillard, 2018; Warr & Mishra, 2021) because the professional activity of PAS is not limited to pedagogical activity but also administrative and scholarly activities.

Conclusion

As PAS at a university-based IEP who have been working with pre-matriculated, international students on the periphery of the academy, our combined 23 years in the field provides us with a robust understanding of what it means to navigate the liminal, third space of an IEP. Privileged with full-time positions for over a decade, we have been afforded the opportunity to develop our professional and scholarly identities, albeit while sometimes juggling heavy class loads, committee work, administrative duties and myriad other tasks related to our ever-changing, ever-reactive roles. Accordingly, we find that we are at a point in our careers where we can and should engage in the important work of making PAS a visible part of the field. Still, when we were first asked to contribute to this edited volume, we were conflicted. While we imagined our contributions could be meaningful, we did not want to perpetuate stereotypes of IEP practitioners as intellectually 'empty' (Turner, 2004: 104) or 'vacuous' (Hadley, 2018: 84). But we eventually realized that these questions were largely a reflection of the stereotypes themselves. To that end, with this chapter, we officially respond to the call from Bond (2020) for EAP practitioners to engage in scholarship that challenges unhelpful representations of EAP practitioners and contributes to improving the position of EAP practitioners in university ecologies as well as within the field of applied linguistics. And, while we concur that this does not occasion a 'quick win' (Bond, 2020: 174), we hope to supplement the contributions set forth by Bond, Ding and Bruce, Hadley, Hamp-Lyons and other 'EAP activists' by submitting our own accounts and reflections as IEP PAS. We encourage other IEP PAS to consider how the liminal space of an IEP allows us to innovate in ways that are not possible for other academic units. Let's reframe the old adage – rather than canaries in the coal mine, we are the miners, the trailblazers, forging ahead, underground but hopefully no longer unseen. Let's push toward a paradigmatic behold-remold of the field and of the theory-practice divide, in particular, in order to arrive at something more integrated and less fragmented, more collaborative and less hierarchical and, ultimately, more inclusive for all.

Acknowledgments

We acknowledge with gratitude all the practitioners and PAS we have worked with as colleagues and friends over the years. Special thanks to Linda Wesley for her comments on earlier versions of the manuscript. Finally, we thank our partners and children for their support and implicit role in this work.

References

Annala, J., Lindén, J., Mäkinen, M. and Henriksson, J. (2021) Understanding academic agency in curriculum change in higher education. *Teaching in Higher Education* 28, 1–18. https://doi.org/10.1080/13562517.2021.1881772.

Bond, B. (2020) *Making Language Visible in the University: English for Academic Purposes and Internationalisation.*. Bristol: Multilingual Matters.

Bragaw, D., O'Keefe, J., Runner, J., Shen, L. and Tang, R. (2010) Final report of the IECP needs assessment committee. [Internal Report] Intensive English Communication Program, The Pennsylvania State University.

Canagarajah, A.S. (2012) Teacher development in a global profession: An autoethnography. *TESOL Quarterly* 46 (2), 258–279. https://doi.org/10.1002/tesq.18.

Carr, J. (2001) Action research and the language classroom. *Counterpoints* 112, 99–111.

Chang, H., Ngunjiri, F.W. and Hernandez, K.-A.C. (2013) *Collaborative Autoethnography*. Walnut Creek, CA: Left Coast Press.

Ding, A. and Bruce, I. (2017) *English for Academic Purposes Operating on the Edge of Academia*. Cham: Palgrave Macmillan.

Fischer, K. (2020) Are declines in English-language programs a sign of trouble to come? *Open Campus*, 24 August. See https://www.opencampusmedia.org/2020/08/24/are-declines-in-english-language-programs-a-sign-of-trouble-to-come/ (accessed March 2022).

Gianico, J.M. (2016) *Pushing the boundaries of oral placement exams: Assessing interactional competence*. Paper presented at the annual meeting of TESOL, April, Baltimore, MD.

Hadley, G. (2015) *English for Academic Purposes in Neoliberal Universities: A Critical Grounded Theory* (22nd vol). Cham: Springer International Publishing. https://doi.org/10.1007/978-3-319-10449-2.

Hadley, G. (2018) Book review. *Journal of English for Academic Purposes* 31, 84–86. https://doi.org/10.1016/j.jeap.2017.11.002.

Holdhus, K., Høisæter, S., Mæland, K., Vangsnes, V., Engelsen, K.S., Espeland, M. and Espeland, Å. (2016) Improvisation in teaching and education – Roots and applications. *Cogent Education* 3 (1), 1–17. https://doi.org/10.1080/2331186X.2016.1204142.

Keles, U. (2022) Autoethnography as a recent methodology in applied linguistics: A methodological review. *The Qualitative Report* 27 (2), 448–474. https://doi.org/10.46743/2160-3715/2022.5131.

Kimura, D., Mattson, N. and Amory, M. (2018) A conversation analytic approach to oral placement test validation: Attending to vertical and horizontal comparisons. *TESOL Journal* 9 (3), 455–480. https://doi.org/10.1002/tesj.335.

Laurillard, D. (2018) Teaching as a design science: Teachers building, testing, and sharing pedagogic ideas. In J. Voogt, G. Knezek, R. Christensen and K.-W. Lai (eds) *Second Handbook of Information Technology in Primary and Secondary Education* (pp. 557–566). Cham: Springer International Publishing. https://doi.org/10.1007/978-3-319-71054-9_108.

Litzenberg, J. (2020) "If I don't do it, somebody else will": Covert neoliberal policy discourses in the decision-making processes of an intensive English program. *TESOL Quarterly* 54 (4), 823–845. https://doi.org/10.1002/tesq.563.

McCloskey, A. and Tanner, S.J. (2019) Ritual and improvisation: Ways of researching, ways of being in mathematics classrooms. *For the Learning of Mathematics* 39 (2), 37–41. https://www.jstor.org/stable/26757471.

Mirhosseini, S. (2018) An Invitation to the less-treaded path of autoethnography in TESOL research. *TESOL Journal* 9 (1), 76–92. https://doi.org/10.1002/tesj.305.

Purdy, J.P. and Walker, J.R. (2013) Liminal spaces and research identity: The construction of introductory composition students as researchers. *Pedagogy Critical Approaches to Teaching Literature Language Composition and Culture* 13 (1), 9–41. https://doi.org/10.1215/15314200-1814260.

Shulte, J. (2013) Reconstructing the theory-to-practice narrative. *CATESOL Journal* 24 (1), 125–136.

Soja, E.W. (1996) *Thirdspace: Journeys to Los Angeles and Other Real-and-Imagined Places*. Cambridge, MA: Blackwell.

Starfield, S. (2020) Autoethnography and critical ethnography. In J. McKinley and H. Rose (eds) *The Routledge Handbook of Research Methods in Applied Linguistics* (pp. 165–175). New York, NY: Routledge.

Tanner, S.J. and McCloskey, A. (2022) Improv theater and whiteness in education: A systematic literature review. *Review of Educational Research* 93 (1), 3–36. https://doi.org/10.3102/00346543221076885.

Turner, J. (2004) Language as academic purpose. *Journal of English for Academic Purposes* 3 (2), 95–109. https://doi.org/10.1016/S1475-1585(03)00054-7.

Waller, L., Wethers, K. and De Costa, P.I. (2017) A critical praxis: Narrowing the gap between identity, theory, and practice. *TESOL Journal* 8 (1), 4–27. https://doi.org/10.1002/tesj.256.

Warr, M. and Mishra, P. (2021) Integrating the discourse on teachers and design: An analysis of ten years of scholarship. *Teaching and Teacher Education* 99, 1–14. https://doi.org/10.1016/j.tate.2020.103274.

8 The Missing Puzzle Piece: Racism and Native-Speakerism Scholarship

JPB Gerald

Nativeness for Whom?

We, in the early 2020s, are engaging in our fifth decade of discourse about native speakers[1] and those outside of the categorization. Let us consider why this problem persists. What is it about the approximation of nativeness that continues to be venerated? Why is it still encouraged, either implicitly or directly, for learners to aspire to membership in this club of ours? And who, precisely, gets to call themselves a *native speaker*? From my vantage point as an educator and scholar with a complex relationship to standardized English, we are often leaving out a key piece of the puzzle even as we engage in useful work wherein we attempt to combat native speakerism.

I started my own career in language education by receiving a job for which I was qualified by virtue of my nationality, despite zero experience in the classroom and nary a credit in the discipline. At the same time, my Blackness has always allowed peers to question my ability and my facility with language, so my status as native has always felt conditional, bestowed upon me when my words are severed from my body, but kept at a remove when my identity is centered. As such, as with all of my work, my own experience is crucial in understanding the points I iterate below, in which I analyze some of the more influential authors on nativeness whose work has substantially advanced discourse. Yet at the same time, as I point out, there is often a piece missing from the puzzle.

Simply put, we will never be rid of native speakerism until we are rid of the concept of the *native speaker*, a category of supremacy by nature and one that exists as a mountaintop for language learners to be told to scale. There is no version of the native speaker that can exist without contributing to harm, and, for English at least, there is no conceptualization of the native speaker that can exist without the twin crutches of whiteness and racism. Any analysis of nativeness and English that fails to consider these ideas in its theorization is doomed to fall short, and the fact that this angle is absent even in some of the more radical scholarship, I would contend, is part of why native speakers continue to reign supreme.

By analyzing scholarship on native speakerism from three different prominent practitioners – particularly, Rampton (1990), Widdowson (1994) and Bonfiglio (2013) – I argue that failing to center the impact of racism and whiteness on perceptions of language learners and teachers has allowed the issue to persist much longer than it should have. I focus less on the actual arguments of the works themselves than on the epistemological basis for the authors' arguments. For instance, what were the questions the authors were asking, and how might they have incorporated the topics that are often lacking from these discussions? I conclude by offering my own perspective on nativeness and related issues, and then by discussing more recent essays that actually do center racism in their analysis of nativeness, offering a few paths forward for the literature and for IEP practitioners and students.

Rampton: Displacing the native speaker

In MBH Rampton's 1990 article, 'Displacing the "Native Speaker"', the author takes a sociolinguistic perspective in examining the issues with the term and the assumptions it implies. The article raises several salient points about the construction of this linguistic identity and the problems with it. Early in the article, Rampton writes, 'It is sociolinguistically inaccurate to think of people belonging to only one social group, once and for all' (1990: 98), going on to explain that language changes just as other markers of group identity and membership change. Note that the word 'race' appears here as one of many factors, though this is one of only two appearances in the article, and both times a single item on a longer list.

Rampton is clear throughout the article that the concept of the native speaker is, on its face, inaccurate, as its static nature fails to capture the relationship most individuals have with language. The idea of linguistic status being conferred by birth or childhood location is, in his view, fundamentally incorrect. With that said, readers can begin to notice the overall thrust of his argument in this early passage, namely the fact that native speaker status falls short of accurately capturing linguistic capability, or, in his words, 'expertise'. In his re-conceptualization, it is less that these terms are inherently harmful but that they are a poor method of creating linguistic hierarchies. Indeed, the claim is that we should not classify people by what we call native speaker status, but we should nonetheless categorize them according to their linguistic ability.

As a metaphor for language proficiency, Rampton lists five advantages of expertise over nativeness:

(1) Although they often do, experts do not have to feel close to what they know a lot about. Expertise is different from identification.
(2) Expertise is learned, not fixed or innate.
(3) Expertise is relative. One person's expert is another person's fool.
(4) Expertise is partial. People can be expert in several fields, but they are never omniscient.
(5) To achieve expertise, one goes through processes of certification, in which one is judged by other people. Their standards of assessment can be reviewed and disputed. There is also a healthy tradition of challenging 'experts'. (Rampton, 1990: 98–99)

There is certainly a persuasive argument to be found among these points, perhaps best summarized as the fact that expertise is supposedly more concrete and more attainable rather than being tied to one's birth. It is true that one of the issues with the concept of native speakers is its dependence on inborn attributes, particularly nationality, and the humility implied by points four and five – 'expertise is partial', 'tradition of challenging experts' – is valuable. The fact that an individual cannot transform oneself into a native speaker is indeed one of its many issues as a concept, and the argument that, having undergone metaphorical certification, any learner could become an 'expert' is appealing. Point three, however, reveals something I suspect Rampton did not intend, but which is important to consider nonetheless. Since expertise is indeed relative, there is always the opportunity for those with more power to classify a burgeoning expert as a 'fool', so to speak. Supposedly objective standards can be crafted, but if built by those whom they flatter, learners classified as outside of the ideal will still struggle to reach 'expert' status in the eyes of those with power who get to define 'expert'.

Rampton pushes against archaic ideas of language as only being connected to certain places, a central component upon which native speakerism depends. He also tackles another oft-assumed component of the native speaker, namely their relatively high proficiency in the given language. His article thereby sought to, as the title suggests, displace the term native speaker and replace it with concepts that he feels would more accurately convey what the term merely implies. It is a valuable effort, and when speaking of an individual's language use, any one of these terms might well be accurate. However, the problem with native speaker is not merely that it is factually incorrect, but also that it renders certain people – and *only* certain people – less valuable, something that unfortunately cannot be surmounted by attaining expertise, or by affiliating oneself with a language over several years or decades.

Even though Rampton's critique begins from a sociolinguistic perspective, it still does not capture what is so insidious about the creation and maintenance of native speaker as a status. He comes somewhat closer at the end of his essay, where he acknowledges that antipathy for certain language users is a factor that is underexplored in the essay, but we do not quite reach a full understanding of *why* certain groups may be seen as less valuable, with their method of communication seen as not just inferior to expertise but almost lacking in language altogether. This and other similar critiques of the concept of nativeness take the term quite literally and challenge the nationality aspect without a consideration of the other forms of hierarchization visited upon those classified as insufficiently native.

Widdowson's plenary

A similarly celebrated publication by H.G. Widdowson (1994) served as a plenary address for the 27th Annual TESOL Convention. Its original provenance is important to note because, regardless of its eventual prominence in the written literature, it was, by definition, consumed by several hundred members of the discipline at the moment when it debuted – indeed, plenary speeches have reach. Whereas some journal publications are seen by very few, even publications that are widely cited, the plenary existed outside of the pages of *TESOL Quarterly*.

Widdowson begins by facetiously arguing that 'proper' English belongs to the residents of England before pointing out how unfashionable it had already become to espouse such a view among ELT practitioners. He goes on to explain that the deification of 'standard' English is tied to an oft-unspoken belief that any changes in the languages must be seen as 'radial', emanating forth from said 'standard' (and indeed, down from the top) rather than independent in development. Native speakers, Widdowson states, 'do not have to be English… but they have to be to the language born' (1994: 379). He provides harsh criticism for spelling pedantry, offers valuable insight into the redundancy of grammar making most language variation comprehensible and, most importantly for my argument here, he elucidates the fact that many writing conventions represent adherence to norms rather than objective quality. The plenary speech is effective in its attempts to puncture the puffery around nativeness and standardization.

By the conclusion of his presentation, Widdowson muses that nonnative speaker teachers may in fact be more appropriate stewards of the language than native speakers, stating that the native speaker 'is the outsider' when it comes to understanding 'the attitudes, beliefs, values and so on of the students' cultural world' (1994: 387). Indeed, as Widdowson (1994: 387) continues:

> To the extent that the design of instruction depends on a familiarity with the student reality which English is to engage with, or on the particular sociocultural situations in which teaching and learning take place, then nonnative teachers have a clear and, indeed, decisive advantage.

This effort is appreciated, but it does leave one wondering precisely what those 'sociocultural situations' might actually be, and against whom they may be unfairly applied. The talk is clear to deconstruct the inherent *value* of nativeness, but still lumps all language users into a native and nonnative dichotomy. Widdowson values very specific aspects of Indian English, for example, but by leaving these innovations outside of the language's center, these groups are still othered. Not too dissimilar to Kachru's (1997) concepts of the inner, outer, and expanding circles, celebrating the 'other' does not remove its status as subordinate. Widdowson's (1994) treatise against the supremacy of the native speaker as English teacher is powerful, but the boundaries remain in place once the argument concludes.

Unlike Rampton, Widdowson does not approach this topic from an explicitly sociolinguistic angle. He travels about as far as one could within the era of his plenary, challenging the field's orthodoxy in a way that must have been thrilling in 1994. I am sympathetic to the view that this was the work that was needed at the time, and frankly I do not actually blame him, or Rampton, or other early professionals of the burgeoning field for not being decades ahead of their time. Yet as bold as this work was (and is), it lacks something important. Namely, while Widdowson and similar pieces critique native supremacy, they rarely engage with who the nonnatives are. What qualities do nonnative speakers tend to share that make them different from native speakers, aside from the language into which they were first initiated? There is a hint at social analysis here, but unfortunately, we are still in realm of disembodied language literature, where the identity of the people in question is only related to how they communicate.

Widdowson (1994: 389) concludes by welcoming TESOL's contemporary 'opposition to discrimination against the nonnative teacher, as a matter of sociopolitical principle', but also warns that:

> if it is to be more than a token gesture, such a move needs to be supported by an enquiry into the nature of the subject we are teaching, what constitutes an appropriate approach, what kinds of competence is required of teachers – in other words an enquiry into matters of pedagogic principle which bring sociopolitical concerns and professional standards into alignment. (1994: 389)

First, TESOL International frequently issues statements about discrimination that have 'no teeth' behind them. As I wrote elsewhere about a statement the organization made in 2020: 'The buzzwords "equity," "diversity," "multilingualism," and "multiculturalism" make appearances, followed by an invocation of Dr. King that manages to also implicitly condemn revolutionary action by urging "peaceful protests," despite King's actual beliefs and words on the subject' (Bryan & Gerald, 2020: para. 10). TESOL remains quick to condemn atrocities, but fails to shift its structures to pursue racial justice effectively. As such, it was interesting for me to learn that this is not a new phenomenon.

It is also clear from his argument (and from the rest of his career!) that Widdowson's (1994) work was rightly celebrated as radical for its era. With hindsight, though, we can look back at his call to action and see where the argument itself might have been something of a token gesture – i.e. the audience might have felt flattered because they, too, oppose the inherent supremacy of native speakers, a stance that takes little self-inquiry and risk. Readers and listeners can easily position themselves as morally superior to the grotesques who espouse the sort of antiquated views Widdowson lampoons at the outset of his piece, and feel comforted as they read the article through to its conclusion. As valuable as Widdowson's discussion was, there is an extra step that the discipline needed to take, one which has mostly eluded scholars until recently. The specter of the native speaker continues to hang over many aspects of the field because we so rarely have painted a full picture of who this native person was, beyond the words they used and how they used them. The whiteness of the native speaker has largely remained unmarked and centered, and even powerful critiques like Widdowson's have had little chance to threaten its hegemony.

Bonfiglio: Getting closer

Let us move a bit closer to what I would argue the target should be. By the time Bonfiglio published 'Inventing the Native Speaker' in 2013, the field had seen celebrated entries from Kubota and Lin (2006) on the field's racism, and, less prominently but just as importantly, other scholars were analyzing the discipline through a lens that included an explicit consideration of race (e.g. Lee, 2009). The work of Phillipson (1992, 2008, among others) had become central to analyses of power and domination in language education, and the ground had been laid for a deeper exploration of what had remained previously unmarked in attempts to challenge the native speaker and the assumptions at its core.

After sharing a story of a Singaporean school that edited an advertisement for new teachers, adding 'Caucasian' to 'native speaker', Bonfiglio (2013: 30) laments the 'ostensible innocence and neutrality' of the term, especially when used to refer to 'someone possessing natural authority in language'. Yet, more importantly, Bonfiglio emphasizes how 'notions of race and ethnicity' are quite clearly embedded within the concept of 'native'. Whereas the connection between nativeness and race was only hinted at by Rampton and Widdowson, Bonfiglio makes the connection explicit.

Bonfiglio (2013) provides a detailed history of how we came to call individuals born in certain locations native speakers, which he credits to maternal religious imagery and epistemology in the medieval era, leading to a still-familiar phrase 'mother tongue'. In his estimation, individuals who eventually came to be understood as native speakers are also those who, implicitly, are closer to godliness and sanctity. He eventually draws a line all the way to the present day, when discourse between mothers and infants can be referred to as 'motherese'. Bonfiglio describes the language between a mother and child as 'one of the most intimate contexts imaginable', and one that is often 'romanticized in a precognitive, emotional, spontaneous, natural, and bodily matrix, one that can move in free association from lactation to language, from breastfeeding to language feeding' (2013: 54). For those who are excluded from nativeness, their own use of the language is implicitly and inherently bastardized, distant from the love that a mother tongue can provide. They can never become native, no matter how hard they study, because they were not granted the opportunity to be fed the language. There is indeed something romantic about a supposed native speaker, an innate gift bestowed only upon those fortunate enough to have been born to certain parents in certain places. Yet nativeness is hardly an objective fact, nor is it anything close to an attribute without societal categorization. Through such discursive means, native speakers are beatified, and associated with a particular sort of maternity, and one can see how nonnatives being categorized as inferior can lead to all sorts of implications, but suffice it to say that a deficit-based mindset (Delpit, 1995) is implied.

The non-linguistic half of the supposedly neutral native speaker equation is nationality or birthplace, yet of course nationality has never been a neutral concept, nor has it ever been fully separated from language. For example, Bonfiglio (2013: 54) describes 'nationalist adhesives that fuse self and nation' as 'fabricated from myriad ideologies of ownership and exclusive possession'. These prejudicial aspects of ideologies, Bonfiglio contends, are 'among the least perceptible and most embedded forms of nationalism'. One conclusion to be drawn from this portion of his argument is that – even leaving aside my own argument about the importance of considering race as a factor in supposed nativeness – categorizing individuals or groups according to their country and language has the capacity to be harmful in itself, as conceptions of nations and the people within them are not without hierarchy. Any argument that rests on uplifting the nonnative rather than seeking to dismantle the concept of nativeness falls short the justice required to push the field farther ahead.

Bonfiglio makes clear that nativeness has been constructed over several centuries, occupying a place in the broader hierarchy from which we continue to struggle to move it, and, on occasion, he brings race into his analysis, certainly much more so than the previous scholars and their contemporaries. It would perhaps be unfair to underline a lack of raciolinguistic analysis when the most influential work in that emerging realm had yet to be published at the time of Bonfiglio's writing. In a way, Bonfiglio's essay represents more or less the best hope for a scholar writing at the time, as it is not a purely language-focused work and does not shy away from racism as an important factor. Nevertheless, the difference is clear when one looks just a few more years into the future at scholars with a full-throated inclusion of race and whiteness in their work on nativeness, some of which is discussed below.

Getting Explicit

We need to be explicit about what we are hoping to counteract; we, for example, cannot be afraid to say the word 'white'. Despite the fact that this concept is certainly defined differently depending on the context, engaging in color-evasiveness serves no one but those who are already in possession of racialized power. Recent works in the field on issues of native speakerism have thankfully moved towards more direct engagement required to dismantle these hierarchies. In these newer pieces, there are lessons for both Intensive English Program (IEP) practitioners and for their students.

Ramjattan (2015, 2018, 2019a, 2019b) details the additional burden placed upon racialized language teachers and speakers in Canada. Particularly zeroing in on the ways that accent-based oppression harms certain language users, he makes clear that racialized speakers have trouble evading these restrictions because 'the pathologizing of immigrants' accents serves to mask the structural racism that they must face when securing employment' (2019a: 12). Indeed, if such linguistic prejudice is not related to language learners in IEPs, they are, arguably, being sold a false bill of goods.

Ruecker and Ives (2015) analyze online advertisements for EFL teachers, focusing on how the images of the people in the advertisements were all young and white, even though the selected marketing materials specified only native speakers rather than particular races. The authors show how this not particularly subtle alignment between languaging and whiteness influences ELT educators worldwide. Regarding one company's advertisements, Ruecker and Ives (2015: 749) observe that the primary themes of several videos are limited in their focus 'on teaching and the dominant presence of whiteness'. For the students whom applicants eventually teach, these EFL teachers represent an early experience with English and its association with whiteness, and articles such as Ruecker and Ives help uncover what is visible yet mostly unsaid before recent years.

Kubota (2021) offers a vision of critical antiracist pedagogy in ELT in which she explains is a necessary path forward for the field if it has any hopes of living up to its supposed ideals of pluralistic language education. Kubota explains that the field must 'question power and ideologies that reproduce the system of domination and subordination and enact antiracism with critical reflexivity on power dynamics, one's own privilege, and potential pitfalls in enactment' (2021: 241). As we have observed by tracking the gradual shifts in scholarly discourse around native speakers, when racism is not included, a vital aspect of power dynamics is left out of the discussion and the problems remain entrenched.

Fraud and Deceit

More recently, my own work (Gerald, 2022) envisions a new path for the field. Using the diagnostic criteria of Antisocial Personality Disorder to 'diagnose' the issues in the language teaching field, one of the issues I examine is how I, like many other English language teachers, fell into this career without qualifications other than my classification as native. There is a complicating factor, however, in that my Blackness occasionally worked against this same assumption that my nativeness was sufficient; nevertheless, broadly speaking, one frequently only needs a certain passport to find their way into the field. Nativeness is clearly not an objective fact, nor would it be different if there were incontrovertible criteria for nativeness that individuals could strive to meet, akin to Rampton's argument in favor of expertise. The binary concept of the native and nonnative is fraudulent – not only in that it is invented, but also in that it makes false promises to teachers and students alike. Both groups are told in one way or another that they may inherently be more valuable depending upon the social-psychological category into which they have been placed, with the caveat being that one's appearance or speech must meet certain qualifications or standards; this is what Ramjattan (2019) referred to as *aesthetic labour*. Aesthetic labor merely serves to reify the fact that nativeness is fraudulent, and, because of its conditionality and subjectivity, it is only useful in creating hierarchies that uphold the *status quo*:

> Ultimately, when a system prioritizes whiteness in determining who is allowed to enter a profession, that system is taking great pains to create inherent value where there is none, and in the process expending effort on convincing the supposed beneficiaries of their deserved success. We needed to believe we were valuable based only on accidents of birth, and that our students' languaging was therefore less valuable than ours. We needed to believe that we brought something to the classroom, that we didn't need any credentials other than who we were. And if it just so happened that we stumbled into the ability to be effective educators, so be it. (Gerald, 2022: 68)

Since much of the earlier literature did not quite draw the connection between nativeness and whiteness, many of us have continued to be told, and unfortunately believe, that to advance in the field, we need to correct whatever problems within us would lead to us being categorized as outside the boundaries of nativeness. One way that this misguided belief manifests is through the deceitful practice of 'accent reduction', pushed onto anyone who does not sound the right way. Companies and institutions frequently advertise quite explicitly that accent reduction will supposedly improve a person's career, and that individuals would be best served by paying large amounts of money to chase this ideal, a burden which inevitably falls more heavily on international students, particularly for those who are participants in IEPs and are being instructed on how they may 'assimilate', 'acculturate' or 'integrate' into English-based higher education. How many IEP curricula include a course with 'pronunciation' as part of the title?

As Ennser-Kananen *et al.* (2021: 337) explain, 'The message to international students is, in turn, that there is almost no limit to the expense and effort they have to invest in order to fit in. While none of this may be the intention of higher education policy makers, it is nonetheless a likely consequence'. Accent reduction is a Sisyphean task forced upon those who will never actually be native enough, as even a 'successful' accent reduction student may be described as having gained or adopted a new accent, like an actor rehearsing for a film. One particular company, Accents Off (n.d.), describes one's native accent as 'part of who you are' and claim that one may 'switch back' into their original accent whenever they want. The goal, according to Accent Off, is to eliminate the 'hard edges' of one's nonnative accent in order to facilitate 'a much smoother cultural and professional transition'. Promoted under the guise of equity and multi- or pluriculturality, language providers argue that 'clear communication is an asset high on every employer's priority list' (Accents Off, n.d.). Participants in such programs are being asked to adopt an aural mask to assuage the impatience of the white perceiving subject (Flores & Rosa, 2015). Since accents are an important aspect of the mirage of the native, practitioners in this field often pretend as though we are benefiting our learners (and our colleagues or institutions) by upholding the idea that there is one right way – or at least a better or more appropriate way – to be an English user. We engage with this hierarchization as if it is just and acceptable, while it continues to transfer money from vulnerable populations to an industry that could make much more equitable choices.

A New Vision

Considering the above discussion, there are several ways that IEPs and IEP practitioners may contribute to changing how the field engages with issues of nativeness and race. First, although as language education practitioners we are often beholden to ideologies that position students as in need of support and 'readiness', we will always fall short if the burden continues to be placed on the learners rather than the schools and/or workplaces into which we hope to send them also assuming some responsibility. IEPs should partner with their host institutions as well as surrounding workplaces to ensure that they are accepting of supposedly nonnative speech rather than the unidirectional placing of expectations upon the learners. The pluralistic values that our field claims to uphold cannot be achieved when the onus is on the racialized; practitioners need ensure that this bridge is built more effectively and multidirectionally.

Second, educators who work in IEPs should receive comprehensive education, either during their formal studies or otherwise, in the intersection of racism, whiteness and language education. Unfortunately, many TESOL (Teaching English to Speakers of Other Language) certification programs still offer language teacher credentials without introducing pre-service professionals to problematizations of nativeness and race or how these concepts overlap. We commit a great disservice the longer we do not take the time to ensure that discussions of nativeness and race are a standard part of teacher education.

Finally, IEPs, like many other aspects of the language field, are constrained by regulations of accreditation bodies and their host institutions, and they therefore often must tie student progress to test results. Nevertheless, practitioners have the freedom to reframe how tests are positioned and utilized within their pedagogy. Instructors should be transparent about the harmful ideologies involved in such assessments and work collectively with students to challenge their deification. Ultimately, the points here revolve around interrogating the assumptions many of us make as members of this field, and if we begin to ask what I believe are the right questions, we stand a much better chance of building a supportive language education structure. Accordingly, the wrong rhetorical battle has been fought, as the role of race has not been considered as a component of the proficiency goals allocated to our students. We must assist our students in attaining their language learning goals while at the same time guiding them to question the racialized constructs that cultivate many of these goals. What does it mean, for instance, to be 'acculturated' to the expectations of US higher education? What are the ideals upon which the expectations are based? We know enough now – and enough has now been published – that we can begin to approach what needs to be done, whether within IEPs, in EFL, or in language education generally. I hope that we make the hard choices we need to.

Note

(1) An earlier version of this chapter employed quotes around the terms *native* and *nonnative*. While the quotes have been removed out of interest of facilitating the readability of this piece, the author would like to acknowledge the capricious inaccuracy of these terms as well as his disagreement with their uncritical usage.

References

Accents Off (n.d.) About accents off. See https://accentsoff.com/about/ (accessed March 2022).
Bonfiglio, T. (2013) Inventing the native speaker. *Critical Multilingualism Studies* 1 (2), 29–58.
Bryan, K. and Gerald, J. (2020) The weaponization of English. *Language Magazine*, 17 August. See https://www.languagemagazine.com/2020/08/17/the-weaponization-of-english/ (accessed March 2022).
Delpit, L. (1995) *Other People's Children: Cultural Conflict in the Classroom*. New York, NY: The New Press.

Gerald, J.P.B. (2022) *Antisocial Language Teaching: English and the Pervasive Pathology of Whiteness.* Bristol: Multilingual Matters.

Ennser-Kananen, J., Halonen, M. and Saarinen, T. (2021) 'Come join us and lose your accent!': Accent modification courses as hierarchization of international students. *Journal of International Students* 11 (2), 322–340.

Flores, N. and Rosa, J. (2015) Undoing appropriateness: Raciolinguistic ideologies and language diversity in education. *Harvard Educational Review* 85 (2), 149–171. https://doi.org/10.17763/0017-8055.85.2.149.

Kachru, B. (1997) World Englishes and English-using communities. *Annual Review of Applied Linguistics* 17, 66–87.

Kubota, R. (2021) Critical antiracist pedagogy in ELT. *ELT Journal* 75 (3), 237–246.

Kubota, R. and Lin, A. (2006) Race and TESOL: Introduction to concepts and theories. *TESOL Quarterly* 40 (3), 471–493.

Lee, I. (2009) Situated globalization and racism: An analysis of Korean high school EFL textbooks. *Language and Literacy* 11 (1), 1–14.

Phillipson, R. (1992) *Linguistic Imperialism.* Oxford: Oxford University Press.

Phillipson, R. (2008) The linguistic imperialism of neoliberal empire. *Critical Inquiry in Language Studies* 5 (1), 1–43.

Ramjattan, V. (2015) Lacking the right aesthetic: Everyday employment discrimination in Toronto private language schools. *Equality, Diversity and Inclusion: An International Journal* 38 (4), 692–704.

Ramjattan, V. (2018) Raciolinguistics and the aesthetic labourer. *Journal of Industrial Relations* 61 (5), 1–13.

Ramjattan, V. (2019a) Racializing the problem of and solution to foreign accent in business. *Applied Linguistics Review* 13 (4), 1–18.

Ramjattan, V. (2019b) The white native speaker and inequality regimes in the private English language school. *Intercultural Education* 30 (2), 126–140.

Rampton, M. (1990) Displacing the 'native speaker': expertise, affiliation, and inheritance. *ELT Journal* 44 (2), 97–101.

Ruecker, T. and Ives, L. (2015) White native English speakers needed: The rhetorical construction of privilege in online teacher recruitment spaces. *TESOL Quarterly* 49 (4), 733–754.

Widdowson, H.G. (1994) The ownership of English. *TESOL Quarterly* 28 (2), 377–389.

9 The Other Side of Community Engagement Projects: Benefits to the Community?

James M. Perren

Introduction

Service learning and civic engagement can be transformative pedagogical tools for learners of English by providing Intensive English Program (IEP) practitioners and their host institutions with opportunities to develop positive connections with their local communities. Historically, the primary duty of an IEP is to prepare English language learners (ELLs) with resources necessary for success in mainstream higher education courses in the United States. While on the one hand IEPs 'are often simultaneously conservative and progressive in their curricular offerings' (Wurr & Perren, 2015: 25), longstanding IEP course offerings have consisted of proficiency-based classes focused on the traditional four language skills of reading, writing, listening and speaking, and oft-times culture as well. English as a second language (ESL) students typically progress along a curriculum path in a somewhat linear and accelerated manner, with targeted language and academic skills designed around courses organized along meaningful proficiency development sequences. The TESOL instructors assigned to these programs are usually supported to innovate and develop the curriculum in order to meet the changing needs of student populations and the interests of government or private industry sponsors. In most cases, IEP pedagogy aligns with student-centered teaching methodologies typifying English language education in the West.

My own institution has various experiences conducting both in-person and virtual service-learning projects within its MA TESOL program, a site of professional training for future IEP practitioners. For example, TESOL faculty and graduate students volunteered to serve meals at a local transition shelter, serving homeless families with children. Students and their families also painted storm drains in a local neighborhood, joining approximately one hundred other volunteers from the community. In another example, TESOL students in an online teaching practicum course created lesson plans and shared teaching responsibilities for an English language class with students from the San Diego area and Mexico. The project was realized in collaboration with the director of a regional employment access organization. Students developed the pedagogical materials and reflected on the entirety of the experience in journals, which was perceived as rewarding.

The purpose of this chapter is to examine many facets of service learning conducted in IEPs by reviewing and integrating from the relevant literature on service-learning pedagogy throughout the United States. Within IEPs service-learning projects can provide authentic learning environments that benefit student acculturation, language skills, interpersonal skills and student identity, as well as foster a sense of language ownership, empowerment and recognition of community membership (Bunning & Kostka, 2018; Cameron, 2015; Collopy *et al.*, 2020; Douglas Jr, 2017; Howlett *et al.*, 2019; Marlow, 2007; Perren *et al.*, 2013; Shannahan *et al.*, 2020; Sousa, 2015). Student benefit is understandably a central concern in the development of these types of projects, yet the impact within the community where these projects occur must also be considered. This chapter provides a brief review of service-learning projects in US-based IEPs, discussing their benefits, limitations and potential for developing collaborative initiatives between an institution and its host community. In doing so, it offers a closer inspection of the impact of service-learning projects within their local communities, considers the obligations of pedagogues to the community when incorporating service-learning projects into curricula, and offers suggestions for guidelines as we move toward the future.

Benefits of Service-Learning Projects in IEPs

Research on service-learning pedagogy in IEPs highlights a broad range of benefits in language skill development gained by English language learners (Askildson *et al.*, 2013; Perren, 2013; Perren *et al.*, 2013; Shannahan *et al.*, 2020). The reported benefits to students' language skills development are substantial. For instance, Shannahan *et al.* (2020) describe how dialogue journal use was examined in the exploration of both IEP learner identity and language development. The researchers analyzed 13 intermediate IEP student dialogue journals in which teachers integrated service learning into writing instruction. Student writing development was monitored by way of 'critical awareness and political awakening' (2020: 88). Findings indicate that teacher-student dialogue in conjunction with service-learning holds promise for permitting students to view multiple perspectives and critical understandings of the writing process as they began to recognize themselves as valued community participants.

Perren (2013) also employs qualitative research methods to interpret student reflections, student presentations, and online survey data. Participants commented on the meaningfulness and importance of learning various language elements such as vocabulary and slang, and they thought highly of communicating with other language users. In another study, Douglas Jr (2017) reports on the effects of a service-learning project that was implemented in a community college IEP among English language learners of three proficiency levels. At the end of the project, participants developed a brochure describing the construction skills that they had acquired by engaging in the service. They also later indicated that they believed the project had increased their English proficiency, boosted confidence in speaking English, and enhanced their desire to participate in future projects. These studies, in other words, demonstrate the engagement of students and benefits of the service-learning interventions.

Another study, Askildson et al. (2013), describes an eight-week intensive course with a service-learning component that was designed to influence students' understanding of US social structures and the associated challenges of these structures. Researchers used quantitative and qualitative data that incorporated pre- and post-language proficiency tests as well as intercultural sensitivity measures, permitting the study to demonstrate students' linguistic development and ability to use language in a socioculturally appropriate manner. Askildson et al. found that averages on pre- to post-test language proficiency measures increased, suggesting how the service-learning component had a favorable effect on students' understanding of social service providers in the community surrounding the host institution, and they report that participants benefited from learning about how social justice issues can be addressed in their home cultures and countries.

Marlow (2007) describes a one-year pilot program in which ESL students were the recipients of a service-learning component of a credit-bearing college course. English speakers from the community worked together with international ESL students in 30 hours of self-selected service and activities, which included campus and community-based events such as museum outings and bowling as well as more practical activities such as apartment searching and banking issues for personal finance. Structured in-class tutoring sessions were centered on language activities. Marlow reports that ESL students were able to apply concepts learned in other university courses with structured assistance from service-learning partners, and they acquired linguistic and cultural knowledge from the project.

IEPs may also incorporate community service opportunities into their programming. Wurr and Perren (2015) discuss the importance of service-learning arrangements for IEP students. They present examples of service-learning projects involving IEPs, their students, and community partners and report on the negotiation of students finding common ground with their community partner service recipients. Community partners express appreciation for the diversity that the IEP students bring and the exposure they gain from the variety of experience levels. There are a range of options available at different stages of development for supporting service learning in IEPs; these innovative practices can structure experiences in which IEP students are both recipients and providers of service at some point in the development of a program.

These studies about language skill development within IEP service-learning initiatives demonstrate several important benefits. The studies show that IEP students can develop English language skills in multiple areas, specifically pertaining to the writing process, listening and speaking, and standardized test-taking skills (Askildson *et al.*, 2013; Perren *et al.*, 2013; Shannahan *et al.*, 2020). Other reported benefits include practical life skills and confidence development, as well as broader applications of content knowledge into real life and employment upon reentry into their home country. A prominent commonality among these studies is the 'sense of empowerment in ESL students', facilitated by their desire to be 'part of their community, allowing them to work cooperatively to develop authorial voice, increasing their audience awareness in writing, and fostering critical reflection that leads to a better understanding of social problems and civic responsibility' (Perren *et al.*, 2013: 463).

Limitations of IEP Service-Learning Projects

Implementing service-learning pedagogies can be a challenging endeavor, and there are multiple limitations related to the practical aspects of implementing service learning in IEPs as well as with conducting research associated with such projects. For example, Bunning and Kostka (2018) note that service-learning participants in different courses with different instructors (even when these courses are within the same program) make it difficult to develop a cohesive analysis of the impact of instruction or students' skills development. Low proficiency of participating students, lack of knowledge of US social problems on the part of IEP participants, limits with transportation, and scheduling challenges with community partners have also been identified as limitations to service-learning projects (Askildson *et al.*, 2013). Transportation is a particular complication, as few IEP students have their own cars, university vehicle systems are not always free, and city bus routes are limited (Sousa, 2015).

A significant barrier is the narrow range of service work available for students to engage with the local community. Institutions must be able to not only identify the needs of community partners but also be able to match what they can offer as far as student service-learning interventions. A non-profit community organization, for example, might prefer a particular skill set or English proficiency level, and participants in the IEP course must therefore also possess the requisite area of expertise. Consideration must be given to the benefits and limitations when coordinating the logistics of potential activities (Perren, 2013), and sufficient time should be reserved for preparation and initial implementation. Douglas Jr (2017: 1096) describes the first time running a service-learning project as 'a bit haphazard' and 'limited to on-campus activities'. Other limitations include students' reluctance to perform a service task that they believe they are ill-prepared to undertake, and instructors should recognize that students might also participate and complete associated assignments in order to earn a grade (Collopy *et al.*, 2020; Perren *et al.*, 2013).

Engagement is an important pedagogical principle to keep in mind when planning service-learning projects. Askildson *et al.* (2013) discuss the importance of the public good through the Campus Compact Principles. Using these principles, Askildson *et al.* ask questions throughout their project, such as *How have campus community boundaries been negotiated? Has the community been consulted?* The importance of presenting information found in projects like that of Askildson *et al.* is a critical part of fostering dialogue between institution and community. Participants in related research also report having limited direct experiences with people from other cultures and little previous learning about people from other cultures (Collopy *et al.*, 2020). Collopy *et al.* (2020) report that intercultural awareness was only occasionally found in self-report measurements for many participants, and in many cases such awareness had primarily taken place through watching television shows and movies about people from other cultures. Moreover, without adequately informed planning, there is danger of implementing underdeveloped reflection methods that do not capture the essence and purpose of critical reflection (Douglas Jr, 2017). Finally, there is risk of reinforcing negative stereotypes and paternalism (Cervantes *et al.*, 2021; Desmond *et al.*, 2011), as well as a risk of reifying psychosocial dichotomies which lead to superficial learning experiences.

In addition to the practical limitations, many practitioners discuss a need to improve research design and methodology. One limitation is the requirement of having projects completed within a one-semester time frame, which is quite short for enacting sustained change (Howlett *et al.*, 2019). Students have provided less-than-favorable reports on the quality and extent of their participation due to the time constraints of the projects. In addition, students may feel obligated to participate in service-learning projects (and in the research). In cases in which the same individual is the researcher, classroom instructor and service-learning site supervisor, evaluations of program efficacy may be biased (Cameron, 2015). Moreover, the frequently low number of participating students provides a relatively small sample size in some projects (Howlett *et al.*, 2019). There is also an overall lack of service-learning research, which impacts the generalizability of the results and the ability of triangulating data. Other limitations, described by Bunning and Kostka (2018), may be an inability to directly observe students at their service site; limited insight from community partner organization management, supervisors, or instructors; and survey data based on students' self-reporting and memory. These limitations are acknowledged in the research design literature (Creswell, 2014; Mackey & Gass, 2015; Mertler, 2021), and they constitute a research design validity and reliability issue necessitating reconsideration of research ethics in applied linguistics research.

Service-Learning Potential for Participants

While the previous section discussed limitations of service-learning pedagogy, the current section presents their potential for positive impact, which includes benefits to cultural development, intercultural communication, and various other skills (e.g. technology use for employment).

The concept of cultural learning is positioned as a critical component in IEP skills development for service-learning projects. To illustrate, Sousa (2015) describes an IEP project that examined student and community partner responses to an upper-intermediate communications course that focused on general English language proficiency, academic writing skills and culture. Sousa reported favorable comments about the curriculum from the participants, but also highlighted student comments about challenges in making cultural connections and 'having difficulty translating words, concepts or cultural perspectives' (2015: 44). Miller and Kostka (2015) provide another example of the potential for cultural development with service-learning projects in IEPs. They describe culture learning through an intercultural and intergenerational oral history project. The researchers demonstrate the benefits and challenges that emerged through the cooperative construction of meaning in the sharing of life stories and how these stories filled linguistic and experience gaps between project stakeholders (i.e. international students, their elderly conversation partners, community partner staff, and university faculty members). Indeed, service learning represents a core learning experience, and increased language development may be only a secondary benefit when considered alongside the experiential intercultural opportunities that students are exposed to (Askildson *et al.*, 2013; Ravina, 2022).

Another example of the potential for cultural learning in IEP service-learning projects comes from Collopy *et al.* (2020), who examined intercultural communication competence by using pre- and post-test questionnaires with IEP students. They utilized a reciprocal service-learning approach to measure foundational attitudes of intercultural competence during a 10-week period of a regular academic semester. The project involved 33 pre-service teachers and 22 international English language learners, all of whom reported little interaction with individuals from other cultures prior to participating. Conversation partner activities were a focus of the service learning. The sessions were shaped by themes of personal identity and the 'exploration of one's own cultural lens and values' (Collopy *et al.*, 2020: 26). Results showed both undergraduate students and international English language learners demonstrated growth. The undergraduate students were provided with opportunities to 'reexamine their biases, deficit-orientation and privileged perspective' (2020: 30), and the IEP students expanded their interactional confidence and tolerance for ambiguity in intercultural interactions.

Service-learning initiatives also have potential to develop other unique skills for participants. Askildson *et al.* (2013) describe the development of appreciation for diversity, understanding of social justice, discernment of vocation, and sense of citizenship by participants in one service-learning project with ESL students. Other skills include the ability to deal with negative people and social learning (Perren, 2013); developing metacognitive skills and communication goal setting (Bunning & Kostka, 2018); learning to participate in campus-based events such as learning academic library skills (Marlow, 2007); and instituting practical skills such as learning to make a brochure or organizing a food inventory (Douglas Jr, 2017). Several of these reports describe the potential of expanding technological skills that can support language learning, which also overlaps with professional skills needed in the workforce and in one's future employment (Cervantes *et al.*, 2021; Howlett *et al.*, 2019; Macknish, 2019). Possibly one of the more critical features of service-learning projects is the significant long-term impact of service-learning pedagogy on relevant stakeholders; participation in service-learning pedagogical activity can lead to future patterns of volunteering in general civic engagement (Cameron, 2015).

Obligations to the Host Community

This section considers the obligations of educators using service-learning pedagogies to their community partner organizations and other stakeholders. While the focus here is more oriented toward the institutional level, they are naturally of relevance to IEP practitioners whose units are housed within a host college or university. Of particular importance are the obligations that educators have to the local communities when structuring and implementing their curriculum offerings via service-learning pedagogies. A cornerstone concept is how the community surrounding an institution is affected by the actions undertaken in service-learning projects. The discussion primarily centers around three separate service-learning projects (Chupp & Joseph, 2010; George-Paschal et al., 2019; Mitchell & Buckingham, 2021), each conducted with substantial institutional support, and each with a distinct focus regarding the university's obligations to the community.

George-Paschal et al. (2019) describe a university-wide service-learning program that was coordinated with the university administration and the institution's core mission and values. The primary purpose of this project was to identify the university's service-learning program by looking at the outcomes upon faculty, students and community partner organizations. The research utilized qualitative research design and data analysis techniques to develop a rich understanding of how service learning impacted stakeholders. George-Paschal et al. outline the benefits of a solid administrative and leadership team for undertaking the tasks of service-learning placements, management of partnerships and program organization. The project also included a professional staff position, the establishment of a university advisory committee, and coordination with an annual fellowship for training service-learning faculty. (This latter point resonates with me personally since I was also extremely fortunate to earn a faculty service-learning fellowship during my second year as a full-time university professor.) Yet despite the distinct benefits for students and faculty in George-Paschal et al.'s study, community partners had difficulty distinguishing different types of service and suggested increasing institutional efforts to educate local partners and to establish clear expectations for partnerships. There also seemed to be an apparent lack of long-term commitment on the part of the university, with many service-learning projects being of a short duration (due to the constraint upon most projects to work within the traditional academic semester). In addition, students should understand the potential impact of their work, and community partners expressed wanting more information about university resources.

Mitchell and Buckingham (2021) provide another relevant study of an institution's obligations to its local community, reporting on the need for a strategic emphasis on service-learning project development, implementation and design. Their purpose was to investigate how service-learning best practices affect the level of strategic impact for community partners. They contend that there is a general lack of thorough empirical testing in educational research, and they point out that most educational service-learning research is directed at what students gain (see also George-Paschal et al., 2019). They indicate the need for examining the impact on community partners with more attention, investment, and evaluation. While Mitchell and Buckingham (2021) found that community partners do benefit from the university-community relationship, this doesn't occur without challenges. However, when the community partner is viewed as a partner rather than a recipient, the university-community relationship can thrive. Mitchell and Buckingham contend that service-learning projects and program design within an institution are related to five separate aspects: individual versus group service learning, length of semester, institutional support, community-partner sectors and community partner capacity. The authors also report that group projects and maintaining a service-learning director were the most beneficial to the community partners. However, Mitchell and Buckingham advise that universities and colleges need to establish service learning to be more than simply a single assignment or course component. They suggest that institutions strategically formulate community involvement, meaning that institutions need to consider a 'community facing' program element which requires 'careful crafting, significant investment, and vigilant evaluation' (2021: 23).

Chupp and Joseph (2010) examine the impact of service-learning in a graduate school of social work in Cleveland, Ohio. They propose intentional focus at three levels for impact of service learning in higher education institutions: students, the institution and the community. They relate how they established their long-standing school of social work and service-learning projects based on the needs of the moderate-to-high poverty neighborhoods that surround their institution, the goal of which was to 'achieve the most substantial and broadly beneficial' service experience outcomes (2010: 191). They noted four approaches to service-learning impact (i.e. traditional, social justice, critical and institutional change), and they emphasized the institution's broader quest for institutional impact through service learning. The authors describe the original pilot project that took place over several years, the communication and interaction with community stakeholders, and the various decisions that were made targeting the development of authentic relationships. Project members determined that maximizing community impact necessitated cultivating trusting relationships between the institution and the community, and increasing cultural competencies for all participants, not just the institution, was prioritized. For instance, community partners were expected to take part in the assessment of activities, and certain community partners were designated as participants with whom to share information, resources, and decision making. A local renovated library and a regional faith-based community organization were identified as meeting places for community residents to brainstorm revitalization strategies. Local government officials (including the mayor) were invited to speak at the kick-off event. Members of the police, fire department, and school as well as city council members took part in the development of the service-learning project and the development of the course. They identified the topic of the course and programs to be shaped around 'predatory lending, foreclosures, and depopulation' with an emphasis on vacant and abandoned properties in the city (Chupp & Joseph, 2010: 201). The institution identified mechanisms in which they could become 'a better neighbor', requiring long-term sustained effort for the application and extension of knowledge within their specific community context. In essence, Chupp and Joseph found that meaningful impact for the local community required community members to be engaged as not just recipients of the service but also as program design and implementation partners. However, the authors also warn that unless there is concentration on a comprehensive institutional structure, processes, culture, and priorities, 'it is quite possible that the very learning and values to which the students are exposed through the service activity are undermined by a contrasting set of values exhibited through some of the institution's structure and practices' (2010: 197).

Universities have an obligation to seek ways to benefit their local communities, thus it is important to determine the impact service-learning projects may have upon them, and pedagogues must consider community impact when incorporating service-learning projects. Scholarship in service learning outside of English language education suggests that educators and institutions need to prioritize learning about the communities in which they are located. This process entails fostering how educational institutions can better understand the complicated issues affecting members of the community in the surrounding area. It also involves instructing community members about how their lives and interactions with the institution and its representatives are connected to the broader issues within society. Chupp and Joseph (2010: 191) argue that 'students, faculty, and universities as a whole could stand to benefit as they engage with residents and other community members to understand the broader context and structural causes of pressing social problems and to seek large-scale community change'. In order to prioritize service learning around critical issues as well as the needs and characteristics of the community requires not only a shift in strategic implementation of resources on the part of an institution, but also a reprioritization of research agendas for those conducting research and the support provided to them.

IEPs and Guidelines for the Future

Suggestions for moving forward with service-learning projects should be understood within both the historical and established research and practices that support English language education and general education. As a practical issue, the filling of critical administrative roles (e.g. a Director of Community Engagement [Chupp & Joseph, 2010], Service-learning Director [Mitchell & Buckingham, 2021], community-based learning coordinator [Askildson *et al.*, 2013]) is part of an institution's obligation to its community; designating an administrative service-learning director can substantially improve community partner outcomes (Askildson *et al.*, 2013; Mitchell & Buckingham, 2020). Institutions and organizations must employ sufficient levels of staff and prioritize resources for their training, and there are financial benefits to ensuring such support takes place: service-learning providers can maintain documentation of the *pro bono* costs provided to the community as a business expense and deduct these costs for tax purposes (Leonard, 2022). Another vital ingredient is to communicate regularly and willingly with community partners regarding a project's purpose and anticipated outcomes; there must be a willingness to meet community partner needs on behalf of the institutional partners (Perren, 2013). Furthermore, being considerate, knowledgeable, and thankful of the community partner's contributions as well as their specific mission and focus is essential (Dowling & Perren, 2021). These related topics of communication and awareness of community partners coincides with other relevant service-learning research in education (see Chupp & Joseph, 2010; George-Paschal *et al.*, 2019).

Institutions are also obligated to sufficiently communicate about research design and disseminate findings to their host communities. Community partners must have voice in the planning, integration and evaluation of service-learning project effectiveness (Chupp & Joseph, 2010; Mitchell & Buckingham, 2021). A relevant objective is to utilize multiple data collection methods to determine what language learners perceive to be important regarding their learning techniques in service-learning encounters in the community (Bunning & Kostka, 2018), and triangulation of this data with 'insights from partner organizations staff and supervisors who interact with students during their service work' (2018: 139) is vital. Future research could include the utilization of various methods of data collection and analysis (e.g. follow-up interviews) that integrate follow-up surveys after the completion of a project in order to better understand the experiences and attitudes students, volunteers, and other community stakeholders in service-learning projects (Bunning & Kostka, 2018). Surveys allow for ascertaining how to improve relationships between students and community participants as well as how to improve program design. Another proposal for future service-learning projects in IEPs is to measure quantitative linguistic competence using standardized English language proficiency exams. Cervantes *et al.* (2021) discusses the possibility that students and programs only participate in service-learning research and respond with surveys and reflection papers because they feel obligated to do so, which more elaborate data collection techniques such as pre- and post-proficiency testing might uncover. Finally, researchers must pay attention to the maintenance of ethical research practices that consistently incorporate inclusive naming and nomenclature practices for stakeholders, adhere to informed consent processes, and secure official approval from university institutional review boards (Perren & Wurr, 2015).

Table 9.1 presents the benchmark topics for future consideration as proposed by George-Paschal *et al.* (2019), Mitchell and Buckingham (2020) and Chupp and Joseph (2010). Clearly, there is a need to weave community voice into the design, planning, and implementation of service-learning projects regardless of whether they take place within the general coursework of a university or college or within an IEP. Moreover, there are innovative service-learning projects taking place in IEPs!

Table 9.1 Obligations to the community: Key points and future research

George-Paschal et al. (2019)	• some anxiety seems to facilitate service experience to have a positive result for students; • students may not fully grasp their potential to cause harm; • community partners eager to transform student preconceptions that prevent learning into unknowns; • recognize service learning in promotion and tenure criteria; • need for faculty preparation and willingness to accept leadership role for successful partnerships; • continue to hold focus groups for all stakeholder groups; • longitudinal study with follow up interviews and surveys focus groups as facilitated interactive discussions between different stakeholder groups to understand both impacts and shortcomings;
Mitchell & Buckingham (2020)	• inclusion of a service-learning director position as the most convincing research result; • teamwork structure is an important topic for service-learning design; • traditional semester time constraints found inconclusive; • explanation of how a service-learning director fosters university–community relationships and positive outcomes for community partners is needed; • teamwork vs. individual should be a continued area of future research; • contradictory 'more time needed' concept warrants further explanation;
Chupp & Joseph (2010)	• capacity, knowledge, and networks among community stakeholders and residents; • access and input to university decision-making processes; • community capacity to manage and sustain investments in revitalization; • Improved quality of life for community residents.

For instance, one example is the California State University (San Marcos), where the IEP offers students service-learning opportunities through a choice of face-to-face, online or a hybrid options.

These objectives may be fostered through open communication and a sharing of resources and expertise among all stakeholders, noting that such efforts in and of themselves facilitate the commitment to reciprocity. Collopy *et al.* (2020: 31) suggest that future projects should also consider the interaction between participants' emotions during service-learning experiences and 'the development of diversity-related attitudes and behaviors'. Research within future service-learning projects should not simply examine language aims, but also explore the language learning outcomes for sociocultural pragmatics and how 'service-learning interactions significantly enrich and advance communicative competence' (Askildson *et al.*, 2013: 430). Finally, the shift to online video conferencing formats that arose during the Covid pandemic have significantly impacted the design and delivery of pedagogical content. Moving forward, virtual educational contexts must also be considered. And, as sites of innovation that have the potential to influence the relationship of their host institutions with the local communities, IEPs can lead the changes. Simple, innovative steps, such as developing faculty positions focused on service learning (e.g. Coordinator of Service

Learning), can position IEPs as campus and community leaders as well as reinvent their relevancy within their host institutions.

Conclusion

This chapter provides a description of the relevant literature on service learning in higher education. It considered the findings from various articles regarding the benefits, boundaries and potential for service-learning pedagogy within US-based IEPs, subsequently looking at the impact of service-learning projects within the local community of an IEP's host institution as well as the obligations of pedagogues when implementing service learning as an experiential form of student engagement. The latter portion of this chapter contained guidelines for moving forward.

One of the most obvious 'take aways' of this review cannot be overstated: in addition to ensuring student learning, university and college-based IEPs have obligations to their local communities that must be part of any service-learning project. These obligations include fulfilling basic social responsibility (e.g. appropriate, equitable and bilateral communication among all stakeholders) as well as demonstrating and building goodwill among partners – actions which lend themselves to more long-term and sustainable community development. IEP practitioners are also responsible for ensuring adherence to ethical and sound research practices, even if they are not immediately involved in a particular project within their program. For instance, if the results of a service-learning initiative are to be used in publication, practitioners have the obligation to follow informed consent practices and obtain official research approval from institutional review boards. By combining resources from the community and the local higher education institution (or an affiliate unit, such as an IEP), service-learning projects have the potential to strengthen bonds between the stakeholders, develop solutions to problems, facilitate economic growth and – perhaps most importantly – educate. All stakeholders in the service-learning process need to understand what *students* bring and can offer to these interactions; similarly, the students, IEP practitioners and the host institution must recognize the significance of a community's willingness to facilitate educational opportunities. It is fundamental that we, as educators, strive to progress the mission of academia to better align with the changing needs of society.

References

Askildson, L.R., Kelly, A.C. and Mick, C.S. (2013) Developing multiple literacies in academic English through service learning and community engagement. *TESOL Journal* 4 (3), 402–438.
Bunning, L. and Kostka, I. (2018) I dare to communicate with strangers: Examining international students' communication goals and strategy use during service learning. *Reading Matrix: An International Online Journal* 18 (2), 117–146.

Cameron, L.M. (2015) Attitude, behaviors, and the longitudinal impact of social justice service learning for language learners. In J.M. Perren and A.J. Wurr (eds) *Learning the Language of Global Citizenship: Strengthening Service Learning in TESOL* (pp. 56–79). Champaign, IL: Common Ground Publishing.

Cervantes, S.E., Chow, K. and Otsuji, S. (2021) CALL in service learning: Innovations to foster second language development. In S.E. Cervantes, K. Chow and S. Otsuji (eds) *CALL Theory Applications for Online TESOL Education* (pp. 203–228). Hershey, PA: IGI Global.

Chupp, M.G. and Joseph, M.L. (2010) Getting the most out of service learning: Maximizing student, university and community impact. *Journal of Community Practice* 18 (2–3), 190–212.

Collopy, R., Tjaden-Glass, S. and McIntosh, N.A. (2020) Attending to conditions that facilitate intercultural competence: A reciprocal service learning approach. *Michigan Journal of Community Service Learning* 26 (1), 18–37.

Creswell, J.W. and Creswell, J.D. (2014) *Research Design: Qualitative, Quantitative, and Mixed Methods Approaches*. Thousand Oaks, CA: SAGE Publications.

Desmond, K.J., Stahl, S.A. and Graham, M.A. (2011) Combining service learning and diversity education. *Making Connections: Interdisciplinary Approaches to Cultural Diversity* 13 (1), 24–30.

Douglas Jr, V. (2017) Service-learning as a useful supplement to intensive English programs. *Journal of Language Teaching and Research* 8 (6), 1090–1099.

Dowling, T. and Perren, J. (2021) *Service-Learning: What Every ESL Teacher Needs to Know*. Ann Arbor, MI: University of Michigan Press.

George-Paschal, L., Hawkins, A. and Graybeal, L. (2019) Investigating the overlapping experiences and impacts of service learning: Juxtaposing perspectives of students, faculty, and community partners. *Michigan Journal of Community Service Learning* 25 (2), 43–61.

Howlett, K.M., Rao, A., Allred, J. and Beck, D. (2019) An English learner service learning project: Preparing education majors using technology and the SAMR model. *Computer Assisted Language Learning Electronic Journal* 20 (2), 128–149.

Leonard, S. (2022) How to calculate the value of volunteer time. *Nonprofit Leadership Center*, 22 April. See https://nlctb.org/tips/value-of-volunteer-time/?gclid=Cj0KCQjwntCVBhDdARIsAMEwACnBR0vnyw-oU_4aPjNXdIOdXPBxDO_-1xyoz187mtLmrYPy4HJB6a4aAv3yEALw_wcB (accessed March 2022).

Mackey, A. and Gass, S.M. (2015) *Second Language Research: Methodology and Design*. New York, NY: Routledge.

Macknish, C.J. (2019) Creating multimodal reflections in an IEP speaking-listening course. *TESL Canada Journal* 36 (3), 173–185.

Marlow, S. (2007) Creating authentic dialog: ESL students as recipients of service learning. *The Internet TESL Journal* 13 (7). http://iteslj.org/Techniques/Marlow-ServiceLearning.html.

Mertler, C.A. (2021) *Introduction to Educational Research*. Thousand Oaks, CA: SAGE Publications.

Miller, J. and Kostka, I. (2015) Bridging cultures and generations: An exploration of intergenerational and intercultural oral history projects with English language learners. In J.M. Perren and A.J. Wurr (eds) *Learning the Language of Global Citizenship: Strengthening Service Learning in TESOL* (pp. 80–108). Champaign, IL: Common Ground Publishing.

Mitchell, D. and Buckingham, G. (2021) Transforming plans into community impact: Strategic planning as service learning in public and nonprofit administration graduate programs. *Teaching Public Administration* 39 (1), 9–25.

Perren, J.M. (2013) Strategic steps to successful service learning in TESOL: From critical to practical. *TESOL Journal* 4 (3), 487–513.

Perren, J.M. and Wurr, A.J. (eds) (2015) *Learning the Language of Global Citizenship: Strengthening Service Learning in TESOL*. Champaign, IL: Common Ground Publishing.

Perren, J.M., Grove, N. and Thornton, J. (2013) Three empowering curricular innovations for service learning in ESL programs. *TESOL Journal* 4 (3), 463–486.

Ravina, E.A. (2022) Service learning (SL) in English language learning: The case of the alternative learning system (ALS) learners. *International Journal of Research* 11 (4), 9–19.

Shannahan, J., Gilliland, B. and Kwon, C. (2020) Dialogue journals for critical reflection on community issues and academic writing. In C.E. Poteau (ed.) *Effects of Service Learning in Foreign and Second Language Courses* (pp. 88–108). New York, NY: Routledge.

Sousa, E.K. (2015) Service-learning as a course component in an intensive English program. In J.M. Perren and A.J. Wurr (eds) *Learning the Language of Global Citizenship: Strengthening Service Learning in TESOL* (pp. 28–55). Champaign, IL: Common Ground Publishing.

Wurr, A.J. and Perren, J.M. (2015) Introduction. In J.M. Perren and A.J. Wurr (eds) *Learning the Language of Global Citizenship: Strengthening Service Learning in TESOL*. Champaign, IL: Common Ground Publishing.

10 Mind the Gap! Voices of Brazilian English Language Teachers in a Continuing Education Intensive English Program in the United States

Kleber Aparecido da Silva, Dllubia Santclair, Lauro Sérgio Machado Pereira, Silvia Penna and Oseas Bezerra Viana-Jr

Introduction

Internationalization practices require a challenging integration of international, intercultural and global dimensions to higher education. Language teachers – particularly English language teachers – maintain a central role in the implementation of language policies for the internationalization of education. This chapter reports on evidence from two continuing education programs for Brazilian English language teachers.

In Brazil, there are at least two continuing professional development programs that have sent English language teachers to the United States to participate in activities provided by Intensive English Programs (IEPs). Their main goal is to support teachers to improve their speaking, listening, reading and writing abilities in English. One of these programs, the Professional Development Program for English Language Teachers (PDPI), has sent hundreds of English Language teachers from public schools to short-term courses in that country. This program is a result of partnerships between the Coordination for the Improvement of Higher Education Personnel (CAPES) in Brazil and the Fulbright Commission in the United States. The other program, known as SETEC-CAPES/ NOSA (Brazil, 2015), is a partnership between the Brazilian government's

Secretariat of Vocational and Technological Education (SETEC) and CAPES and the Northeastern State Community College (NOSA, pseudonym) consortium in the United States. This program focused on Brazilian English language teachers from the Vocational, Scientific and Technological Education Federal Network (EPCT Network).

This chapter analyzes the SETEC-CAPES/NOSA Program, considering internationalization of education mobility policies and practices as a strategy for the continuing professional development of English language teachers. In the present discussion, we interpret internationalization of education from the local experiences of two teachers, who are also co-authors of this chapter; one teacher participated in the first year of the program and the other teacher participated in the second. Lundgren *et al.* (2020) state that a benefit of internationalization of education is the promotion of cognitive and social justice, as it provides opportunities for the development of global citizens and individuals who can work actively in local and global communities. This perspective questions the coloniality of knowledge; it searches for alternatives to Eurocentric and non-Eurocentric knowledge, prestigious and subaltern languages, and other dichotomizing classifications. Following de Wit *et al.* (2015), our position is that teachers should be encouraged to critically integrate global, intercultural and international perspectives in their practices and activities.

The study considers implications for the continuing education of language teachers in the Global South and provides suggestions for decolonial internationalization. It employs a theoretical framework that incorporates concepts from critical approaches such as the locus of enunciation (Mignolo, 2017), decoloniality (Pennycook & Makoni, 2020), critical internationalization (de Wit *et al.*, 2015; Pereira *et al.*, 2021) and discursive representations in the internationalization of English teachers continuing education (Pereira & Silva, 2021). This decolonial perspective considers the underlying politics and ideologies of a historically uneven relationship between the Global North (in this case, represented by the United States) and the Global South (such as Latin American countries, and more specifically in this case, Brazil). It reveals an unequal distribution of both resources and power in these internationalization of education encounters. Through analysis of the SETEC-CAPES/NOSA Program, we problematize how these unbalanced relations affect the interaction among Latin American and North American language teachers within international education. Each group's different positionalities are simply a reflection of the centuries of Eurocentric-oriented views of knowledge and power (Walsh *et al.*, 2018), and, consequently, these internationalization initiatives risk becoming unilateral, reproducing and perpetuating a model that needs re-evaluation.

The following sections first provide an overview of the SETEC-CAPES/NOSA Program for language teachers' continuing education, methodological procedures, and results. Subsequent discussion and analysis suggest that the internationalization of English teachers' continuing education should be reevaluated and conceived from a bottom-up perspective that considers local issues and centers teacher voices.

Background of the SETEC-CAPES/NOSA Program

In this section, we present some considerations about bilateral diplomatic relations between Brazil and the United States in the 21st century, focusing on the agenda of internationalization of Brazilian education that was supported by the government of former President Dilma Rousseff. We reflect on the SETEC-CAPES/NOSA program's relevance for the internationalization of teacher education and for the improvement of English language teaching and learning practices that are guided by intercultural and collaborative dimensions.

While there are asymmetries involved in the bilateral relations between Brazil and the United States, both countries have political and economic relevance for one another (Peres Milani, 2021). According to Pecequilo (2014: 11), the United States has 'political, economic, strategic and ideological weight' in the Brazilian foreign policy agenda, marked by complex factors such as 'the nature of North American power resources, their projection capacity and Brazil's perception of itself and of this partner'. When Rousseff took power in 2011, her government benefited from the plan of her predecessor, Luis Inácio Lula da Silva, who had served as President from 2003 to 2010. Lula provided an agenda that allowed Brazil's diplomacy to become truly global via the country's material capacities as well as its diplomatic corps and strategic guidelines for humanism and solidarity (Milani, 2011). Indeed, in the administrations of both Lula and Rousseff, Brazilian foreign policy relied mainly on *soft power* (Peres Milani, 2021) – that is, the capability of a country to indirectly attract and influence other countries through actions of education, media and tourism.

In 2010, less than a year before the election of Rousseff, former President Lula signed a decree between Brazil and the United States that provided for the continuation and expansion of programs to promote mutual understanding 'through an educational, cultural, scientific, technical and professional exchange' (Brazil, 2010: 1–2). In a section of the decree that concerns the purpose of the funds being made available, a key objective is described as financing 'visits and exchanges between students, professors, researchers and professionals from the United States and Brazil' (2010: 2). Rousseff defended the continuity of this educational policy, as domestic and international educational cooperation was defined as a priority of her government.

In 2011, the Federal Government launched the Science Without Borders Program (Brazil, 2011), which sought to insert Brazil as a protagonist in the international education scenario by promoting 'the consolidation, expansion, and internationalization of science and technology, innovation and Brazilian competitiveness through exchange and international mobility' (Stallivieri, 2017: 130). On the one hand, the Science Without Borders Program achieved positive results by increasing the number of Brazilian students and researchers with access to international academic mobility. It interjected Brazil into the world and opened paths for dialogue between Brazilian educational institutions and similar institutions around the globe. On the other hand, the program also brought to the fore Brazilian participants' challenges with effective communication in non-national languages, a necessary component to applying for a scholarship from the program (Stallivieri, 2017). As a response, the Brazilian government created the English without Borders Program (Brazil, 2012) to promote the linguistic development of university students who were applying for scholarships, and this initiative also necessitated investment in Brazilian English teachers' continuing education. The English without Borders Program offered free English language courses and language proficiency tests (e.g. TOEFL [Test of English for Speakers of Other Languages]) for students and researchers (Abreu-e-Lima & Moraes Filho, 2016); it was later expanded to the Language without Borders Program (Brazil, 2014b) to include languages other than English. Thousands of participants in this program were sent to the United States to study in IEPs, but the linguistic and educational quality was not guaranteed or rigorously monitored (Abreu-e-Lima *et al.*, 2016). The English without Borders eventually became referred to by United States-based IEP practitioners as the 'Brazilian Teachers Program' and served as an important source of revenue for many IEPs for almost half a decade.

In this scenario, a relevant document was The National Plan for Education (Brazil, 2014a). It consists of 20 goals with the purpose of expanding 'the Higher Education System by increasing access to educational institutions and by improving graduation rates' (Abreu-e-Lima & Moraes Filho, 2016: 102). The National Plan for Education sought to: (1) consolidate and expand programs and actions that stimulate national and international mobility for both educational professionals as well as undergraduate and graduate students; (2) consolidate the internationalization of Brazilian graduate studies and research programs and groups, which included the promotion of scientific and technological exchange experiences between national and international institutions in the fields of teaching, research and service, and the raising of scientific and technological competitiveness of national research; and (3) institute a program for granting scholarships to language teachers from public elementary schools in order to provide them opportunity to study abroad and gain linguistic, intercultural and pedagogical experience regarding the language they teach. These goals make the National Plan for Education an important legislation that guarantees that Brazilian English teachers have experiences that might reflect in the language education offered in the EPCT Network. The SETEC-CAPES/NOSA Program resulted from these initiatives to develop the quality of language education in Brazil by investing in the continuing education of language teachers. This chapter reviews the experiences of two participants in this program.

Research Methods and Participants

The perceptions of two English language teacher participants in the SETEC-CAPES/NOSA Program problematize modern scientific-academic mobility from a decolonial perspective (Mignolo, 2017). The study follows Walsh *et al*. (2018: 3), who encourage 'critical thinking based on those subordinated by European capitalist modernity and a theoretical project aimed at critical and transdisciplinary rethinking'. It seeks to decolonize knowledge construction 'among thinkers outside the modern western canons' as a contrast to 'dominant academic trends of a Eurocentric perspective' (Walsh *et al*., 2018: 3). The research is part of the qualitative interpretive paradigm that considers 'the socially constructed nature of reality, the relationship between researchers and what is studied, and the situational limitations that influence the investigation' (Denzin & Lincoln, 2006: 23). The methodology allows the exploration of various epistemic possibilities for a critical interpretation of experiences.

Data originate from a series of dialogues between two Latin American teachers who participated in the so-called 'Brazilian Teachers Program' at NOSA, a United States-based IEP. The discussions allowed the teacher participants to (re)construct knowledge related to their impressions, feelings and perspectives of the experience. The first participant, Lauro, is a tenured English language teacher at the Northern Minas Gerais Federal Institute (IFNMG), Janaúba branch campus. Lauro participated in a TESOL training course as part of the SETEC-CAPES/NOSA Program in 2016. The second participant, Silvia, is a tenured English Language teacher at the Federal Institute of Minas Gerais (IFMG), Ouro Preto campus. Silvia participated in the same program in 2017, but at a different NOSA campus.

The second source of data is the responses of these teacher participants to the Program Evaluation Questionnaire, which was an official formal assessment of the SETEC-CAPES/NOSA Program for understanding participants' experiences upon return to their home country.

Table 10.1 SETEC-CAPES/NOSA Program evaluation questions (Likert and open ended)

5. Evaluate the Pedagogical Activities:
   5.1. Positive aspects.
   5.2. Negative aspects.
6. Contents and/or tools covered in the program:
   6.1. Describe if the contents and tools were more relevant in the formation as an educator and if, after this experience, they consider themself able to use them in the improvement of the teaching within the scope of their institution.
   6.2. Do you consider yourself willing to act as a multiplier of the knowledge acquired in training, whether at a local or national level?
   6.3. Overall, your level of satisfaction with the program was ___
   6.4. What suggestions for improvement do I consider important for new classes in the program?
7. The SETEC-CAPES/NOSA Program aims to:
   7.1. Value the professionals who work in the Federal EPCT Network.
   7.2. Strengthen the mastery of the four language skills – understanding, speaking, reading, and writing in English – of English language teachers working in the Federal Network.
   7.3. Expose teachers from the Federal Network to the pedagogical practices of North American Community Colleges, with a focus on teaching English.
   7.4. Share experiences of teaching English as a second language, proposing activities that encourage student participation in the classroom.
   7.5. Encourage the use of online resources and other tools in the continuing education of teachers and the development of new methodologies and teaching materials for use in the classroom.
   7.6. Stimulate the use of technologies for the development of projects, with a special focus on projects developed by students from the Federal Network.
   7.7. Provide an on-site experience in English language proficiency, considering the cultural, local, and social aspects of the United States of America.
8. Has your experience in the program contributed to the development of your educational skills in Vocational Education?

(Potential Likert responses were: *1 – Did not reach the goal, 2 – Partially achieved the goal, 3 – Reasonably achieved the objective, 4 – Fully achieved the goal, and 5 – Exceeded the goal*)

Adapted from Brazil (2015: 3)

Participants provided responses on both a five-point Likert scale as well as qualitative responses when appropriate. These data were particularly useful for their reflections on the IEP curriculum and pedagogical activities. Table 10.1 shows selected questions concerning formative, pedagogical, and linguistic dimensions.

The last source of data is a series of conversation circles between the co-author participants and their co-author colleagues. These circles enable formative experiences because they encourage reflection, creating a space for the confrontation of the participants' points of view (Warschauer, 2017).

Throughout the analysis, we assume a questioning approach that enables 'continued dialogic mediation between teachers when they engage in activities directed toward a specific goal' (Johnson, 2006: 95). This type of analysis enables participants to understand their actions and perceptions. The first task consisted of categorizing the answers of the participants, followed by a process of establishing relationships and making inferences, all of which were informed by critical internationalization studies, and a decolonial stance. Analysis was guided by the following questions: what conception of internationalization of education permeated the program? In what aspects has the program impacted the discursive representations of two Brazilian English teachers? And, to what extent has the program reproduced a colonial relationship of internationalization of education? The data analysis process was iterative and cyclical among all the co-authors, and they illuminate the uneven relations between the Global North and the Global South and their underlying politics and ideologies.

Analysis

This section provides an overview of several (but not all!) key findings from the data. It is divided into two subsections, the first one looks at how the idea of internationalization is conceptualized within the SETEC-CAPES/NOSA Program. The second subsection provides a broader overview of the impact of the program, and the final subsection looks more specifically at the experiences of the two co-author teacher participants.

'Internationalization' as conceptualized within SETEC-CAPES/NOSA

The SETEC-CAPES/NOSA Program was an eight-week TESOL training program sponsored by the Brazilian government and hosted by NOSA in the United States. The program was designed to internationalize Brazilian education, develop the linguistic and communicative knowledge of the English teacher participants, and improve their communication in the target language as well as their teaching methodologies and autonomy. The full set of objectives of the program is presented in Table 10.2.

Table 10.2 Objectives of the SETEC-CAPES/NOSA Program

2.1. To value the professionals who work in the EPCT Network.
2.2. Strengthen the mastery of the four language skills – listening, speaking, reading, and writing in English – of English language teachers working in the EPCT Network.
2.3. Expose teachers from the EPCT Network to the pedagogical practices of North American Community Colleges, with a focus on teaching English.
2.4. Share experiences of teaching English as a second language, proposing activities that encourage student participation in the classroom.
2.5. Encourage the use of online resources and other tools in the continuing education of teachers and the development of new methodologies and teaching materials for use in the classroom.
2.6. Stimulate the use of technologies to develop projects, with a particular focus on projects developed by students from the Federal Network.
2.7. Provide an on-site experience in English language proficiency, considering the cultural, local, and social aspects of the United States of America.
2.8. Encourage partnerships with North American teachers, with a view to future exchanges of teachers and students between the two countries.

Adapted from Brazil (2015: 2)

The program's objectives primarily represent linguistic, pedagogical, intercultural, technological, interpersonal and diplomatic dimensions to be developed among the English teachers in the training course, and all objectives are connected via the dimension of internationalization. As a number of these dimensions relate to issues outside of the teaching profession, we consider that some in-advance orientation before heading to the United States was necessary. In particular, the objective to 'encourage partnerships with North American teachers' places participants in a diplomatic position that requires training on how to approach the possible partner teachers and institutions and on which formal mechanisms are available to put the partnership into practice.

The internationalization perspective is central to all objectives of the SETEC-CAPES/NOSA initiative, as demonstrated by the following excerpt from a 2015 public announcement of the program:

> In return for participating in the Program, selected candidates must *work through a work plan*, for a minimum period of one year, in the actions of the Languages without Borders Program of the Ministry of Education, in their institution of the Federal Network or other public schools in Brazil, in order to *apply the acquired knowledge and contribute to teaching, research, service, innovation and internationalization actions and activities* ... (Brazil, 2015: 1–2, emphasis added)

In this excerpt, the verbs 'apply' and 'contribute' suggest actions of the English teachers for reflecting on educational quality. And, while internationalization is directly expressed in the verb 'internationalize', the action it implies appears as a secondary 'backdrop' strategy that occurs through teachers' participation in the activities their local institutional campuses develop. Internationalization is positioned as one of the axes to be benefited by the teaching work rather than as a valued dimension and consistent topic of the program. It is positioned as a process for which mainly teachers are responsible for carrying out the practical actions, without any systematization and guidance strategy by a specialized team, government agency, or dialogue with the international relations office of the participating institutions.

The voices of two English teacher participants

Teachers' continued professional development can be considered successful not only by the influence of the activities included in it, but also by the teachers' previous professional experiences and beliefs, their personal circumstances at the time, and instructional and sociocultural contexts. The positive outcomes of a continued professional development program depend on teachers' willingness to critically engage in their activities and on the personal meaning it has for them (Heyes, 2019). While a continuing professional development program must promote professional learning, participation in a continuing professional development program is no guarantee of an impact on practice (Heyes, 2019). Thus, discussions around the critical education of English language teachers should consider two fundamental elements – namely, people's subjectivities and the contexts in which they operate. This requires a dialogic dimension (Freire, 1987), for whom dialogue mediates the relationship of teachers with the world and is responsible for the meanings they construct (Pessoa, 2018).

The impact of the program upon participants divides into four assessment themes: (i) pedagogical activities, (ii) contents and/or tools covered in the program, (iii) program objectives and (iv) the development of the participating teachers' pedagogical skills. This section focuses on the first of these dimensions, the pedagogical activities, which was constituted by several themes – namely, classroom observations at the local IEP, participant subjectivity and a disregard for the local Brazilian teachers' contexts.

The first of these themes – class observations at the local IEP at NOSA – was a meaningful practical activity for the participating co-authors, as demonstrated in the following excerpts:

> I was able to observe classes at the [IEP], where students from a variety of language backgrounds are taught ESL classes. The goal of such observations was to compare teaching techniques and methodologies from that context to my context in Brazil and envision ways of adapting and applying these new ideas to the language classes at my Institute. [Lauro, 2016]
>
> The class observations at the [IEP] as well as the practicum activities fostered my reflection on my teaching practice reinforcing some of the techniques and methods I already use and bringing new ideas that can be adapted to my classes, even though it was an ESL context. [Silvia, 2017]

Successes of the SETEC-CAPES/NOSA Program (i.e. evidence of meeting program objectives) were identified in the participants' subjectivity in which they describe their knowledge construction process. In the excerpts that follow, comments emphasize the benefits of participants' exposure to 'pedagogical practices of North American Community Colleges'.

> [T]he experiences in the program indeed contributed to developing my educational skills in Vocational Education. I felt more confident after the experience abroad. [Lauro, 2016]
>
> I could give other meanings to the methodological approaches I learned at NOSA, so they became applicable to the reality of the campus where I work in Brazil. [Silvia, 2017]

Unfortunately, however, participants also describe impressions of disregard for their professional knowledge and contexts.

> The idea of sharing experiences was a very frustrating aspect of the experience ... there was a general attitude, on the part of the instructors and organizers, that we were there in a more passive position, observing and listening. [Silvia, 2017]

> I strongly believe that listening to what the prospective students [teachers in service] have to say is the first step to developing a well-grounded program from which we could all benefit. This is necessary to design a program that would aim at the demands of the groups considering their professional experience, their academic background, as well as the specificities of their teaching contexts. Promoting interactions among the professionals that will develop the program and the Brazilian language teachers who will take part in the training, will certainly contribute to a remarkable exchange experience. [Lauro, 2016]

> As there was no previous contact between the staff at the [IEP] and the members of the Brazilian groups, they did not have a clear idea of the groups' demands, needs, or expectations [...] It was somewhat frustrating to find out that the program was planned exclusively as a teaching preparation for an ESL context, which greatly differs from the EFL teaching context at the federal institutes in Brazil. [Silvia, 2017]

A lack of input regarding the content of the professional development is exemplified in participants' comments about the methodologies and the topics of program content. For example, participants expressed dissatisfaction with the choice of Task-Based Language Teaching (Ellis, 2003) as a methodological focus of the program contents:

> The classes were mostly focused on how to apply the Task-Based Language Teaching (TBLT) methodology for ESL students, so it seemed that the program was designed for pre-service ESL instructors. [Silvia, 2017]

> The focus on TBLT was not much suitable to our reality ... [Lauro, 2016]

TBLT is known for being efficient in the English classroom, however, it is not a one-size-fits-all method and such an emphasis on TBLT suggests an attempt to export a methodology that disregards the local context of the course participants. According to Lauro, TBLT is a less effective methodology for regions such as Brazil:

> It fails by not highlighting other dimensions manifested in the language learning process, that is social, economic, political, and cultural aspects under a critical perspective. Since the participants of the program were English teachers from Brazil, a country with high discrepancies in income distribution and increasing poverty, learning a foreign language is not only

a matter of communicating or doing things, but much more it means to use the language for creating another legitimate way or existing in an oppressive context. [Lauro, 2016]

In his answer, the participant points out that there are internal and external factors that directly impact the teaching/learning process of a language and these factors can be very different from country to country. The comments of these teacher participants bring to light their frustration with their lack of input in the curriculum content and design. Pennycook (1999: 332) points to the relationship between English and colonial ideologies by discussing the hegemonic constructs of colonialism and the 'multiple ways in which power may operate in social life'. Indeed, 'languages have no borders' (Pessoa, 2018: 194), and English is not the prerogative of one nation or people. Rather, English is a part of users' plurilingual repertoire in the everyday lives of people all over the world, and this observation is no less true in contexts in which English is not a dominant language of the local population.

This lack of regard for the program participants' professional knowledge and contexts is highlighted by the participants from the assessment questionnaire comments on the use of digital tools. According to them:

> The classes on digital tools were a remarkable learning experience. This content, which is directly applicable to my classes at the institute, will make the classroom a more dynamic environment, encouraging students to have a more active role in their learning process by being able to use the tools that are part of their everyday lives. [Silvia, 2017]

> The use of digital tools was the focus of some of the classes and that was something that added to my teaching practice. I had already used a few of the apps and digital tools presented in class, however, I had not had contact with most of them. I learned a lot from those classes, and I especially appreciated that the teachers would guide us through which tools were free and which were not, considering the tight budgets available to the Education sector in Brazil. [Lauro, 2016]

The participants embrace digital tools, and they even suggest including them in their future pedagogical activities, even though access to the internet and electronic devices in classrooms is more difficult in Brazil than in the United States. Enormous income and social inequalities in Brazil (Chancel *et al.*, 2022) prevent access for a large portion of the population to the internet and to electronic devices, and many regions may have only a single computer connected to the internet in most schools. Not all students own a smartphone (even though they may want one!). Nevertheless, it is important that they have chances to function in a digital world, as digital tools are a productive way to engage students and teachers in the process of internationalization of education.

Yet the dissatisfaction that these teacher participants express may not have been so profound if they had been provided more opportunity to shape the program contents. As professional instructors, they possess a wealth of experience and knowledge that could contribute to their hosts' understanding of the field and provide for more bilateral exchange:

> As experienced teachers, we wanted to discuss new techniques and methodologies as well as the ones we had been using in our classes. Neither the experience and knowledge of the group nor the context in which we work were really taken into consideration. [Silvia, 2017]
>
> [...] they should have given us the chance to be in touch with multiple teaching approaches and methodologies, so we could critically reflect on the most suitable ones for an English class in Brazil. [Lauro, 2016]

According to Heyes (2019: 166), continuing professional development must 'go beyond the externally mandated face-to-face short course focusing on introducing a new curriculum or some other educational innovation' and instead enable teachers to develop a meaningful pedagogical work based on practices with which they can identify. This researcher explains that professional development should 'encompass a range of practices focused on the collaborative understanding of classroom issues which teachers recognize as important to their own sense of self-efficacy as facilitators of their students' learning' (2019: 166). Participants' dissatisfaction with some aspects of the continuing professional development was that it seemed to lack acknowledgment of their own teaching contexts in Brazil. Critical linguistic education practitioners must recognize that 'language is about social practice' (Urzêda Freitas & Pessoa, 2012), and language and pedagogical approaches cannot be detached from all those elements.

The excerpts presented in this section demonstrate the benefits and challenges of the SETEC-CAPES/NOSA Program. Benefits, for instance, include the IEP class observations and evidence of the participants' knowledge construction processes. However, it is also noticeable that the previous knowledge of these teacher participants is not embraced by their peers from the United States. The contents and methodology seemed to already be waiting for the teachers upon their arrival, and it was difficult to modify or adapt. The participating teachers did not have the opportunity to discuss their own context in relation to the ways of learning from another culture or other perspectives of life. The expectations of Brazilian and American teacher colleagues who were part of the SETEC-CAPES/NOSA were not bilateral in nature, revealing an asymmetry between countries. Indeed, the hegemonic/non-hegemonic position of these countries in the Global North/Global South relations perpetuates an imbalance throughout the collaboration, particularly in its extent and type. This imbalance creates a missed opportunity within this continued professional development program.

A Decolonial Perspective of Internationalization

This chapter considered the internationalization of education policies through the innovative initiative of the SETEC-CAPES/NOSA Program. By presenting the program background and design, we attempted to shed some light on our object of study and to guide our discussion which ranged from the diplomatic relations between Brazil and the United States and the concept of internationalization of education upon which the policies were based. The analysis covered the pedagogical and methodological dimensions of the program. Another important aspect of our analysis was the focus on the impressions of two Brazilian English language teachers who evaluated their own experience as participants of the NOSA's IEP. The analysis of their answers to the program questionnaire provided information that helped pinpoint the positive and the conflicting aspects of this program.

This research assumes a decolonial perspective to consider the underlying politics and ideologies of the North-South relationship, revealing the unequal distribution of resources and power. The inequalities are revealed in the fact that Latin American institutions have been sending their teachers to the northern hemisphere *not* for *exchange* but for the sole purpose of *learning*. This approach to the program design reflects a form of epistemicide, as it fails to recognize teacher participants' own knowledge and local professional contexts. It is, in this way, associated with the exercises of power and violence against knowledge called subaltern or abyssal (Grosfoguel, 2012; Santos, 1998).

Although the term *internationalization* means a variety of things to a multitude of people (Teferra, 2019), the results of this study suggest a coercive and passive conception of internationalization that permeates the program. This was evidenced in the program's objectives, which prioritized the cultural, local and social aspects of the country of destination to the detriment of a dialogue with the real needs of the contexts in which teachers work in Brazil, as well as foreseeing that these professionals would 'apply' the knowledge 'acquired' (and not 'collaboratively constructed') in the different lines of action of the EPCT Network. The reports of the participating teachers, when explaining that both their knowledge and their local realities were disregarded in the approach of the course, go back to the idea of a passive internationalization in which those involved must consume and reproduce North-Global practices without any kind of problematization.

The participants' discursive representations were impacted in different ways. Through a critical reflection on the formative process, the teachers advanced from a developmental vision of abilities provided by the program, towards other possibilities directed to untested feasibility[1] (Freire, 1987) and to the critical re-signification of foreign language teaching-learning. In other words, the participants appropriated the program's knowledge and experiences, but at the same time constructed problematizations that would make its applicability in the Brazilian educational context feasible. Excerpts such as 'to apply the acquired knowledge' (Brazil, 2015: 1–2) and 'considering the cultural, local, and social aspects of the United States of America' (Brazil, 2015: 2) demonstrate that the internationalization of education proposed by the program reproduced colonial relations, since there was no symmetry in valuing the culture and educational system of the participants' country of origin.

The pedagogical diplomacy between the United States of America and Brazil has agreements, policies and official documents which denote different attempts to establish internationalization through solid partnerships that could be beneficial for both countries, and the programs were well funded. Nevertheless, the analysis of the SETEC-CAPES/NOSA Program revealed important asymmetries, such as unilateral, top-down decisions that mismatched some of the Brazilian language teachers' needs. Participant expectations of the program were built upon the notion that a relationship is a two-way street, especially it comes to sharing knowledge, but the reality did not meet this expectation. A decolonial lens allows us to articulate the problems of unidirectional program design, demonstrating through the experiences described in this chapter that the 'one size fits all' notion must be problematized. Specificities must be considered when designing a program, especially the voices of teachers who have already participated in continuing education initiatives.

Note

(1) The untested feasibility can be understood as a force that allows the individual to act in the face of threshold situations, which, if noticed from another perspective, would paralyze and not motivate transformative action.

References

Abreu-e-Lima, D.M. and Moraes Filho, W.B. (2016) Languages without Borders Program (LwB): Building a Brazilian policy for teaching languages towards internationalization. In K.R. Finardi (ed.) *English in Brazil: Views, Policies and Programs* (pp. 97–123). Londrina: Editora Eduel.

Abreu-e-Lima, D.M., Moraes Filho, W.B., Barbosa, W.J.C. and Blum, A.S. (2016) O Programa Inglês sem Fronteiras e a política de incentivo à internacionalização do ensino superior brasileiro. In S. Sarmento, D.M. Abreu-e-Lima and W.B. Moraes Filho (eds). *Do Inglês sem Fronteiras ao Idiomas sem Fronteiras: A construção de uma política linguística para a internacionalização* (pp. 19–46). Belo Horizonte: Editora UFMG.

Brazil (2010) *Decreto nº 7.176, de 12 de maio de 2010*. Promulga o Acordo entre o Governo da República Federativa do Brasil e o Governo dos Estados Unidos da América para Programas Educacionais e de Intercâmbio Cultural. See http://www.planalto.gov.br/ccivil_03/_ato2007-2010/2010/decreto/D7176.htm (accessed February 2022).

Brazil (2011) *Decreto nº 7.642, de 13 de dezembro de 2011*. Institui o programa Ciência sem Fronteiras. See http://www.planalto.gov.br/ccivil_03/_ato2011-2014/2011/decreto/d7642.htm (accessed February 2022).

Brazil (2012) *Portaria n° 1.466, de 18 de dezembro de 2012*. Institui o Programa Inglês sem Fronteiras. See http://isf.mec.gov.br/images/pdf/portaria_normativa_1466_2012.pdf (accessed February 2022).

Brazil (2014a) *Lei n° 13.005, de 25 de junho de 2014*. Aprova o Plano Nacional de Educação - PNE e dá outras providências, 2014. See https://www.planalto.gov.br/ccivil_03/_ato2011-2014/2014/lei/l13005.htm (accessed February 2022).

Brazil (2014b) *Portaria n° 973, de 14 de novembro de 2014*. Institui o Programa Idiomas sem Fronteiras. See http://isf.mec.gov.br/images/pdf/novembro/Portaria_973_Idiomas_sem_Fronteiras.pdf (accessed February 2022).

Brazil (2015) *Chamada Publica SETEC/MEC n° 01/2015, de 22 de setembro de 2015, RETIFICAÇÃO de 01 de junho de 2016. Programa Setec-Capes/NOSA de capacitação para Professores da Rede Federal de Educação Profissional, Científica e Tecnológica*. See http://portal.mec.gov.br/escola-de-gestores-da-educacao-basica/190-secretarias-112877938/setec-1749372213/46021-editais-setec-2015 (accessed February 2022).

Chancel, L., Piketty, T., Saez, E. and Zucman, G. (2022) World inequality report 2022. See https://wir2022.wid.world/www-site/uploads/2022/03/0098-21_WIL_RIM_RAPPORT_A4.pdf (accessed February 2022).

de Wit, H., Hunter, F., Howard, L. and Egron-Polak, E. (2015) Internationalisation of higher education. *Directorate-General for Internal Policies on Culture and Education*. Brussels: European Union. https://doi.org/10.2861/444393 (accessed February 2022).

Denzin, N.K. and Lincoln, Y.S. (2006) *O planejamento da pesquisa qualitativa*. Porto Alegre: Artmed.

Ellis, R. (2003) *Task-Based Language Learning and Teaching*. Oxford: Oxford University Press.

Freire, P. (1987) *Pedagogia do oprimido* (11th edn). Rio de Janeiro: Paz e Terra.

Grosfoguel, R. (2012) Decolonizing western universalisms: Decolonial pluri-versalism from Aimé Césaire to the Zapatistas. *Transmodernity: Journal of Peripheral Cultural Production of the Luso-Hispanic World* 1 (3), 88–104. https://escholarship.org/uc/item/01w7163v.

Heyes, D. (2019) Continuing professional development/continuous professional learning for English language teachers. In S. Walsh and S. Mann (eds) *The Routledge Handbook of English Language Teacher Education* (pp. 155–168). New York, NY: Routledge.

Johnson, K.E. (2006) The sociocultural turn and its challenges for second language teacher education. *TESOL Quarterly* 40 (1), 235–257. https://doi.org/10.2307/40264518.

Lundgren, U., Castro, P. and Woodin, J. (2020) *Educational Approaches to Internationalization through Intercultural Dialogue: Reflections on Theory and Practice*. New York, NY: Routledge.

Mignolo, W. (2017) Desafios decoloniais hoje. *Epistemologias do Sul* 1 (1), 12–32. https://revistas.unila.edu.br/epistemologiasdosul/article/view/772.

Milani, C.R.S. (2011) A importância das relações Brasil-Estados Unidos na política externa brasileira. *Boletim de economia e política internacional* June (6), 69–85. http://repositorio.ipea.gov.br/handle/11058/4674.

Pecequilo, C.S. (2014) As relações bilaterais Brasil-Estados Unidos no governo Dilma Rousseff, 2011–2014. *Austral: Revista Brasileira de Estratégia e Relações Internacionais* 3 (6), 11–36. https://doi.org/10.22456/2238-6912.49932.

Pennycook, A. (1999) Introduction: Critical approaches to TESOL. *TESOL Quarterly* 33 (3), 329–348. https://doi.org/10.2307/3587668.

Pennycook, A. and Makoni, S. (2020) *Innovations and Challenges in Applied Linguistics from the Global South*. New York, NY: Routledge.

Pereira, L.S.M. and Silva, K.A. (2021) Discursive representations about internationalization by English teachers in continuing education. *Revista Educação Em Questão* 59 (59), 1–23. https://doi.org/10.21680/1981-1802.2021v59n59ID25293.

Pereira, L.S.M., Costa, S.M. and Silva, K.A. (2021) Internacionalização e políticas linguísticas: As percepções de professores de línguas de um instituto federal. In

R.R. Pessoa, K.A. Silva and C.C. Freitas (eds) *Praxiologias do Brasil Central sobre educação linguística crítica* (pp. 109–134). São Paulo: Pá de Palavra.

Peres Milani, L. (2021) Brasil e Estados Unidos: Cooperação em defesa e busca de autonomia (2003-2010). *Carta Internacional* 16 (1), 1–25. https://doi.org/10.21530/ci.v16n1.2021.1091.

Pessoa, R.R. (2018) Movimentos críticos de uma prática docente. In R.R. Pessoa, V.P.V. Silvestre and W. Monte-Mór (eds) *Perspectivas críticas de educação linguística no Brasil: Trajetórias e práticas de professoras/es universitárias/os de Inglês* (pp. 187–200). São Paulo: Pá de Palavra.

Santos, B.S. (1998) *La Globalización del derecho: Los nuevos caminos de la regulación y la emancipación*. Bogotá: Universidad Nacional de Colombia.

Stallivieri, L. (2017) *Internacionalização e intercâmbio: Dimensões e perspectivas* (1st edn). Curitiba: Appris.

Teferra, D. (2019) Defining internationalisation – Intention versus coercion. *University World News*. See https://www.universityworldnews.com/post.php?story=20190821145329703 (accessed February 2022).

Urzêda Freitas, M.T. and Pessoa, R.R. (2012) Rupturas e continuidades na linguística aplicada crítica: Uma abordagem historiográfica. *Calidoscópio* 10 (2), 225–238. https://revistas.unisinos.br/index.php/calidoscopio/article/view/cld.2012.102.09.

Walsh, C., Oliveira, L.F. and Candau, V.M. (2018) Colonialidade e pedagogia decolonial: Para pensar uma educação outra. *Arquivos Analíticos de Políticas Educativas* 26 (83), 1–16. https://epaa.asu.edu/ojs/article/view/3874.

Warschauer, C. (2017) *Rodas em rede: Oportunidades formativas na escola e fora dela*. Rio de Janeiro: Paz e Terra.

11 Over a Decade of Third-Party Pathway Programs in the United States

Carter A. Winkle

Introduction

Partnerships between universities and corporate-sector education service providers for the purposes of recruitment and development of matriculation pathway programs for English-learning international students have now been part of the Intensive English Program (IEP) landscape in the United States for more than a decade. Often sold to university presidents, provosts, and academic deans as a proprietary 'innovation' by third-party pathway providers, English language program administrators have been quick to recognize the pitch as *appropriation* of a model rather than a model of innovation: many IEPs and their host institutions have or had previously had their own, in-house variations of bridge or pathway programs which provide early access to credit-bearing coursework and matriculation into degree-conferring programs (Winkle, 2014) to the English-learning international students they serve. A notable departure from the in-house pathway program models includes international recruitment through in-country agent systems and, in some cases, the infusion of corporate-sector capital craved by institutions suffering from declining state financial support and falling enrollments (Winkle & Algren, 2018).

The Pathway Program

As institutions of higher education experience budget decreases from previously reliable funding sources, they are forced to seek alternative channels for generating revenue (Choudaha, 2017a). IEPs have long had reputations on their campuses as being the university's 'cash cow' (Clark *et al.*, 2021) whose coffers are there for the raiding. This mindset has expanded markedly with an increased push to recruit international students (Choudaha, 2017a), often within the pretext of institutional efforts toward internationalization (Winkle & Algren, 2018). An unspoken query within university leadership boardrooms frequently seems to be: 'how can we get more international students with their full-freight tuition and fees onto campus sooner?'. Matriculation bridge or pathway programs are one answer to this question.

Undergraduate and graduate pathway programs generally afford international students whose English language proficiency does not meet the university's direct-admissions requirements a first-year experience in which they are simultaneously enrolled in English language courses – oftentimes facilitated by an existing IEP – and in credit-bearing, academic content courses which may or may not be in sections restricted to pathway program students and facilitated by academic units (Winkle & Algren, 2018). Offering a pathway year or semester to English-learning international students can support their understanding of both academic and cultural expectations in US higher education learning contexts. Pathways afford early-access to academic credits that are recognized within degree programs once pathway students matriculate (Klahr, 2015). Apropos to university administrators' unspoken desires: pathway programs also bring full tuition and fee-paying international students to campuses sooner.

The 'innovative' notion of universities developing systems and programs to provide international English-learning students early-access to credit-bearing coursework is clever, but universities and their IEPs have been developing matriculation programs and creating opportunities for conditional university admission for decades without partnering with corporate entities (Bowman, 2019; Winkle, 2014; Winkle & Algren, 2018). In Winkle (2014: 247–265), I include descriptions of a number of universities' 'home-grown' alternatives to corporate-sector, third-party pathway program partnerships, most of which continue to this day. A significant exception is that of George Mason University's ACCESS and BRIDGE pathway programs. George Mason University had very robust in-house pathway programs for both undergraduate and graduate students, but after a number of courtships with a third-party provider, they ultimately made the decision to partner with INTO University Partnerships just as my book was going to press (Redden, 2013). Still, the descriptions of George Mason University's programs – as well as programs at DePaul University, Rowan University at Camden, University of Delaware and Drexel University – provide possible roadmaps for IEP practitioners' development of in-house pathway programs.

Corporate-sector partnerships between universities and third-party educational service providers began to appear in US contexts in fall 2007 with Northeastern University's partnership with Kaplan (Lewin, 2008), and such partnerships have increased steadily in both the number of university partnerships as well as the quantity of third-party providers operating in the United States, with varying results (Redden, 2018b). The phenomenon of partnerships between universities and third-party pathway providers already had prevalence in the United Kingdom and Australia, where such partnerships are relatively well established (Choudaha, 2017b) and where a number of the providers are domiciled. Prior to 2011, these kinds of partnerships received primarily journalistic attention (Graves, 2008; Levin, 2010; Lewin, 2008; Moser, 2008; Redden, 2010[1]), with only minimal empirical research in United Kingdom (Fulcher, 2007, 2009) and Australian (Dooey, 2010) contexts. At the time, published literature examining the impact of such partnerships on faculty status or implications for curricular and pedagogical autonomy in US contexts was nonexistent.

By the late 2000s, US universities with university-governed IEPs were being targeted by pathway providers to set up partnerships incorporating functions of existing IEPs (Reeves, 2011; Winkle & Algren, 2018). These events sparked high levels of anxiety within professional English language teaching (ELT) communities due, in part, to the perceived top-down strategy of third-party providers first obtaining 'buy in' from university provosts and presidents, intentionally circumventing IEP administrators and faculty who were often unaware of the discussions (Mullooly, 2009; Winkle, 2010).

Partnership models, their 'wrap-around services', and contractual agreements (i.e. duration of partnership, expense and revenue sharing, etc.) vary widely. While providers court university presidents and provosts with a ready-made, 'proprietary' partnership frameworks, agreements are ultimately independently negotiated with host institutions and both models and contractual agreements, therefore, vary widely – even when negotiated by the same pathway provider (Choudaha, 2017a; Redden, 2018a, 2018c; Winkle, 2011a, 2014). Nevertheless, such third-party agreements characteristically include a provider's responsibility for recruitment of English-learning international students who do not yet meet host institutions' minimum English proficiency scores for direct admission (Choudaha, 2017b; Klahr, 2015). Beyond recruitment through virtual or technological means, most pathway providers have cadres of in-country recruiting agents (Redden, 2018d). Immediate access to well-established recruitment networks has been a significant motivator for universities partnering with third-party pathway providers (Choudaha, 2017a, 2017b), though there remains controversy over the competitive, commercialized and commission-based nature of this aspect of pathway providers' services (Redden, 2018d).

The provider is further responsible for the development, management, and administration of the university's pathway services, where students are afforded early access to credit-bearing, disciplinary content courses while concurrently enrolled in English for Academic Purposes (EAP) language support courses. In some models, the disciplinary content course sections are restricted to pathway students but taught by academic departments or similar units while others integrate the international pathway students into sections inclusive of domestic or non-pathway students. In a few cases, the corporate-sector partner hires its own academic-content teaching faculty to facilitate pathway-only course sections (Winkle, 2011a, 2014). In some cases, the corporate partner augments or even replaces existing English language curriculum and programs at the host institution. In other cases, the IEP or EAP faculty within the host institution retain curricular and instructional autonomy in supporting both pathway and non-pathway English-learning students. Some programs have seen growth in the number of full-time EAP faculty positions due to initial influx of pathway program students (Winkle, 2014), though some of these gains may be lost due to the Covid pandemic's impact on international student enrollments overall (Redden, 2020a, 2021).

Third-party providers are also responsible for monitoring pathway students' progress and matriculation into degree programs. A number have convinced host institutions to restructure admissions and progression requirements (Winkle, 2014), and some are involved in curricular programming, either through adopting or adapting existing curriculum from the host institution's IEP.

While not all third-party providers offer such arrangements, those that do usually enter multi-year profit-sharing arrangements tied to international student tuition and fees. For example, corporate-sector educational service providers within US contexts include Cambridge Education Group, INTO University Partnerships, Kaplan International Pathways, Kings Education, Navitas, Shorelight and Study Group. Shorelight and INTO University Partnerships are the most dominate players in the United States (Redden, 2018a).

Illuminating Experiences of Pathway Program Stakeholders

My original exploratory study into the phenomenon of third-party, pathway program partnerships was sparked by Sheila Mullooly, a former instructor with the Oregon State University's English Language Institute. Mullooly (2009) presented findings from a research inquiry of four IEP Directors' attitudes vis-à-vis partnerships between third-party pathway providers and universities that already had IEPs prior to the partnership. The underlying message was clearly received by all who attended the session: 'this is what is coming. Beware'.

Fear of the unknown was a dominant theme within my exploratory inquiry (Winkle, 2010) at an IEP whose host-institution was actively being courted by a third-party pathway provider. This fear was intensified through ELT administrators' and faculty's perceptions of poor communication and secrecy from the host-institution and the new partners, as well as threats to the rigor and quality of their existing programs. Yet counter to these concerns, I was left with a sense of optimism by a number of the administrative 'knowers' that – at least for teachers – things might not be as dire as they envisioned. Still, I was curious if perceptions of poorly managed explorations and negotiations leading up to the university-third party partnership would have a lingering effect on the IEP practitioners who were on the receiving end of the top-down leadership approach they had described. How, I wondered, were university faculty who teach disciplinary, academic content responding to this fast-approaching partnership? These questions led me to my narrative inquiry dissertation (Winkle, 2011a).[2]

The intent of my previous research was to examine issues related to the targeting of colleges and universities with institution-administered IEPs by for-profit third-party pathway providers for corporate-sector partnerships. Specifically, the focus was the partnership's impact on faculty perceptions of professional status, as well as faculty decision-making autonomy and perceived impact to their students and university. I have followed up on this research focus at various times over the past decade, gaining evolving insight each time. Twelve participants were interviewed in the initial inquiry, consisting of four self-identified as English language program administrators who – depending upon the organizational location of their program – had the potential to have university-recognized faculty appointments. In all cases, these individuals had 12-month full-time contracts which included university benefits such as healthcare, paid time off and disability insurance. Among the participants were three individuals who self-identified as English language teaching professionals, two of whom were full-time instructors with university benefits. Four participants described their institutional roles as being split between administrative and language teaching domains of their institutions' English language programs, and I classified these individuals as being English language program administrator/English language teacher border crossers (see discussion of practitioner-administrator-scholars [PAS] in Mattson & Gianico, this volume). Two disciplinary faculty members teaching academic content in pathway programs also were among the participants. Neither of these participants held terminal degrees in their academic fields: one was a full-time instructor, and the second was an adjunct faculty member specifically hired to teach credit-bearing disciplinary-content pathway courses.

The inquiry was broadly situated from a perspective that views these types of partnerships as an extension of a general trend toward a corporatization of higher education through privatization and outsourcing. The most salient findings from the study (Winkle, 2011a, 2014[3]) concern the following themes, each of which I briefly discuss in the subsequent sections:

- continued feelings of marginalization by English language teaching professionals;
- retention of curricular and pedagogical autonomy counter-balanced by concerns that 'too much' autonomy in credit-bearing academic-content

pathway courses may result in non-equivalence with their mainstream counterparts, potentially risking accreditation of academic programs and institutions;
- observations that content-teaching disciplinary faculty lack professional development support in meeting English language learners' cultural and linguistic needs, yet the perceived lower status of English language professionals may be inhibiting utilization of this skilled resource;
- perceptions that English language learner pathway students recruited by the corporate partner are not prepared for credit-bearing academic work; and
- the refrain that universities could have created matriculation pathway programs themselves without having to engage an outside corporate partner.

Marginalization of ELTs and ELT as a profession

All ELT faculty and administrator participants acknowledged the historically marginalized status of both English language programs and the academic standing of ELT professionals. 'This profession is a funny thing: working in university-based English programs throughout the world has kept me on the margin – within, but on the margins of academia for my 20 years of working', suggested one administrator/ELT border crosser. Most ELTs and border-crossing participants did not feel that their status had been elevated as a result of the implementation of their institutions' pathway programs. On their campuses they remained 'stepchildren', perhaps elevated to the state of recognition of their existence, but outwardly no more respected or valued by the leadership of their universities or the faculty teaching in the content disciplines. Indeed, one participant suggested at the time of our interview that 'it's definitely a one hundred percent negative perception of us, of our students, of our program, of what we do and who we are: "oh, you work in the PassageMaker Center? Ugh!" There's all this negative connotation …'. While there was acknowledgement that 'maybe some are starting to see us as more than just service providers', others were less certain regarding the English language teaching faculty, even though they suggested that the status of the language center had been elevated as a result of the partnership with the third-party provider ('As soon as the senior management of the university had invested in this joint-venture idea, [the language center] rocketed up the agenda').

The two disciplinary content teaching faculty participants, however, were less so aware of the historical marginalization of the profession. An adjunct faculty member hired to teach business content in pathway courses reflected on the possibility that – beyond his frustrations with seemingly being viewed as only an adjunct by the program's host institution – his affiliation with what he now understood to be a marginalized class of faculty may be impacting how he is perceived by colleagues within his academic discipline. Sadly, this sense of marginalization-by-association was perhaps an additional justification for his maintaining a 'don't ask, don't tell' policy with colleagues regarding his teaching assignments in the university's pathway program, preferring not to disclose the fact he was teaching in the institution's pathway programs. In contrast, another full-time faculty member teaching pathway-only sections of communications courses seemed rather to embrace dual membership in both his academic discipline and the adopted world of English language teaching: 'I straddle these two worlds where I'm satisfying the department's equivalency standards and the standards of my field and translating those so that they make sense for the pathway students. I think everyone's quite happy. I feel respected. I'm actually embracing the fact that I'm straddling two identities here'.

A positive outcome in a number of ELT research participants' worksites was an increase in student enrollments stemming from their institution's corporate sector partnership, and this resulted in the emergence of new full-time teaching lines for some institutions. However, while many of the interviewed ELT professionals expressed enthusiastic appreciation for the new full-time lines, faculty from all categories of this inquiry recognized that the academic professionalism of ELTs was not being acknowledged by their university administration, nor by the corporate partners.

Some IEP practitioners described their work environments as becoming more corporatized – for example, corporate branding through logo-emblazed polo shirts, increased teaching assignments, and a move toward 12-month contracts that emulate staff appointments with eight-to-five workday expectations and limited or no release time for scholarly pursuits. These changes reinforce an inaccurate view of ELT professionals as merely service providers rather than as academic professionals with the capacity to engage with academic colleagues and contribute to the knowledge base of second-language acquisition, pedagogy and curriculum. While not all ELT participants from this inquiry expressed a desire to become 'more academic' or professorial (in fact, several specifically rejected this identity), all professionals engaged in academic activities that sustain the mission and goals of the university should – in my judgement – be respected and supported through opportunities for professional development, research remits for those who are interested, and financial reimbursement when pursuing advanced academic degrees and attending and participating in discipline-specific professional conferences.

Preservation of curricular and pedagogical autonomy

None of the participants indicated that curricular and pedagogical autonomy and decision-making was adversely impacted by the corporate sector partnership. In several contexts, it appears that the corporate partner attempted to make tentative advances toward standardizing curriculum in such a way as to allow for transfers of students among its partner universities. But English language program faculty and administrators – and in some cases, academic deans or university provosts – held firm in retaining full control over academic standards in all university courses and programs.

Nevertheless, several participants described mismatches between the curricular objectives and performance expectations in pathway-only 'segregated' course sections and those of their 'mainstream' university counterparts. This mismatch could raise significant accreditation issues for academic disciplines' degree programs, as well as for universities overall in terms of maintaining their regional accreditation: segregated course sections for pathway program students of credit-bearing courses must be appropriately aligned to mainstream courses in terms of measurable outcomes and objectives. Traditional academic governance systems generally provide for a faculty-driven program review processes through undergraduate and graduate councils or curriculum committees, and the curricula for credit-bearing pathway courses and programs must be similarly vetted through these collaborative faculty systems. Assurances must be made that the objectives, outcomes and standards for the curriculum of integrated content courses are not adapted to align the perceived abilities of enrolled English language students. In short, universities and their faculties must retain complete control over the academic curriculum for all programs within the institution and not subordinate this responsibility to a corporate partner or privileged team of university administrators.

Professional development for disciplinary content teaching faculty

Participant narratives suggest that some disciplinary content teaching faculty were not adequately prepared to address the cultural and, specifically, linguistic needs of international English language students. Their universities and the affiliated third-party providers seemed unwilling to utilize the professional, academic and experiential knowledge of the ELT practitioners in professional development of disciplinary instructors teaching in the pathway programs. Some participants suggested that this unwillingness was related to the perceived low status of ELT. While not all institutions may be able to provide ELTs with opportunities for academic mobility into tenured lines – which potentially could result in a professional collaboration among 'equals' – targeted efforts by university administration to foster symbiotic relationships among faculty in academic disciplines and those in English language programs will ultimately benefit the institution and the students it serves. In the meantime, IEP administrators and faculty may do well to make strides to develop or further advance interdisciplinary relationships among themselves and administrators and faculty in academic units. Many US states require PK–12 teachers to have in-service hours or endorsements demonstrating preparation for working with English language learners; professional development modules focused on the pedagogy of teaching and assessing English language learners could also be required of higher education faculty teaching disciplinary content in pathway program contexts. I would argue that administrators and faculty within universities' existing IEPs – perhaps with the support of their universities' English, World Languages, or Applied Linguistics units or departments – might be able to forge internal partnerships for the development of such professional learning modules.

Pathway students characterized as ill prepared

Numerous participants expressed concerns over admission and exit criteria for the pathway programs. While the number of recruited students was generally reported as high, the quality and preparedness of pathways students were considered lacking. This brought into question whether financially incentivized recruitment agents are serving the best interests of the academic programs, or indeed, the university.

Diversity of students, both by country of origin and gender, were also concerns raised by participants. Several of the faculty shared stories of students who had been admitted with appropriate transcripts and IELTs or TOEFL scores, but after arrival were found to have a level of language proficiency that was significantly below that which had been represented in their applications. One participant shared that within the first few months after their program's transition to the partnership, the corporate partner was trying to make exceptions to the admissions criteria. Similar exceptions were reported by other participants, although two participants reported that the students recruited were generally better than expected in both academic and linguistic performance.

Programs differed in their exit requirements, yet a similarity across most contexts was that pathway students often did not have an accurate understanding of the expectations they would encounter once enrolled in the pathway program. Perhaps influenced by the corporate partners' recruiting agents and marketing materials, many students were unaware admission to academic degree programs was not assured merely because they had been admitted to the pathway program. In cases where completion of the program did translate into automatic matriculation, the admission of domestic students was at times jeopardized since the limited numbers of slots for new students were potentially being taken up by pathway-matriculating international students whose academic qualifications were often inferior to those of their domestic counterparts.

Nearly all participants shared stories which revealed that high numbers of international students recruited by the third-party provider were not prepared for credit-bearing academic work. In a number of contexts, such issues only became apparent following the growing pains associated with the partnership's hasty implementation. While generally measures were implemented to address matters of instructional quality over matters of enrollment quantity, in some cases the promise of tuition revenues appears to have overridden other educational priorities for both corporate and university administrators, exemplified through a reluctance to cap admissions to the pathway programs. Additional concerns were raised by several participants about domestic students and direct-admission international students being unfairly displaced because of guaranteed admission for pathway students. It may be argued that the identification or development of appropriate pre-admission assessments, as well as the development, implementation and adherence to set policies, need to be cooperatively addressed by university administrators, disciplinary faculty and IEP practitioners prior to a pathway program implementation, third-party or otherwise.

Universities could create their own pathway programs

English language teachers and program administrators in this inquiry recognized that their universities could have developed matriculation pathway programs independently without third-party providers. As one participant pointed out, 'The idea of a pathway for English language learners is an excellent idea … but it isn't [the corporate partner's] idea … The most significant thing that [the corporate partner] brought to the table – something I don't know how we at the ELI could have done – they brought leverage'. In the case of one administrator's institution, the ELI apparently already had matriculation agreements in the form of a bridge program, but 'nobody else in the university seemed to know that … we didn't have any recruitment. We just could have used help identifying students'.

Beyond support with recruitment, the primary obstacles were not external to the university; rather, they were university admissions-related issues such as SAT or TOEFL waivers. Universities and colleges are staffed by intelligent and resourceful academic and administrative professionals with experience in curriculum and program development, and so IEP administrators may wish to consider working with deans and faculty from their institution's academic units to develop proposals for their own in-house pathway programs rather than outsourcing these to a private service provider who links them to international recruitment services. Developing such proposals in university settings can be a significant hurdle to overcome, but IEP administrators may be able to make the case that the revenue which would have been shared with corporate partners could instead be directed toward the hiring of short-term contracted consultants or full-time university-employed human resources who can provide the needed skills, competencies, or experience. Further, this retained revenue would support fees associated with international student recruitment through an experienced, quality vendor. In other words, leave the academics to the academic professionals on campus, and utilize the third-party provider solely for recruitment. Conferring with colleagues from institutions that have successfully developed such programs would be advised, and the University and College Intensive English Program (UCIEP) and TESOL International Association may be appropriate avenues for making such connections.

Limitations to Researching Third-Party Pathway Partnerships

My earlier inquiries contributed to the limited empirical scholarship in the areas of English language teaching as a marginalized profession, the outsourcing and instructional privatization in higher education, and pathway programs in US contexts, yet there were naturally limitations. I had responsibility, for instance, to protect research participants' privacy and identities, especially since this study involved their professional livelihoods, and the interviews occurred during a time of significant turmoil for a number of them. As a result, I was unable to include explicit detailing of the various third-party pathway providers' models because such specificity might facilitate connections between the research and the real-life participants. Likewise, the inquiry does not include any form of evaluative judgment or assessment in terms of model or program quality or partnership agreement equity for any of the partnerships within which the study participants worked. Just as third-party pathway providers and their programmatic frameworks are not all the same, nor are the host universities which independently negotiate their institutions' partnership agreements; each collaborative partnership is unique to its context. There were substantial differences among the host universities and the third-party partnership models that were in place at the time of my research, and these differences have led to a range of experiences among research participants. The benefits and challenges described by inquiry participants should not be considered representative of all such pathway programs, nor are such benefits and challenges necessarily attributable to a corporate vendor.

While initial inquiries into the phenomenon of universities with third-party, corporate-sector pathway programs provided insight into the lived experiences of ELT administrators, ELT faculty and content-area teaching faculty, absent from these inquiries were individuals who participated in the decision to partner. With the hope of expanding my work into the realm of decision-makers such as university presidents, provosts and academic deans – and including opportunity to 'follow up' with ELT administrators, ELT faculty and content-area teaching faculty – I subsequently developed and administered another brief survey and recruitment instrument in 2016. The return rate for participants was disappointing (N=10), as was interest among participants to be interviewed (N=2). Throughout these recruitment attempts I relied on direct emails to presidents, provosts and academic deans (addresses which I obtained through time-consuming and tedious searches) and placed calls for ELT professionals through the *MyTESOL* professional networks hosted by TESOL International Association. Academic content-teaching faculty were sought via snowball sampling, as I was and continue to be unable to identify content faculty in pathway programs through publicly available sources, yet this method was largely insufficient for reaching content-teaching faculty. With the exception of a single dean who provided no narrative data, responses from the target demographic of upper institutional administration (i.e. university presidents, provosts and academic deans) were not forthcoming.

When invited to contribute to the present volume, I modified my recruitment strategy to additionally include direct emails to faculty senators from institutions which had third-party pathway program partnerships, with the request that they forward the call for participants to colleagues. Thus far, responses have been equally disappointing (N=8), with only two individuals willing to being interviewed. Yet even within these limited data, a qualitative response provided by an academic dean offers insight into decision-makers' reluctance to participate in this research: 'we're under a gag order, and we really can't discuss any details about the pathway program or [the third-party provider]'. One interviewee – an English program administrator – similarly shared when asked what they knew of the profit-sharing arrangements between the third-party provider and the university, 'Yes, I may know something, but I'm not at liberty to discuss'. Journalists who report on higher education (e.g. Elisabeth Redden and others) seem better able to gain responses than researchers when it comes to interacting with university administrators. Their access may in part result from fewer information-gathering constraints (i.e. IRB) in terms of how they contact and interact with university decision-makers, as well as the silent leverage wielded through journalistic reporting: 'president so-and-so did not respond to my interview request'.

Notwithstanding my limited data vis-à-vis open-ended survey items of eight respondents and an interview with one English language program administrator, some *preliminary* findings of this revived inquiry once again provide a picture of non-involvement by IEP administrators and faculty in the vetting or decision-making regarding their institutions' partnership with a third-party pathway program provider. One ELT shared, 'We were just told it was happening. There was no negotiation. Our former provost met with someone from Shorelight, and they just jumped at the chance'. Interestingly, a university provost – who did not agree to be interviewed – noted they were 'not involved in the vetting process, as this was done through enrollment management', and only became involved during the final negotiations. Participants' beliefs as to why their university elected to partner with a third-party provider rather than develop in-house pathway programs converged on access to international networks of recruiters and the lack of human resources within their universities to develop and maintain such networks on their own. When presented with eight potential reasons why their university might have elected to develop pathway programs through a third-party provider, the top three responses were the desire (1) to recruit full tuition paying students; (2) to 'internationalize' their university communities; and (3) to avoid financial exigency.

Only two of the eight survey participants expressed the opinion that students being recruited for their pathway program by the third-party provider were academically and linguistically prepared. This included one English language program administrator – previously employed by the host university, but now employed by the third-party provider – who shared that the corporate partner recruits all categories of international students for the university (i.e. pathway program eligible L2 English speakers; 'direct-admit' L2 English speakers; and L1 English speakers) and, therefore, recruited students whose placement scores were below that of the pathway program would be admitted into the university's existing IEP.

When asked to consider what was 'working well' with the pathway program and the university's partnership, relatively robust student recruitment was cited by several (not withstanding a global pandemic), though some remarked that undergraduate student recruitment was lower than promised or expected. Two ELTs noted strong institutional support, and one proudly shared their positive 'track record of successfully matriculating students from the pathway program to the university'. Among the 'remaining challenges' expressed by the provost who participated in the survey were the need for the partner to balance 'the approach to not simply be market driven. The focus on the company leans heavily toward markets, not success and thriving'. IEP administrator comments included a concern that the partner is 'recruiting students who are unaware of the requirements' and that 'declining international enrollments, especially in English-prep programs, threaten the future viability of this enterprise'.

One of the final open-ended items included on my recruitment survey asked participants to reflect upon their past and present experiences with the third-party partnership and – if they could go back in time to the conference room of stakeholders where the decision to enter into the partnership was made – would they advocate for their institution to enter into this agreement? In short, would they do it all again? Of the eight respondents, four would have pushed for the partnership agreement. Among those who would not was the provost participant, who remarked, 'I would target recruitment and do everything else in house. We already had infrastructure. The additional structure tends to get in the way more than it supports it'.

Concluding Remarks

I am heartened knowing that a growing number of established and emerging scholars are now exploring the pathway program phenomenon. A number of studies have illuminated the experiences of students while engaged in pathway programs (Elturki *et al.*, 2019; Randall, 2016), with two specifically focused on Chinese international students' experiences (Norstrand, 2020; Xue, 2021). Findings reiterate the need for quality ancillary services to support students engaged concurrently in discipline-related content courses while developing their English language skills. A quantitative study by Holmes (2014) examined the experiences of direct-admit and pathway-admit international students – specifically finding that pathway students perceived more positive experiences during their initial month of study at their university than did direct-admit students, and these increased over time. Miller *et al.* (2015) described the impact of service-learning experiences within pathway programs, and several studies (Benzie, 2015; Kaktins, 2017; Lantz-Wagner, 2022; Mendez, 2021) examine the critical periods when students formally matriculate from their pathway program to degree-granting academic programs. Kaktins (2017) identified incongruities among the pedagogical approaches of instructors of pathway and mainstream course delivery, specifically a propensity for collaborative group-work assignments and activity in academic coursework which challenged students. Lantz-Wagner's (2022: 122) recently defended doctoral dissertation includes salient findings vis-à-vis the oft-contested questions related to 'sheltered spaces' – instructional and non-instructional – and their capacity to strengthen belonging and connectedness for undergraduate pathway students. Finally, I have been and continue to be privileged to consult with a number of teacher-scholars and doctoral students, formally and informally, over the years, suggesting that there may be sustained interest in empirically understanding the impact of pathway programs – both in house and third party – as we move into the future.

During my initial empirical inquiry into the phenomenon of pathway programs (Winkle, 2010), I very nearly assigned the pseudonym, 'Cassandra' – the Greek mythological princess of Troy – to an IEP administrator who described herself as having been given the gift of prophesy in relation to the turmoil and challenges a third-party partnership would bring to her long-standing and successful IEP, but that this gift came with the curse of not being believed when she tried to communicate her concerns to university decision-makers at the time partnership agreements were being finalized. At the risk of mixing metaphors – over a decade hence – the sky hasn't fallen, yet some turbulent clouds clearly remain.

The so-called 'innovative' trend of pathway programs will surely continue, as they are arguably harmonious with universities' goals related to internationalization. Whether or not private, for-profit corporate entities need to be involved beyond student recruitment remains a persistent question for me, personally. Those who view higher education as a public good rather than profit center are naturally skeptical as to how corporate entities, whose main goal is the generation of revenue, cannot be in conflict with educational goals. As a Cassandra-like advocate for the English language teaching profession, I argue that – rather than promoting the professionalization of English language teaching – the corporatization of instruction or services to international students further risks the deprofessionalization of English language teaching. I have lingering concerns that the rapid influx of English-learning students may result in the lowering of minimum standards for ELT professionals hired for such contexts, thereby potentially exacerbating the deprofessionalization of this type of work.

Yet it is true that blame for the commodification of English language programs in tertiary settings cannot solely be laid at the feet of the corporate sector: many universities continue to view their IEPs as profit-generating service centers staffed by non-academicians. That being said, there are strong arguments for the collaborative efforts of university administrators, faculty and non-teaching staff in the development in-house pathway programs for English-learning international students. The IEP and its administrative leadership have an opportunity to be at the forefront of such work.

Notes

(1) Journalist Elizabeth Redden with *Inside Higher Ed* has reported extensively and effectively on the pathway program phenomenon; her comprehensive 2018 *Third-Party Pathways: A Series* articles are cited widely throughout this chapter.
(2) See also the companion YouTube channel (Winkle, 2011b) where administrators and faculty share stories of working in institutions with corporate sector partnership matriculation pathway programs through restoried narratives: http://www.youtube.com/user/WinkleAtBarryU.
(3) All direct quotations and assertions included within the five findings discussion sections are findings attributable to Winkle (2011a, 2014).

References

Benzie, H. (2015) Third space strategists: International students negotiating the transition from pathway program to postgraduate coursework degree. *The International Educational Journal: Comparative Perspectives* 14 (3), 17–31.
Bowman, K.D. (2019) Recruiting with pathway programs. *International Educator* 28 (2), 40–42.
Choudaha, R. (2017a) Are international students 'cash cows'? *International Higher Education* 90 (2017), 56.
Choudaha, R. (2017b) *Landscape of Third-Party Pathway Partnerships in U.S.* Washington, DC: NAFSA.
Clark, A.T., Lippincott, D. and Kim, J. (2021) More than learning English? The impact of university intensive English language program attendance on international student academic achievement. *Education Policy Analysis Archives* 29 (43), 1–19.

Dooey, P. (2010) Students' perspectives of an EAP pathway program. *Journal of English for Academic Purposes* 9 (3), 184–97.

Elturki, E., Liu, Y., Hjeltness, J. and Hellman, K. (2019) Needs, expectations, and experiences of international students in pathway programs in the United States. *Journal of International Students* 9 (1), 192–210.

Fulcher, G. (2007) Universities undermine their own foundations: Contracting out English preparation courses in Britain is a short-term fix. *The Guardian*, 13 April. See http://education.guardian.co.uk/tefl/comment/story/0,,2055735,00.html (accessed March 2022).

Fulcher, G. (2009) The commercialisation of language provision at university. In J.C. Alderson (ed.) *The Politics of Language Education: Individuals and Institutions* (pp. 125–146). Bristol: Multilingual Matters.

Graves, B. (2008) Oregon State University and a British company court international students – And controversy. *The Oregonian*, 12 August. See http://www.oregonlive.com/education/oregonian/index.ssf?/base/news/1218511504125970.xml&coll=7 (accessed March 2022).

Holmes, M.S. (2014) International students in a pathway program: Perceived experiences in transitioning to U.S. higher education. See https://ir.library.oregonstate.edu/concern/graduate_thesis_or_dissertations/5m60qx210 (accessed March 2022).

Kaktins, L. (2017) The international students' transition from pathway program to mainstream university: Insights and challenges. *Proceedings of the International Institute of Social and Economic Sciences Conference* 34, 109–119. https://doi.org/10.20472/IAC.2017.034.024.

Klahr, S.C. (2015) Pathway provider partnerships in higher education: What institutions should consider. *International Educator* 24 (5), 44.

Lantz-Wagner, S. (2022) Paths to pathways: Exploring lived experiences of international students to and through third-party pathway programs. Unpublished doctoral dissertation, University of Dayton.

Levin, D. (2010) The China boom. *The New York Times*, 5 November. See http://www.nytimes.com/2010/11/07/education/07china-thtml?_r=1&pagewanted=1 (accessed March 2022).

Lewin, T. (2008) College and company link up to lure foreigners. *The New York Times*, 7 August. See https://www.nytimes.com/2008/08/08/education/08kaplan.html#:~:text=In%20an%20unusual%20partnership%20that,higher%20education%2C%20before%20starting%20one.

Mendez, A. (2021) Pathway provider programs: The international student experience. *Capstone Collection* 3227. https://digitalcollections/capstones/3227.

Miller, J., Berkey, B. and Griffin, F. (2015) International students in American pathway programs: Learning English and culture through service learning. *Journal of International Students* 5 (4), 334–352.

Moser, K. (2008) New model for recruitment of foreign students sparks debate. *Chronicle of Higher Education*, 27 June. See https://chronicle.com/article/New-Model-for-Recruitment-of/10321/.

Mullooly, S. (2009) Privatization of IEPs. Paper presented at TESOL's 43rd Annual Convention and Exhibit, 26 March, Denver, CO.

Norstrand, L. (2020) Chinese international students' narratives of their experiences in a graduate pathway program: An exploratory study. ProQuest Dissertations and Theses database. (UMI No. 28154459). https://www.proquest.com/openview/72f36d6c3484e4a319d7382f5fd86ab9/1.pdf?pq-origsite=gscholar&cbl=18750&diss=y.

Randall, S.J. (2016) An exploration of an academic bridge program for English language learners. Unpublished doctoral thesis, The University of Arizona.

Redden, E. (2010) Privatized pathways for foreign students. *Inside Higher Ed*, 3 August. See https://www.insidehighered.com/news/2010/08/04/pathways (accessed February 2022).

Redden, E. (2013) Going it alone no longer. *Inside Higher Ed*, 31 October. See https://www.insidehighered.com/news/2013/11/01/george-mason-turns-corporate-partner-grow-international-enrollments-and-programs.

Redden, E. (2018a) Overview of the third-party pathway program landscape. *Inside Higher Ed*, 18 June. See https://www.insidehighered.com/news/2018/06/19/overview-third-party-pathway-program-landscape.

Redden, E. (2018b) More colleges hire corporate partners for international student pathway programs, with mixed results. *Inside Higher Ed*, 18 June. See https://www.insidehighered.com/news/2018/06/19/more-colleges-hire-corporate-partners-international-student-pathway-programs-mixed.

Redden, E. (2018c) A pathway model that differs from the rest. *Inside Higher Ed*, 18 June. See https://www.insidehighered.com/news/2018/06/19/pathway-model-differs-rest.

Redden, E. (2018d) Corporate pathway providers shake up international student landscape and up ante on compensation for agents. *Inside Higher Ed*, 19 June. See https://www.insidehighered.com/news/2018/06/20/corporate-pathway-providers-shake-international-student-landscape-and-ante.

Redden, E. (2020) International student numbers decline. *Inside Higher Ed*, 15 November. See https://www.insidehighered.com/news/2020/11/16/survey-new-international-enrollments-drop-43-percent-fall.

Redden, E. (2021) Intensive English enrollments fell by half in 2020. *Inside Higher Ed*, 2 June. See https://www.insidehighered.com/quicktakes/2021/06/03/intensive-english-enrollments-fell-half-2020.

Reeves, M. (2011) Private schools. In M.A. Christison and F.L. Stoller (eds) *A Handbook for Language Program Administrators* (2nd edn, pp. 345–352). Palm Springs, CA: Alta English.

Winkle, C.A. (2010) Into the corporate unknown: Targeted for privatization in an academic intensive English language program. Paper presentation at Southeast TESOL Regional Conference, 24 September, 2010, Miami, FL.

Winkle, C.A. (2011a) A narrative inquiry into the corporate unknowns: Faculty experiences concerning privatized-partnership matriculation pathway programs. Unpublished doctoral thesis. ProQuest Dissertations and Theses database. (UMI No. 3525011). https://www.proquest.com/openview/7e26965882e4edd12f440c4c02d2be9b/1?pq-origsite=gscholar&cbl=18750.

Winkle, C.A. (2011b) Into corporate unknowns. *WinkleAtBarryU's Channel*. See http://www.youtube.com/user/WinkleAtBarryU.

Winkle, C.A. (2014) *University Partnerships with the Corporate Sector: Faculty Experiences With For-Profit Matriculation Pathway Programs*. Leiden: Brill.

Winkle, C.A. and Algren, M.S. (2018) Current trends in IEPs. In J. Liontas (ed.) *TESOL Encyclopedia of English Language Teaching*. Hoboken, NJ: Wiley.

Xue, L.Y. (2021) Preparing Chinese international students for graduate studies in a US university through a pathway program: A case study. ProQuest Dissertations and Theses database. (UMI No. 28319200). See https://www.proquest.com/openview/a89232717afbee23911932a5493b7030/1.pdf?pq-origsite=gscholar&cbl=18750&diss=y.

12 Brave New Classrooms: On the Role of Technology in IEPs

Ekaterina Arshavskaya and Marta Halaczkiewicz

Introduction

As Aldous Huxley famously imagined in his dystopian novel, *Brave New World*, humans have gradually been outsourcing the inconvenient aspects of our lives to technology. In education, technology has made learning convenient, accessible and democratic (Diem, 2006; Prensky, 2005). Yet it often hinders connections that humans so crave and allows for a level of detachment (Dumford & Miller, 2018; Kryeziu *et al.*, 2021). During the Covid pandemic, this has been most evident in mental issues that both teachers and students suffered due to the isolation and lack of simple human connection (Perkins *et al.*, 2021; Zahrin *et al.*, 2021). Yet we bravely push onward, harnessing the affordances of technology to bring education to more students. For decades, technology has been cited among the more common examples for innovation in Intensive English Programs (IEPs) (Stoller, 1994). Indeed, in 2008, TESOL introduced the *TESOL Technology Standards Framework* (Healey *et al.*, 2008) for the main stakeholders such as program administrators, students and teachers; the standards have since been revised and expanded. Ray Clifford from the Defense Language Institute, as cited in Healey *et al.* (2008: 2), states: 'Computers will not replace teachers. However, teachers who use computers will replace teachers who don't'. Indeed, language educators must embrace new technology or face irrelevancy (Blake *et al.*, 2020). This ominous threat, akin to Huxley's famous narrative, persists in IEPs, where instructors exert much effort in order to keep pace with digital native students expecting engagement through technology. Given the many disruptions caused by Covid to the educational sphere as well as the unprecedented speed at which technology develops and enters our lives, we can undoubtedly concur with this observation.

In this chapter, we review a major framework for understanding the use of technology in modern language classrooms and present multiple examples illustrating the theoretical points discussed in the framework. While the technology and digital resources will undoubtedly change, we argue that the model itself, with some possible considerations, can nevertheless serve as a tool for IEP professionals to reflect on how technology is used in their classrooms and to guide their pedagogical decisions for incorporating instructional technology.

TPACK Framework and IEP Practitioners

While the Covid pandemic forced IEP instructors to embrace technology in ways that may have been unforeseeable previously, many of these innovations are integral parts of IEPs today. Among the many affordances of instructional tools for language learning, Healey (2016) names *connectivity*, *mobility* and *gaming*. Connectivity means people being able to connect to their mobile phones, laptops, tablets and other devices on a constant basis, while mobility allows us to stay connected with family, friends, and colleagues while on the move. Classroom assignments can move in new ways beyond physical classrooms as students join classes and accomplish projects on mobile devices.

The pedagogical augmentation via technology must occur in sound and purposeful ways. Many IEPs are nested within larger institutions such as colleges and universities and therefore often have robust instructional technology support. Yet it is important that the programs avoid technology integration 'for the sake of it', as such an approach can drain resources and lead to student and faculty burnout (Cross & Polk, 2018; Hira, 2021). The Technological Pedagogical and Content Knowledge (TPACK) framework allows IEP professionals to craft strategies for technology integration that are rooted in both pedagogical need and student benefit. TPACK was first described by Mishra and Kohler (2006) as a conceptual framework for educational technology. It is a way to think about technology integration as ecology of knowledge. The framework outlines not only the elements that should be considered but also their interrelation and interdependence. Educational researchers (Willermark, 2018) have noted an increased interest in the TPACK model over time. For example, a study by Tai (2015) showed that in-service language teachers were able to improve their knowledge and applications of computer-assisted language learning in teaching as a result of participation in a TPACK-based workshop developed around the idea of learning-by-doing (Chapelle & Hegelheimer, 2004). Participants first experienced and analyzed the use of the TPACK model by an expert English instructor in designing a class, then applied the same ideas in planning their own technology-supported language classes. All participating teachers reported a positive impact of the workshop, which was evidenced in their teaching.

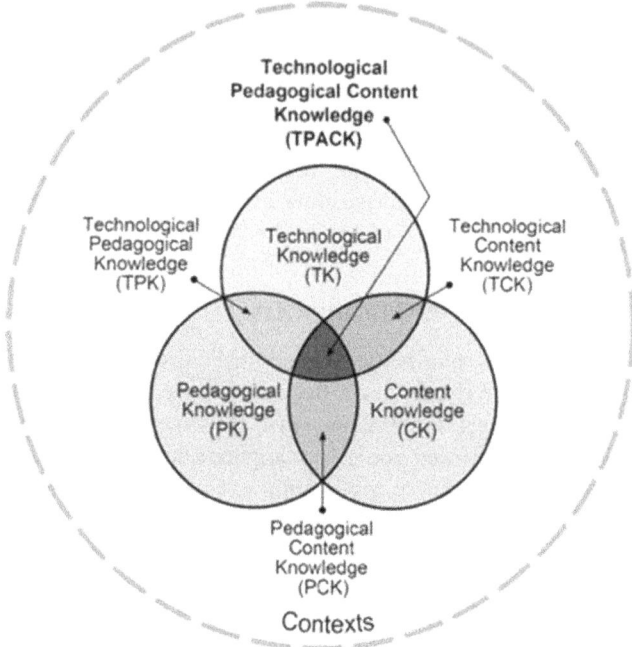

Figure 12.1 The TPACK Framework Model. Areas of interdependence (TPK, TCK and PCK) are represented as overlapping circles

Source: Image reproduced by permission of the publisher, © 2012 by tpack.org.

The framework is based on three types of knowledge: technology, pedagogy and content. This framework evolved from Lees Shulman's (1986) Pedagogical Content Knowledge (PCK) model from the 1980s, which illustrates a longer history to studying teacher knowledge. The three knowledge forms combine to become the Technological Pedagogical and Content Knowledge (TPACK). Each of these elements refers to the knowledge that an instructor brings at an onset of instructional technology integration. Figure 12.1 below presents a visual illustration of the framework and how its elements interplay.

Three types of knowledge

Content Knowledge (CK) refers to what the teacher knows about the subject being taught. In general, teachers at an IEP are well versed in teaching English language and academic skills. However, they may tap into each of those content knowledges at different levels depending on the focus of a course being taught. For example, while teaching a writing course, the instructor may need to access the knowledge of academic genres, academic word lists and English grammar, but in a course on academic reading, that same instructor may rely less on their knowledge of grammar and more on reading and note-taking strategies as well as academic, technical, and general English vocabulary. CK not only changes with the subject being taught but also with the level of instruction. The content knowledge necessary for teaching advanced speaking courses, for instance, is vast in scope and may include knowledge of argumentation or persuasion on academic and cultural topics, public speaking strategies or effective use of visuals. On the other hand, teaching a beginning level speaking course may require the knowledge of context-specific phrases, conversation discourse patterns or general vocabulary. Overall, CK differs from course to course according to its subject, skill, or proficiency level.

Pedagogical Knowledge (PK) encompasses the 'how' of teaching and learning. In the context of an IEP, teachers' knowledge of this type includes methodology of teaching English language skills, curriculum design, student assessments and classroom management. An instructor, for instance, may decide to use a lecture to present a set of new technical terms and ask students to take notes on it to assess their comprehension. IEP teachers' PK consists also of strategies to assist in delivering instruction in heterogeneous classrooms where learners come from a variety of linguistic and cultural backgrounds. In this context, decisions of arranging a class discussion as group or pair work as well as how students are assigned to discussions may have a perceptible impact on the level of student participation. For example, early in a new semester, group work may be a more appropriate pedagogical choice than pair work as students are better able to familiarize themselves with their classmates and develop trust and confidence.

The final element of the framework is *Technological Knowledge* (TK), the knowledge of tools that are available to teachers as well as the ability to adapt as technologies evolve. IEP teachers need to make decisions about applications based on the availability, capabilities, adaptability and efficacy of each tool at their disposal, as well as consider their own level of comfort using the resources and guiding students in using them. An important factor that IEP instructors have to consider is the professional development time and effort they will need to devote. Even using familiar resources takes considerable time to develop instruction (and this time expands considerably if the tool is unfamiliar!), and students may require additional training when familiar tools are used in novel ways by the instructor. Such interventions take time away from content instruction, so IEP practitioners must be ready to provide both training and troubleshooting support when implementing instructional technology.

Each of these three knowledges plays a role in educational technology integration. They interact with each other in ways that create additional 'overlap' areas which play a role in technology implementation. The next sections consider these overlapping areas.

Element overlap areas

The TPACK framework becomes most helpful for making instructional decisions when both the educational context as well as the areas of interdependence are taken into consideration. Those areas of interdependence include Pedagogical Content Knowledge (PCK), Technological Pedagogical Knowledge (TPK) and Technological Content Knowledge (TCK). While the framework is general and may be applied to a variety of contexts, it is best visualized with examples; so, for the purpose of the present discussion, we use examples applicable to the context of IEPs.

Pedagogical Content Knowledge (PCK)

PCK includes both the *what* and the *how* of teaching. The instructor has the expert knowledge of the content that they teach and can make curriculum choices of how to deliver or assess that knowledge depending on the instructional context. For example, an IEP instructor teaching note-taking skills necessary for college approaches instruction differently when the notes are taken during reading rather than during listening. That is, students learning how to take notes during reading might need to recognize keywords in text, cues such as bold, italic or color font, and they might need to annotate the text. In contrast, students taking notes from listening might require instruction on recognizing signal words that mark new points or emphasis. Because of the speed of listening text, they may also need to learn how to use symbols, abbreviations or other shorthand for note taking. And, of course, these approaches change depending on the level of the learners, such as through the pace of instruction or the amount of text being used. Students in advanced-level courses might be able to take notes on longer text (written or audio) excerpts while lower-level students might be able to focus only on shorter chunks of text. Since PCK includes recognition of the students' prior knowledge, instructors might prioritize the content accordingly. When teaching note-taking skills, for instance, students in lower-level courses might learn basic common abbreviations and symbols and be introduced to simple visual organizers such as t-charts or Venn diagrams. On the other hand, students in advanced-level courses might be introduced to annotating skills as well as study skills such as the Cornell method. IEP curricula require vast expertise in PCK. Instructors may specialize in a particular pedagogical approach, yet the IEP needs a variety of experts to be able to support learners at all levels and skills.

Technological Pedagogical Knowledge (TPK)

TPK refers to the instructional decisions of teachers on how technology applications influence the process of teaching and learning. It requires that instructors weigh the positive and negative effects that technology may have on pedagogical approaches. Instructors may choose to use technology as enhancement of instruction or avoid it as an unnecessary complication.

Continuing with the previous note-taking example, open educational resources (OER) materials (e.g. textbooks, newspaper or magazine articles, recorded lectures, TED Talks and podcasts) are a reservoir for teachers to find written and audio texts for note-taking. Instructors can select level-appropriate materials of varying length and linguistics complexity. In case of video or audio recordings, the pacing and speed of recordings can also be adjusted, which can be helpful for students in lower levels who might need to work through a text in chunks. On the other hand, introducing technology as a way to take notes, such as word processing applications, may unnecessarily overburden lower-proficiency students. The cognitive load of comprehension, using new abbreviations and acquiring visual organizers may become too great – especially for students with less word processing experience – when computers are used to accomplish those tasks. Yet with improved comprehension level and familiarity with basic note-taking techniques, the added layer of technology can become a convenience rather than a hindrance.

Technological Content Knowledge (TCK)

The final area of knowledge that plays a role in a teacher's instructional choices, TCK, concerns instructors' understanding of how content and technology influence one another. Using technology may change how students interact with content but also it may change the content itself. And, content changes technology, too. Educational technology developed for delivering content includes learning management systems and vocabulary tools such as *Quizlet*. Digital technologies can assist in the process of teaching note-taking skills, for example, by presenting a text (such as a video recording) live while simultaneously showing a side-by-side view of someone taking notes on the text by typing on-screen. Similarly, teachers can record a screencast video of a textbook passage they are reading while simultaneously annotating the text.

The technology tools made specifically for the purpose of note taking have transformed how we not only teach but also how we take notes. Video annotation tools such as *Voicethread* and *GoReact* allow the student to type time-stamped notes side by side with the video. Students can also use doodling and other features to mark directly on the video. These features allow students to create notes directly over the recording that they are annotating. Some annotation tools, like *Notability* or *OneNote,* let students keep their notes on digital written texts such as documents, pdfs and websites. Mobile applications and browser extensions give students the ability to make comments, highlight and hyperlink texts, make drawings, or attach images. All of these features eliminate the need to create a separate document (digital or hard copy) with notes. Digital technology has transformed the art of taking notes and the teaching of note-taking skills. TCK allows instructors to understand how technology and content are interrelated and helps them make pedagogical decisions. For IEP students, whose minimum course hours almost always necessitate a heavier course load than matriculated college students, the ability to keep track of one's materials and notes is crucial. Acquiring a skill that allows them to eliminate paper notes might prove beneficial in their IEP studies and beyond.

TCK can also develop students' digital literacy skills as both consumers and creators of content through more easily accessible technological tools. For example, in IEP classrooms, teachers often engage students with wikis, blogs, personal websites and/or podcasts. Apart from the aforementioned benefits, these tools create a sense of a more 'real' audience for the students. In one of the classes at our IEP, for example, students created personal websites focused on their life experiences, hobbies and goals. While these websites were not publicly available, the students could share these projects with their peers and/or family members to get more ideas or feedback about how to improve.

A TPACK Sociocultural Layer

The TPACK model can be effectively used in various educational contexts, including IEPs. It can guide instructors' decisions in regards to instructional technology, while highlighting the need to start at the foundation, i.e. the pedagogical objectives of a class activity. Educational researchers (Figg & Jaipal, 2012; Tai, 2015) argue for the use of TPACK-informed approaches as a basis for technology workshops for teachers. While navigating all the complexity of IEP contexts and their associated challenges, even experienced instructors in IEPs can rely on this model to guide their thinking about instructional technology.

A case in point is a recent visit to a local art museum with a group of IEP students. The purpose of the visit was twofold: (1) review the academic vocabulary from a previous class unit; (2) connect students to the university resources in the form of a local art museum. As a teacher contemplates the best ways to achieve these goals, she starts with the content objectives. Then, she uses her pedagogical knowledge about the use of scavenger hunts. She decides to use students' photos with the words and art objects as proof of their accomplishing the activity goals. As she shares her thoughts with a colleague, the latter suggests the use of the *GooseChase* mobile app to accomplish all these goals. As a result of this interaction, the instructor decides to use the *GooseChase* mobile app, as it allows instructors to easily design and customize scavenger hunts and other similar learning activities. Students enjoy the friendly, dynamic interface that includes augmented reality tools, video and audio tools and other options. The activity was carried out with great success and engagement from the students who used their mobile phones to accomplish the tasks. The model guides teachers' thinking about instructional technology tools throughout the contextual changes and challenges of IEP work.

Despite these advantages, the model fails to acknowledge the co-constructed and dynamic nature of teacher knowledge. It suggests that the control for integrating technology happens inside an instructor's head. However, there are many communities of practice that engage IEPs and influence decisions about technology. In most universities, there are exclusive centers that offer this kind of guidance to instructors. From a sociocultural perspective, learning is social (Cole, 1996) and is often facilitated by communities of practice (Firth & Wagner, 2007; Lave & Wenger, 1991). TPACK would benefit with greater consideration of the contextual realities of the various communities of practice. While the model does incorporate the idea of contexts (see Figure 12.1), integrating the concept of communities of practice (Lave & Wenger, 1991) into the current model would better reflect the social nature of all learning, including teacher learning-to-teach. Within the 'multi-splendored, many-faceted' (Kaplan, 1997: 3) IEP community of practice, programs can engage the expertise and knowledge of its various local and global stakeholders. IEP communities of practice are involved in activities such as teaching grammar, academic skills and pragmatics; offering academic and personal counseling services; providing teacher training; developing teaching and assessment materials; maintaining technology; training international teaching assistants; engaging in the pursuit of funding; recruiting students and teachers; interacting with other units; interacting with foreign and domestic educational agencies; and a multiplicity of other activities (Kaplan, 1997). The multifaceted nature of these programs can only be reflected by adding an additional layer of sociocultural knowledge and contexts over the model. Broader social contextualization should extend to educational programs and contexts beyond IEPs.

Instructor and student experiences in pandemic-hit IEPs exemplify the need for a sociocultural layer. During the early stages of the Covid pandemic, technological support provided by the host institution's instructional designers was particularly necessary and welcomed by many teaching professionals, including IEP instructors. For example, attending a workshop using *Zoom* led by one of the instructional designers at the onset of the pandemic allowed participating instructors not only learn the basics of using *Zoom* and some of its interactive features, but also experience an online class as one of their students would and thus share some of the frustration and isolation moments that can occur in technology-facilitated spaces.

While the TPACK model features the areas of interdependence of a teacher's knowledge (*Pedagogical Content Knowledge, Technological Pedagogical Knowledge* and *Technological Content Knowledge*), a sociocultural layer exemplified by various communities of practices

(Lave & Wenger, 1991) integrated into and/or communicating with IEPs, in our opinion, makes the model more comprehensive. Consider the following example from our practice. An instructor working with a group of lower-proficiency IEP students aims to create an active student-centered learning environment. Using the PCK, she sees an opportunity to introduce her students to the course syllabus through a digital annotation tool. In this activity, students collaboratively read and annotate the course syllabus while answering the following prompts: 'what questions do you have about the syllabus?; What seems unclear/confusing in this document?'; 'what important course policies and/or deadlines should be noted?'; 'how/when can you get in touch with your instructor?', etc. A sociocultural layer in this case may involve the instructor's consultation with a university instructional designer to learn more about a specific digital annotation app (e.g. the Hypothes.is app) to accomplish her goal, attending a professional conference session on the same topic, and/or finding a tutorial on YouTube about the pedagogical use of this tool. While the use of such tools may be new and intimidating to the lower-proficiency students, the instructor sees more positive sides to the use of a digital annotation tool (the TPK), i.e. providing students with a collaborative e-learning environment where every student can contribute a thought. This collaborative nature of the assignment again speaks to the sociocultural layer inherent in all learning. Finally, the TCK here encompasses use of a digital (rather than a paper-based) syllabus that can be collaboratively and digitally annotated and saved for future reference.

Overall, given the nature of the learning and work environments within and beyond IEPs, it seems necessary to entertain the possibility of adding this extra sociocultural layer to the TPACK model. Taken further, we can see the necessity of using this layer to contextualize IEPs and the kinds of knowledge and skills necessary to run and to work at an IEP. These knowledge and skills, for instance, differ from the knowledge and skills of teachers working with younger English learners in K-12 settings or with students in community colleges. English language teachers develop knowledge and skills that are particularly effective in their own contexts. Thus, while these teachers' knowledge can be also seen as *Technological Knowledge*, *Pedagogical Knowledge* and/or *Content Knowledge*, it will be specific to the contexts of their work. Therefore, the concept of communities of practice (Lave & Wenger, 1991) seems so crucial and yet missing in the current model. While we concur with the model in that the various areas of a teacher's knowledge are interrelated and interdependent, we propose to stress the contextualized nature of this knowledge acquired/developed through socialization in various communities of practice (Lave & Wenger, 1991), especially if we focus on English language teachers working in IEPs, community colleges, K-12 and other contexts.

The next section further illustrates the ways in which technology was crucial in helping IEPs navigate the changes brought by Covid.

The Future of Technology in IEPs

When instruction was forced online due to the Covid pandemic, many IEP instructors experienced anxiety. The transition was overwhelming even for professionals who were avid instructional technology users. Indeed, IEP professionals had to pivot on a spot to convert in-person teaching to online instruction, often resulting in chaos and a sense of loss for students. Yet in this constantly connected and mobile world, students are exposed to an almost dizzying amount of information, resources and tools, which makes it hard for them to stay focused. Thus, games have found their way into educational environments as a way to engage often-distracted students in meaningful ways. Oftentimes, players start to play these games with the purpose of entertainment; however, through playing the game, they learn many other practical skills, including the English language skills, among many others (Sykes *et al.*, 2008; Thorne & Reinhardt, 2008). Augmented reality tools (e.g. *Google AR, Google lens, Translate App*) have been used to create meaningful interactive language experiences for students (Kessler, 2019). One of the best examples in this category is *Pokémon Go!*, a 2016 augmented reality mobile game that has fascinated the world for a number of years. Language teachers have used *Pokémon Go!* to teach vocabulary, digital storytelling and other skills to language learners of various ages and backgrounds (Halaczkiewicz, 2020). IEP instructors have certainly embraced the many technological tools that reflect the connected, mobile and gamified (Healey, 2016) nature of today's world. IEP programs have also utilized the opportunity to connect to wider audiences by making their promotional materials, samples of video-recorded lessons, and other information digitized and available on the programs' websites. In this way, students can develop a better idea of what their classes may look like and decide whether a particular program would be a good fit for them, and in the short term, these digitized resources certainly help increase programs' visibility, even within universities themselves.

The interconnected nature of today's world cultivates new collaborative professional development opportunities. The Covid pandemic triggered many professional teacher organizations (TESOL, TESOL affiliates, etc.) to offer free professional webinars for teachers during this time. Throughout these times, we certainly witnessed teachers' (including IEP teachers') resilience and creativity facilitated through technology. For example, during the summer of 2020 the Intermountain TESOL organization hosted a series of free webinars on instructional online tools for teachers in the region and throughout the world. Such kinds of efforts demonstrate teachers' dedication to their profession and communities even through the challenging times of the pandemic. Nowadays, both TESOL affiliates and Interest Sections continue to offer free webinars on various topics, including instructional technologies. Another example is the spread of OER materials for English professionals (Thoms *et al.*, 2018). While commercial materials for IEPs can be expensive and not always relevant, teachers' own materials available online can be easily adapted, changed, or simply adopted in a different program. The inclusion and adaptation of OERs over commercial materials provides opportunity for teachers to demonstrate the development of their TPACK.

Despite certain concerns over the scope and sometimes quality of these materials, the OER movement is growing and becoming global in nature (Filatova, 2019; Weller *et al.*, 2015). Some of these concerns are centered on less experienced teachers' use of OER materials. These teachers may need more guidance about how to use these materials in a classroom, since unlike the more traditional textbooks that often have a special companion book with explanations for teachers, the OER materials do not usually feature those.

Another pedagogical imperative today concerns helping students become lifelong and autonomous learners, and we can certainly see that happening with our students being equipped with various mobile apps for language learning (*Quizlet, Flipgrid, Grammarly*, to name a few). Within IEPs, instructors have found ways to engage learners in language learning experiences both inside and outside the classroom in meaningful, authentic and creative ways, putting their TCK and TPK into practice. For example, writing experiences that have traditionally happened in the silos of a classroom, can now reach wide audiences, facilitated by online spaces and practices (Halaczkiewicz, 2019). Technology has also enabled us to re-imagine what a class field trip may look like and how it is carried out. While IEPs give students an advantage of learning the language in an immersive environment, the global pandemic demonstrated that such benefit of IEPs cannot always be taken advantage of. With the advancement of technology and the internet, virtual field trips to museums, organizations and art galleries have become possible (Kung, 2001), along with virtual reality educational opportunities (Jung, 2002). IEP instructors with their TCK acumen can continue to allow a level of immersion by facilitating those virtual experiences. In our own IEP classes, for example, we explored the virtual features of a local art museum and the Metropolitan Museum of Art in New York. Of particular interest were the video and audio files representing interviews with artists and regular visitors to 'the Met' that provided additional listening practice to the students. In other words, together with the students, we were able to explore one of the best museums in the world without leaving the classroom in Utah. Supporting students' curiosity through engagement with quality online sources is one of the practices IEP instructors have long engaged with and we hope we will continue to do.

This switch to e-learning impacted students in both negative and positive ways. At our IEP, it offered some benefits to ESL students. For example, students who lived in remote areas of our state and before the pandemic could not complete English language instruction because of the face-to-face nature of IEP courses, after the pandemic removed of the in-person requirement, however, they were able to join courses online, complete their English training, and move on to the university. The IEP instructors tapping into their TCK and TPK helped those students to reach their academic goals. Nevertheless, there do seem to be students who value in-person immersion, as some students returned to their home countries, waiting to continue their English training until they would be able to do so in person. Informal feedback to our IEP's office indicated that those students wanted the immersive experience of living in the target language country and that they preferred in-person instruction to online experiences.

In the context of our own program, we utilize the PCK expertise of our instructors in teaching English in the academic contexts to develop and to launch a new certificate program within our IEP aimed to train new professionals interested in teaching English in US private institutions and abroad. The curriculum of the certificate is strengthened by augmenting instruction with TCK and TPK to prepare its students for their future jobs. This is just one of the many solutions. Among other alternatives can be re-designing IEPs to better meet the needs of the more proficient yet less numerous student populations. Online conversation classes can be a valuable option for foreign professionals seeking to improve their English skills, while online writing labs can be more useful for international students seeking to enter US universities. Within our IEP, we were also recently able to re-purpose the former academic writing skills and speaking skills courses originally designed for international students to better serve the needs of local (domestic) multilingual students. All of these curricular innovations can be facilitated through technology. For example, local students may prefer online classes facilitated through *Zoom* or a similar video-based communication platform due to busy schedules at work and family obligations. Such innovations are made possible on the basis of teachers' TPACK.

With the rapid development of technology (including language learning apps and translation tools) will students still need intensive training in English in IEPs in the future? Will technology itself be sufficient in helping students become successful language users? Perhaps in the foreseeable future technology is insufficient to fully threaten the need for IEP services, but IEP practitioners need to recognize and acknowledge changes in educational landscapes. Changes may include the format of the classes (online/hybrid/face-to-face), varying student populations due to various changes in the economies, and English language instruction improvements facilitated through technology in students' home countries. Needless to say, these changes also impact the job security of IEP practitioners.

Another concern that is often voiced among IEP instructors today is our extreme fascination with technology and forgetting to connect with students more personally, perhaps also forgetting to utilize the available community and university resources. However, effective and thoughtful use of instructional technology, on the other hand, can allow us to better connect to both students and available resources. For example, IEP professionals often find their TPK helpful in exploring ways to connect to students via phone apps or social networks rather than the more traditional way of using learning management systems or email. Also, community and university organizations welcome the contributions of 'digital natives' (Prensky, 2001), i.e. students who grew up in the information age. For instance, community-engaged service projects can involve IEP students in designing social media and website posts for local communities in students' native languages and in English. For this to happen, of course, IEP practitioners need to be the facilitators.

Research on post-secondary digital native students highlights a desire for 'frequent educational opportunities that use technology and visual media' (Mohr & Mohr, 2017: 92). Many of the recommendations about how to work with the younger generations of students revolve around digital literacy skills (Mohr & Mohr, 2017). Cook (2015: para. 11) describes this same generation, noting that they 'write and communicate in new ways with new syntax using multi-modal approaches'. Indeed, while many IEP students can be considered digital natives or digital integrators, some students nevertheless still arrive in IEPs with less proficiency in technology, such as students from socioeconomically disadvantaged backgrounds or refugees. These individuals may require greater support and more time to learn the various technological tools used in today's classrooms. This calls for instructors with not only the TCK know how, but in particular for those having the TPK acumen as well as patience and understanding of how to train technology 'newcomers' to become digital citizens of US academia. In our own program, we have witnessed successful language learning against the backdrop of collaborative technology-facilitated spaces, such as through digital storytelling, *Canva*, personal websites and other multimodal approaches. As these technologies grow and change, IEP practitioners must be prepared to adapt their TCK and TPK to the new opportunities.

Speaking of the future that may await intensive language programs, Healey (2016: 21) suggests that students may not wish to spend extensive time in these educational institutions if they can access high-quality translations and information digitally via the internet. This may be particularly true for 'self-directed language learners' capable of creating 'their own pathways to learning language' (Healey, 2016: 21). This assumption seems reasonable, especially given the possibilities that online social media tools offer to today's learners in terms of communication and opportunities for creating and publishing one's own content online as information-creators. At the same time, those learners 'not skilled at language learning' (Healey, 2016: 21) may need extra guidance and support in choosing the right materials, resources, and so forth. The future role of teachers may be helping these kinds of learners understand the resources available to them (Healey, 2016). We agree – even today, IEP teachers often find themselves in the role of facilitators. A case in point is the use of digital storytelling and websites. Based on our experiences, students oftentimes learn new technologies necessary for class projects with ease and enjoy the individual creativity and space that these tools allow.

Huff (2010) states that technology 'is easy to talk about. But it is much more difficult to use it effectively' (2010: 3, as cited in Lee & Egbert, 2016: 195). We can safely assume that technology use in IEPs, and most learning, is here to stay. Students expect technology integration, and even instructors formerly not apt in using technology have successfully tamed it, at least to some degree. Careful consideration needs to be given to whether and how to use technology in IEP classrooms. The present chapter demonstrates how the TPACK model helps IEP educators navigate the dense web of instructional technology tools, guiding the instructional decisions of instructors with consideration of different types of knowledge and skills. It elaborates on a sociocultural layer of the model in order to more accurately represent professionals' lifelong quests to improve their teaching. Instructors must be intentional about the choice of technologies against the backdrop of their work contexts, students' needs, and other factors. While the chapter is hardly comprehensive, we hope that it offers examples that will assist in deciding on the role of technology in instructional design. In our pursuit of teaching excellence facilitated through instructional technology, we hope not to lose sight of our bigger goals in education and our humanity, as ominously predicted in *Brave New World*.

References

Blake, R.J., Thorne, S.L. and Guillen, G.A. (2020) *Brave New Digital Classroom: Technology and Foreign Language Learning* (3rd edn). Washington, DC: Georgetown University Press.

Chapelle, C. and Hegelheimer, V. (2004) The English language teacher in the 21st century. In S. Fotos and C. Browne (eds) *New Perspectives on CALL for Second Language Classrooms* (pp. 299–316). Mahwah, NJ: Lawrence Erlbaum.

Cole, M. (1996) *Cultural Psychology: A Once and Future Discipline*. Cambridge, MA: Harvard University Press.

Cook, V.S. (2015) Engaging generation Z students. Center for Online Learning Research and Service, University of Illinois Springfield. See https://sites.google.com/a/uis.edu/colrs_cook/home/engaging-generation-z-students-1 (accessed July 2022).

Cross, T. and Polk, L. (2018) Burn bright, not out: Tips for managing online teaching. *Journal of Educators Online* 15 (3), 1–6. https://doi.org/10.9743/jeo.2018.15.3.1.

Diem, R.A. (2006) A positive or negative force for democracy: The technology instructional paradox. *International Journal of Social Education* 21 (1), 148–154.

Dumford, A.D. and Miller, A.L. (2018) Online learning in higher education: Exploring advantages and disadvantages for engagement. *Journal of Computing in Higher Education* 30 (3), 452–465.

Figg, C. and Jaipal, K. (2012) TPACK-in-practice: Developing 21st century teacher knowledge. Society for Information Technology & Teacher Education International Conference Proceedings. See https://www.learntechlib.org/p/40349/ (accessed October 2022).

Filatova, O. (2019) The use of electronic Open Educational Resources to teach college writing to ESL students. Paper presented at *TESOL CALL Electronic Village Events*, Atlanta, GA.

Firth, A. and Wagner, J. (2007) Second/foreign language learning as a social accomplishment: Elaborations on a reconceptualized SLA. *Modern Language Journal* 91 (1), 800–819.

Halaczkiewicz, M.D. (2019) Harnessing writing in the wild: Practical applications of affinity spaces for English language instruction. *TESOL Journal* 11 (1), 1–10. https://doi.org/10.1002/tesj.453.

Halaczkiewicz, M.D. (2020) "Let's go on a gym raid tonight!": Video game affinity spaces in English language instruction. *TESL Electronic Journal* 25 (2).

Healey, D. (2016) Language learning and technology: Past, present, and future. In F. Farr and L. Murray (eds) *The Routledge Handbook of Language Learning and Technology* (pp. 9–23). New York, NY: Routledge.

Healey, D., Hanson-smith, E., Hubbard, P., Ioannou-Georgiou, S., Kessler, G. and Ware, P. (2008) *TESOL Technology Standards Framework*. Alexandria, VA: TESOL.

Hira, S. (2021) Mental stress due to technological difficulties in online education: Observations from a Saudi college. *International Journal of Current Research* 12 (12), 15305–15308. https://doi.org/10.24941/ijcr.40397.12.2020.

Huff, L. (2010) "There's too much stuff": Professional development. In J. Egbert (ed.) *CALL in Limited Technology Contexts* (pp. 31–41). San Macros, TX: CALICO.

Jung, H.J. (2002) Virtual reality for ESL students. *The Internet TESL Journal* 8 (10). http://iteslj.org/Articles/Jung-VR.

Kaplan, R.B. (1997) An IEP as a many-splendored thing. In M.A. Christison and F.L. Stoller (eds) *A Handbook for Language Program Administrators* (pp. 3–21). Burlington, CA: Alta Book Center Publishers.

Kessler, G. (2019) Augmented reality for language learning. See http://blog.tesol.org/augmented-reality-for-language-learning/ (accessed July 2022).

Kryeziu, S.A., Avdiu, T.A. and Avdiu, A. (2021) Examining the teachers, administrators and parents' view on drawbacks of technology use in education. *Ilkogretim Online* 20 (2), 206–215. https://doi.org/10.17051/ilkonline.2021.02.26.

Kung, S-C. (2001) A virtual visit to the Guggenheim museum in New York. *The Internet TESL Journal* 7 (7). http://iteslj.org/Lessons/Kung-Guggenheim.html.

Lave, J. and Wenger, E. (1991) *Situated Learning: Legitimate Peripheral Participation*. Cambridge: Cambridge University Press.

Lee, H.G. and Egbert, J. (2016) Language learning and technology in varied technology contexts. In F. Farr and L. Murray (eds) *Handbook of Language Learning and Technology* (pp. 185–197). Florence, KY: Routledge.

Mishra, P. and Koehler, M. (2006) Technological pedagogical content knowledge: A framework for teacher knowledge. *Teachers College Record* 108 (6), 1017–1054.

Mohr, K.A.J. and Mohr, E.S. (2017) Understanding generation Z students to promote a contemporary learning environment. *Journal on Empowering Teaching Excellence* 1 (1), Article 9. https://doi.org/10.15142/T3M05T.

Perkins, K.N., Carey, K., Lincoln, E., Shih, A., Donalds, R., Kessel Schneider, S., Holt, M.K. and Green, J.G. (2021) School connectedness still matters: The association of school connectedness and mental health during remote learning due to Covid. *The Journal of Primary Prevention* 42 (6), 641–648. https://doi.org/10.1007/s10935-021-00649-w.

Prensky, M. (2001) Digital natives, digital immigrants part 1. *On the Horizon* 9 (5), 1–6. https://doi.org/10.1108/10748120110424816.

Prensky, M. (2005) "Engage me or enrage me": What today's learners demand. *Educause Review* 40 (5), 60.

Shulman, L.S. (1986) Those who understand, knowledge growth in teaching. *Educational Researcher* 15 (2), 4–14. https://dx.doi.org/10.3102/0013189X015002004.

Stoller, F.L. (1994) The diffusion of innovations in intensive ESL programs. *Applied Linguistics* 15 (3), 300–327. https://doi.org/10.1093/applin/15.3.300.

Sykes, J.M., Oskoz, A. and Thorne, S.L. (2008) Web 2.0, synthetic immersive environments, and mobile resources for language education. *CALICO Journal* 25 (3), 528–546.

Tai, S.-J.D. (2015) From TPACK-in-action workshops to classrooms: CALL competency developed and integrated. *Language Learning & Technology* 19 (1), 139–164. https://llt.msu.edu/issues/february2015/tai.pdf.

TESOL Technology Standards Framework (2008) https://www.tesol.org/docs/default-source/books/bk_technologystandards_framework_721.pdf?sfvrsn=4bd0bee6_2 (accessed July 2022).

Thoms, J., Arshavskaya, E. and Poole, F. (2018) Open educational resources and ESL education: Insights from educators in the United States. *TESL-EJ* 22 (2). https://tesl-ej.org/wordpress/issues/volume22/ej86/ej86a2/.

Thorne, S.L. and Reinhardt, J. (2008) "Bridging activities," New media literacies, and advanced foreign language proficiency. *CALICO Journal* 25 (3), 558–572. http://dx.doi.org/10.1558/cj.v25i3.558-572.

Weller, M., de los Arcos, B., Farrow, R., Pitt, B. and McAndrew, P. (2015) The impact of OER on teaching and learning practice. *Open Praxis* 7 (4), 351–361. https://proxy.qualtrics.com/proxy/?url=http%3A%2F%2Foro.open.ac.uk%2F44963%2F1%2F227-1106-2-PB-3.pdf&token=qWHfwYA68m%2FSQBW9D6Kt8FVI8EJQaxfore1t1HsAo7k%3D.

Willermark, S. (2018) Technological pedagogical and content knowledge: A review of empirical studies published from 2011 to 2016. *Journal of Educational Computing Research* 56 (3), 315–343.

Zahrin, S.N.A., Sawai, R.P., Sawai, J.P., Ab Rahman, Z. and Samsudin, M.Z. (2021) Emotion, mental and spiritual regulation of the higher education community during the Covid-19 pandemic. *ASEAN Journal of Teaching & Learning in Higher Education* 13 (2), 1–24.

13 Where to From Here? Continuing to Innovate, Respond and Reform in IEPs

Crystal Bock Thiessen

Innovating from the Periphery

Innovation is one of those buzzwords that businesses and institutions of higher education love to use, and which people engaged in the process often hate to hear. We're told that we must innovate to survive and to remain relevant in these times of rapid change, but what does it actually mean to innovate? Is it creating a brand-new product or service? Is it the excellent execution of a brilliant idea? Can it be anything other than another neoliberal pursuit? Does it, instead, transcend all of these concepts to reflect a complete and often uncomfortable change in the status quo altogether? The chapters in this volume present the idea of innovation – along with varying interpretations of its somewhat vague meaning – as something that has come to define Intensive English Programs (IEPs) in their very essence by examining both the historical underpinnings of IEPs and in wondering how they can, yet again, innovate to survive an uncertain future.

As a physical embodiment of the intersection of applied linguistics, TESOL and English language education as a whole, IEPs have a distinctive history, role and position in their respective host institutions that has always hinged on the concept of innovation. In what is frequently described as 'just being flexible', IEP practitioners and administrators are often faced with changing policy or practice in order to meet varying demands of the institutions, governments and students that seek their services. Yet the research on innovation in IEPs remains surprisingly low, and the 'zone of innovation' – that window for meaningful changes to be made within IEPs – is open for just a brief moment before interested stakeholders become chary of its implementation (Litzenberg, Introduction). We are reminded that, between innovation and change, it is only change that is inevitable. While innovation is connected with education as a whole, without both change and innovation, IEPs would not have survived the historical tides and liminal position of their existence.

The role of professionals working in IEPs has been shaped by two primary views: that of providing a support service, and that of scholarly participation in an academic field (Mattson & Gianico, Chapter 7). In the former, practitioners are usually assigned heavy teaching loads with the singular goal of advancing international multilingual students' English language to the level required for matriculation into tertiary education in the United States. Under this view, practitioners are seen merely as providing a support service to students wanting to further their education in the United States, yet at the same time they are not considered a viable part of the academic world for which they are preparing students to enter. In the academic field view, however, continuing education that further develops the connection between praxis and scholarship is encouraged, and IEP practitioners are expected to be contributing members to a scholarly community of practice, an endeavor that can be difficult considering their larger teaching loads and the multitude of roles they must accept within their programs. IEP practitioners and administrators, thus, need to better understand how their unique positioning can facilitate innovation in ways that are difficult or impossible for more traditional academic units in their host institutions.

Caught somewhere between service unit, academic component, and neoliberal industry, IEPs have almost become accepting of their disposition on the peripheries of both their literal placement on campuses and as contributing academics among their faculty peers. The experts in the field who have contributed to this volume examine the past (including both program development and the more sociocultural and problematic history of colonization) present and future of IEPs in order to challenge this positioning and help bring attention to a field that, historically, arose out of a need to innovate and has continuously pursued its identity as an innovator, meeting ever-changing needs and demands of those to whom they provide learning and services.

How We Got Here

Awareness of the history of IEPs can help us to better understand how the past has formed (and continues to form) the relationships they generally have with their host institutions, the culturally varied students they serve, and the governments and institutions to which they often must respond and for which they have often must reshape. In Chapter 1, Diane Larsen-Freeman provides a comprehensive historical overview of University of Michigan's English Language Institute (ELI), which was established in 1941 and is widely regarded as the first IEP.

This contribution offers a concrete record for how IEPs as we know them today came to be. The ELI's dual mission of conducting research and developing materials in English language teaching led to the creation of more communicative and immersive language teaching pedagogies. Eventually, the publication of the very first academic English language journal, *Language Learning: A Journal of Applied Linguistics*, contributed to Michigan being credited with first using the term *applied linguistics*. The journal has a continued academic standing, celebrating its 75th year at the time of this publication. Larsen-Freeman's account details how the ELI was chosen as the site for English teaching training for participants in President Kennedy's newest effort at the time to improve American perception and leadership in the world via the Peace Corps, making it a historic player in a government program that has sent over 240,000 citizens on volunteering missions in 142 countries (Peace Corps, n.d.). With more programming and higher enrollment, the ELI led advancements in curricula and methodologies, as well as developing innovative ways to produce and publish new teaching materials. Continuing to strive to meet the needs of international multilingual students on campus while remaining committed to the fusion of research and practice resulted in international graduate teaching assistant training, the development of English language corpora, a host of EAP courses and more innovative practices. The ELI's status as a leader in English language teaching and learning innovation helped to advance its reputation and relationship with the University of Michigan itself.

In the ELI at University of Michigan, IEPS have a strong model of service and innovation upon which they are based and which has served to contribute to their own history as centers for methodological and pedagogical innovation, applied linguistics research and support and employment opportunities. As IEPs began to take a more unified shape across the United States in the 1970s and early 1980s, they were further innovated by the development of an MA TESOL program at Michigan in 1976, the creation of an annual conference in applied linguistics, and the development of the second language acquisition (SLA) subfield (Larsen-Freeman, Chapter 1). Applied linguistics research and IEPs share a more than 50 year history of mutually benefitting one another throughout this development yet, just like their status in their home institutions, IEPs have often been overlooked in the crucial and supporting role they have in helping to advance the field (Litzenberg & Kim, Chapter 2).The pinnacle of IEP-supported applied linguistics publications show a majority of them appearing across three main journals between 1976–1987 (Litzenberg & Kim, Chapter 2). It was around this time that many former directors of IEP programs got their start in the field, coming of age in a 'Wild West' of IEP development, research, and implementation (Cavusgil *et al.*, Chapter 3). As was the trend with IEP programs of the time, many IEP educators and administrators did not train specifically for a career in TESOL but became involved in the field due to a love of languages, experience in the English or foreign language departments, time in the Peace Corps or abroad, or by being in the right (or wrong) place at the right time. In a sense, anyone who could speak English presumably natively or with a native-like command was thought to be able to teach English, contributing to a lineage of problematic thought that is often reflected in sentiments towards TESOL practitioners and the profession today.

The ELI in Michigan set the stage for a wave of IEPs at higher educational institutions to be initiated, although many of these earlier IEPs were low on trained faculty and appropriate materials, making resourcefulness a necessary component to the innovative base from which these programs took root. Practices of IEPs and IEP educators themselves were both proactive and reactive (Litzenberg, Introduction) as programs were built from the ground-up or completely overhauled in order to best meet student learning goals while proving relevance through stakeholder requests. It is this 'free-for-all' stacking of IEPs that has perhaps led to the residual perception of IEP educators as second-rate academics to their peers in their host institution, and explains the later rush to 'professionalize' the programs through specific MA and doctoral degrees in the field for both educators and administrators (Slagoski, Chapter 4), a practice that pushed many qualified educators with years of English language teaching experience out the door or hanging on the edges of the field looking for work elsewhere. Many directors who were especially active during the 1980s and 1990s in IEPs acknowledge that, despite their years of work in shaping, teaching, and leading IEPs, they would not be able to hire themselves nowadays for a position in the IEP due to a lack of a professional degree in the field (Cavusgil *et al.*, Chapter 3), signifying a marked change in IEPs and the profession as a whole.

By the late-1980s and continuing through the 2000s, IEPs began to encounter more neoliberal challenges at their host institutions, often needing to innovate, change, or both as a means of proving their relevance and justify their existence. Morphing into revenue-generating service units under the ascendancy of their host institutions, IEPs became less central to applied linguistics research (Litzenberg & Kim, Chapter 2). Most IEPs came to be generally self-supporting programs positioned on the margins of institutions of higher education, which developed a view of them as service or support units rather than an integral part of the greater academy of scholars, despite decades of innovative scholarship in teaching and learning, the fostering and support of greater internationalization on US campuses, and practical development and support of the broader field of applied linguistics.

When times are good, like they were during the era of globalization after the Cold War, IEPs are a welcomed source of revenue through international students on campus. When times are more trying – such as after 9/11 in 2001, the financial crisis of 2007–2008 and, most recently, during the global pandemic of 2020–2021 – and with increased isolationist and nationalist sentiments (Slagoski, Chapter 4), IEP educators and administrators find themselves scrambling to prove their relevance and put market value on their existence to their host institutions by demonstrating innovation of services, programming and curricula – while also maintaining themselves as academic professionals. This reality has resulted in many IEP educators taking on something of 'a hybrid professional identity on the periphery of the academy' (Mattson & Gianico, Chapter 7) and adopting the multiple roles of practitioner-administrator-scholar. More accurately described by Mattson and Gianico as Blended EAP Professionals (or BLEAPs), they must navigate the unique tensions that accompany their IEP's reputations at their host institutions. By posturing IEPs as operating within an important 'third space' of innovation, collaboration and academic influence, negative perceptions of IEPs can be reframed instead. Just like many IEP educators who initially fell into their roles in the field and found themselves both creating and taking on multiple roles in their programs during the early years of the field (Cavusgil *et al.*, Chapter 3), Mattson and Gianico describe what it means for IEP professionals to be accidental practitioners turned accidental administrators, who became more impassioned with their roles in the IEP as opportunities for academic, social and cultural support of international multilingual students grew, even in the face of adversity. With the addition of third-party pathway programs vying to compete for IEP revenue (Winkle, Chapter 11), many BLEAPs find themselves consumed with the business strategist role, reducing the time spent on actual applied innovation and student learning in the classroom.

In more recent years, IEPs have experienced major setbacks, with some never really recovering and others hanging on and weathering the proverbial storms. IEP employment trends from 2010–2021 reflect the tenuous existence of opportunities within the field, giving us a more modern history on which to theorize their future (Slagoski, Chapter 4). Currently, IEPs have to contend with reductions in foreign government support for English language study abroad and more and better opportunities for English language education in students' home countries. Additionally, rising tuition fees in the United States compared with their international competitors as well as government, social and internal pressures or expectations from their own home institutions contribute to the threat of their existence. It is especially imperative, then, that IEPs acknowledge and face changing trends that will affect their sustainability in the future. Problems, nevertheless, are generally catalysts for creativity and innovation. An understanding of the histories that contributed to the impetus of IEP development, structure and relationships with their host institutions, as well as an understanding of where we are today, can help position for future innovation (Litzenberg & Kim, Chapter 2), which will be vital to future directions of programs and their success.

Innovate to Create, Relate and Survive

One of the ways that many IEPs are currently working to not only engage in innovation, but to also further position themselves as academics and experts in multicultural communication and multilingual language support is through the development of partnerships at their host institutions. This volume provides chapters that specifically look closer at how IEPs can and do expand their impact beyond just the immediate students with whom they work to create wider university appreciation and reputation (see Grosik, Chapter 5; Anderson & Godfrey, Chapter 6; Winkle, Chapter 11). These endeavors can be especially challenging as IEP educators are often more passionate about and dedicated to their actual teaching roles than they are to the neoliberal tasks of marketing, strategizing and actively responding to the current buzzwords that supposedly ensure their department's survival (Grosik, Chapter 5; Litzenberg, 2020). IEPs can do more than just serve their students; they can also be of value and support to international multilingual learners of English as they advance through their degree programs. The best way to establish IEPs as outward support units is undoubtedly through campus partnerships. Grosik (Chapter 5) argues that this is best achieved through higher administrative outreach through their diversity, equity, and inclusion efforts rather than be left to IEP administrators and educators alone. Anderson and Berger Godfrey (Chapter 6) suggest the need for the creation of a new campus position to facilitate these kinds of connections specifically.

By providing language and academic support, through workshops on multiculturalism and inclusive access, and with the creation of teacher training workshops for their faculty peers, IEPs can essentially work to increase access to second language education and understanding. This role is especially important as teaching faculty on campus often do not feel prepared to both address and understand cultural differences and linguistic endeavors of their international multilingual students. In this sense, fostering interdisciplinary relationships among IEP and course content faculty would be symbiotic in nature for all involved. The need to continue to be a revenue-generating source on campus in times of decreasing international student enrollment can be supported through a campus/IEP partnership in the form of pathway programs (Winkle, Chapter 11), in which pre-matriculated international multilingual learners of English are provided with a credit-bearing first year experience supported by the IEP. Although this kind of partnership opportunity is often overlooked by higher administrators who are wooed by 'innovative' touts from third-party pathway program providers, a partnership of this nature aligns with campus efforts to internationalize, and IEPs would do well in promoting themselves as the more affordable in-house experts for the job.

The notion of IEP partnerships can be taken a step further (or actually, off campus altogether) to include community partnerships through service-learning initiatives (Perren, Chapter 9). As a way to disrupt the linear curriculum pattern in which language learners in IEPs often take, he presents community service learning as a way for students to engage in authentic language learning and use while developing a better understanding of their roles and responsibilities towards the greater community in which they live. Although this model offers what could be considered innovative, meaningful language learning through community connections and service, it is not without major challenges, including international student transport, understanding of social problems and histories in the United States, language proficiency, limited exposure to the various communities themselves and a risk of perpetuating stereotypes through limited engagement, among others. Still, Perren asserts that when university (including IEP) educators and administrators place importance on learning about and engaging with the communities around them – and when those communities are indeed viewed as partners that are given a voice in the service-learning activity project – partnerships based in social responsibility can benefit everyone involved.

As with other areas of education, innovation in IEPs cannot be fully addressed without acknowledging the important role technology has and will continue to have in both teaching and learning. English language educators often find themselves wading through dense layers of educational technology tools and strategies while trying to encourage and manage actual human interaction and the sociocultural aspects of language learning and intercultural communication in their classrooms. They are faced with needing to both teach skills in technology and use educational technology with students who are digital natives yet who are not always necessarily digitally literate. Digital literacies need to be integrated as core components in the English as a Second Language/English as an Academic Language curriculum for students to better understand how digital spaces and the social contexts that inform digital practices work to shape, influence, and even change language (Tour, 2020). The very aspects of connectability that entice us as users of technology, however, quite often contribute to isolation and disconnection, and the pervasiveness of our virtual endeavors can most certainly be challenging in a language classroom focused on meaningful interaction and engagement with others. Nevertheless, IEPs that are unwilling or unable to keep up with technological shifts will most likely eventually render themselves irrelevant.

Gaining a particular boost during the global pandemic, technology has served as a catalyst for innovation in IEPs. Because L2 motivation is both shaped by and shapes meaningful and agent-driven engagement with the target language, when paired with virtual and other tech-driven media practices, it has powerful implications for English language teaching (Henry, 2019) that can be both exciting and overwhelming for IEP practitioners (especially those who take on the multifaceted role of a BLEAP). The Technological Pedagogical Content Knowledge (TPACK) framework serves as a guide for both supporting English language educators in navigating these endeavors and also in facilitating innovation as they use technology in new ways to support learners' language-learning goals (Arshavskaya & Halaczkiewicz, Chapter 12). IEP educators must not only embrace new technologies and strategies in education, but they must continue to do so throughout their careers if they are to remain pertinent in their positions. To better reflect a more sociocultural stance on language learning (and the social aspect to all forms of learning in general), Arshavskaya and Halaczkiewicz suggest the addition of communities of practice into the TPACK framework, something which IEPs especially cultivate and gravitate towards given their periphery status at many of their home institutions. While educational technology can connect and engage learners in new, exciting and very relevant ways, especially through the TPACK framework, the authors remind readers that IEPs also need to face realities of how advances in educational technology impact their relevance and their revenue, and practitioners must understand the ways in which their units need to adapt and change in order to acknowledge the changing global technological landscape.

Innovate to Critically Reform from Within

A volume on innovation in IEPs would be remiss if it didn't include calls for more radical reform, especially as the profession of English language education and its underlying ideologies stem from even earlier histories of colonization and racialization, and the more modern practices of neo-colonization. Although L2 education (which includes IEPs as well as TESOL) is a field that attracts *nice* professionals who are interested in working in a *nice* internationalized field that promotes the *nice* idea of multiculturalism across races, this should 'not make the field devoid of the responsibility to examine how racism or any other injustices influence its knowledge' (Kubota 2002: 86). In this case, innovation means acknowledging hard and honest truths in order to engage in the critical reflection needed for actual meaningful reform.

Through scholarship on native speakerism and on how the concepts of race and ethnicity are intertwined with the notion of *native*, failing to acknowledge the racism and whiteness that is perpetuated through the idea of a native speaker greatly affects all involved with and impacted by TESOL (Gerald, Chapter 8). In the United States, where language (especially standardized, native and 'white' English) has been commodified as an asset for self-development and belonging as a 'true' citizen, a neoliberal approach to language teaching and learning has further entrenched complex social hierarchies that contribute to inequitable social and economic opportunities. Gerald argues that there is essentially 'no conceptualization of the native speaker that can exist without the twin crutches of whiteness and racism' (p. 132–3), yet the absence of this theory in some of the most radical writings about the profession has only helped to keep the field from actually and meaningfully moving ahead. In university IEPs in the United States, where the majority of the educators are white, the ideal or 'perfect' native English speaker is white and being both white *and* a native speaker of English garner a certain globalized status of privilege and power, these ideologies are not only replicated, but also maintained and promoted. This reality is evidenced through neoliberal competition for international student enrollment and through recruitment images of white (implied native English speaking) educators.

Although quick to revise mission statements that include more 'innovative' DEI efforts in the wake of Black Lives Matter, IEPs have actually fallen short in the critical consciousness needed to begin to implement any valid change. A historical preoccupation in IEPs with strategies for uplifting (i.e. saving, helping or successfully assimilating) non-native English speakers and teachers shadows the real issue at hand, which is confronting uncomfortable truths in pursuit of real justice (Gerald, Chapter 8). IEP directors and educators often do not engage in robust and sustained critical analysis of how race, ethnicity, culture and (English) language teaching practices have been used to continue colonized and imperial oppression throughout modern history. The result is the perpetuation of dominant, racist epistemologies wrapped in a guise of 'multiculturalism' and 'opportunity' within IEPs and their respective host institutions that, in reality, instead *others* and often isolates those it claims to be helping. This creates an unbalanced – or colonized – relationship when IEPs seek to partner with other international institutions, resulting in study abroad and continuing education opportunities for their global peers that are not true exchanges, but instead foster 'a form of epistemicide' (Silva *et al.*, Chapter 10). In a field that works with populations from a diverse array of cultures, races and ideologies, simply grasping onto the multicultural nature of the profession as *proof of virtue* is not enough to push back on linguistic colonization or to truly innovate the field. Our current understanding of globalization and multiculturalism – concepts which should promote and seek inter-connected and inter-exchanged ideas and experiences – has instead morphed into competition and marketability for profit (Berry, 2017). The Western capitalism that seeks homogenization and conformity as the path to being 'successful' or to having 'more opportunity' within dominant systems is a framework under which many IEPs have had to operate. To truly innovate is to challenge this model. Acknowledging that there are multiple stories, approaches and perspectives (epistemologies) that are just as valuable as the valued and unquestioned standards (Silva *et al.*, Chapter 10), is the only way to move those involved in English language education towards more equitable positionings.

Continuing to Make History: Towards Innovating IEPs for the Future

Through multiple historical accounts on how IEPs came to be, this volume serves as an important record for their growth, which further contributes to a better understanding of where IEPs are currently as well as informing directions that they can and should take in the future. The identity of IEPs as flexible innovators occupying liminal spaces – both literally and figuratively – has afforded them the wherewithal to be able to adapt as necessary to survive. In looking to the future, perhaps the three areas where IEPs can most tangibly innovate is through reimagined partnerships, applied technology skills development, and in critical examination and work to decolonize the field of TESOL as a whole. More specific suggestions for innovation in these areas are discussed below.

Reimagined partnerships

IEPs can truly innovate and tackle their periphery positionings on campus by partnering with other campus units to democratize language learning and to help develop more interdisciplinary understanding of multiculturalism and cross-cultural communication. It is not enough to position themselves internally as experts in language learning, intercultural communication and multiculturalism; IEPs also need to advertise themselves as such through workshops for their greater faculty peers, open language labs for matriculated students, pathway programs, and in departmental support. Understanding the importance of host institution partnerships is not in of itself an innovative idea, as 'working in a vacuum as an English program without connections to the surrounding territory is a recipe for disaster' (Cavusgil *et al.*, Chapter 3). Conscientious practitioners, however, can be quite innovative if they are willing to employ a fresh approach to the kinds of partnerships available through language, multiculturalism, and internationalism.

IEPs are in a unique position to be leaders in taking an anticolonial stance on multilingual education by partnering with other units dedicated to communication and departments or colleges that have components of global outreach in their disciplines. Often considered to be the world's lingua franca, English has nearly three times the number of speakers who have learned it in addition to a primary home language as it does native[1] speakers (Ethnologue, 2022). It is the non-native speakers of English, however, who are consistently pushed and expected to reduce their accent to sound more native-like and be able to 'more successfully' communicate and integrate with native speakers. Institutes of higher education seek to 'internationalize' and prepare students for global endeavors, yet native English-speaking students, especially those who are monolingual themselves, greatly lack training in and understanding of the variety of World English dialects (Kubota, 2001) and 'accents' uttered by the majority of the world's English-speakers, making them among the worst communicators in English worldwide (Morrison, 2016; Sweeney & Hua, 2010). Given the fact that native English speakers are in the vast minority globally, it would only make sense that IEPs partner with communication departments to help develop listening training for native speakers of English who are often disadvantaged when it comes to understanding multiple cultural perspectives and the various accents of the more widely spoken World Englishes. These labs could contain recordings of participants from all around the world who share their stories, insights, and perspectives in English. Not only would this listening training benefit native English speakers in their understanding of and empathy towards their non-native counterparts, it would also highlight the valuing of World Englishes for international multilingual English learners themselves and the greater educational community as a whole. The teaching of world Englishes in the IEP classroom, and more exposure to and valuing of 'accented' English in native English-speaking settings truly brings a more anticolonial and multicultural dimension to English language education (Kubota, 2019). This example is but one of a reimagined and more innovative IEP partnership in which multiculturalism – one where exchange of perspectives and mutual valuation coexist – can not only thrive, but actively push back on dominant narratives and standards.

Applied technology skills and integration to meet a new era

Most IEPs in the United States have embraced, to varying extents, the degree to which technology is an integral part of education today and in the future, so it's not too far of a stretch to state that any future considerations for innovation in IEPs must include this area. The global pandemic gave many who were reluctant to veer too far from traditional language teaching methods the push (or rather, a giant kick) into new ways of teaching language in completely virtual settings. Although they may use technology such as innovative apps or online tools with their students as well as LMS systems for assignments and grading, many English language teachers are still not confident problem solvers when it comes to computers, and many still have only basic technology use and integration skills (Andrei, 2017). Without a doubt, technology and education are here to stay, but more should be done to both prepare pre-service teachers and continuously train in-service educators in not only effectively and meaningfully using technology with their students, but also in advancing their own technology skills. Some educators fear that an overemphasis on technology overshadows other traditional and perhaps more communicative strategies in language teaching and learning (Arshavskaya & Halaczkiewicz, Chapter 12), yet these approaches are not mutually exclusive. Having a strong foundation in technology skills is the key to being able to more successfully navigate both traditional and tech-based approaches to teaching and learning, to understanding in which contexts one may be more effective than the other, and in knowing when and how to interweave the two (Tondeur *et al.*, 2019). Language teachers nowadays have an understanding of why tech skills and tech literacy are important; however, they should also be tech literate themselves, an idea in which IEPs could help lead the way in terms of research – something which is greatly lacking in this area.

Technological approaches to innovation in IEPs simply cannot ignore the fact that, not only are advances in technology changing at paces unprecedented, but they are bringing with them whole new worlds and challenging our knowledge like never before. Uni-directional media (books, newspapers, tv, radio, etc.) once dominated not only how we received information about the world around us, but also shaped how we think about and teach literacy. With more interactive, user-driven and democratized forms of media (e.g. social media, streaming platforms, blogs, video-sharing sites, etc.) constantly at our disposal on the small computers that many of us carry around in our hands, a new way of thinking about literacy is upon us and demands attention, especially in IEPs, where an almost proprietary approach to what English language literacy is exists. These new media platforms require an understanding of new media literacies, as communication becomes more fluid and a range of affordances is needed to traverse them (Olmanson & Falls, 2016). Many students nowadays are digital natives and have cultivated an entrenched online presence, yet they are not necessarily digitally literate or tech savvy (Beavis, 2013). As new media becomes increasingly commonplace at institutions of higher education and the societies in which they are positioned, IEPs cannot truly and fully prepare their students for communicative and linguistic success solely by focusing on their program's traditional language learning goals while ignoring the importance of developing these new media literacies. As we are on the cusp of yet another digital era, moving out of Web 2.0 and into Web 3.0, new media literacies are adding even more dimensions, blending the traditional and physical with incredible virtual experiences and becoming just another part of daily life. The increasing number of developers moving into the Web 3.0 space (Filipčić, 2022) is reminiscent of the early days of the internet; we know something exciting (and, for some, scary) is taking place, yet we cannot even imagine where it will take us in only a few years. Many jobs and academic disciplines that many of our students will have do not even exist yet. The metaverse is a reality for our sociocultural and sociolinguistic future (Mustafa, 2022), and will greatly impact how language is taught, learned and experienced. With many IEPs and English language educators still trying to catch up with Web 2.0 technology, looking towards and preparing themselves for this new era is the only way to ensure that any innovations they contribute remain relevant.

Radical decolonization of a historically colonized field

True innovation within IEPs needs to include deep critical and reflexive analysis on the part of IEP educators and administrators that challenge the status quo and the field's colonial and neo-colonial capacities. Despite arguments and attempts to the contrary, the act of teaching itself is not and cannot be neutral; it is a political act where what and how teachers teach, what information is included or excluded from the syllabi, materials and objectives, and how classroom policies and procedures are carried out all reflect personal beliefs, values and prejudices that are informed by (often dominant) epistemologies (Howard & Rodriguez-Minkoff, 2017; Mortenson, 2021). Since they are engaged in teaching a language of historic colonizers – and with it epistemologies that have neutralized and naturalized colonizing ideologies – it's imperative that educators in IEPs be involved in anticolonial and antiracist examinations of their field, practice and position within it (Chan & Coney, 2020; Kubota, 2019). Kubota (2002) summarizes it simply: *being a nice person/educator won't end (colonial-induced) racism.* Scheurich and Young (1997: 12) state that 'we can be strongly anti-racist in our own minds but be promulgating racism in profound ways we do not understand' and they claim that invisible racism – one in which we unconsciously know and participate in – is one of the worst racisms of all. In the wake of the capricious Trump presidency and the renewed calling out of racial injustice and sense of activism sparked by Black Lives Matter, Americans who have never had to be concerned with race before are now either learning more about engaging with antiracism measures or are engaging in politicized measures against the movement in order to preserve the status quo. Learning more about systemic, systematic and colonized structures of racism requires a deeper look at biased practices in TESOL and the colonized proliferation of English through native speakerism and whiteness, which is often unconsciously replicated in university IEPs.

Merely relying on the multicultural makeup of students in traditional English language classrooms and supposed altruistic endeavors of educators as 'proof' of antiracist diversity and inclusivity actually keeps

TESOL operating as a white-dominant, neocolonial field. Without a full understanding of the epistemologies of those who both control and are controlled, and without seeking the critical consciousness needed to engage with more critical pedagogies in the classroom, TESOL's *niceness* only works in continuing to whitewash oppression and inequity. Moving from ideologies and pedagogies that are primarily focused on what we do or don't do in the classroom towards ones that also are critically focused on how we think (about valued knowledge, our students, our epistemologies and our practice) is the only way we will be able to move the field and the profession into an actual anticolonial, antiracist and equitable realm. This would be a move of true innovation given the field's past. More TESOL educators partaking in critical consciousness are needed to transform from a colonizing field to one committed to anticolonial and antiracist pedagogies and practices (Gerald, Chapter 8). By thoroughly looking at how other ways of being and knowing are (un)welcomed, (mis)communicated, and (de)valued in the field (including within scholarly research, teacher education, materials and classroom practices), inequities at the micro and macro levels may be revealed.

In this sense, culture and critically examined histories become center to curricula and professional education, allowing people from diverse backgrounds to better work together and co-create knowledge for problem-solving, empathy and understanding (Berry, 2017; Bhattacharya, 2016; Chan & Coney, 2020; Mortenson, 2021). Detaching from the feel-good multicultural aspects of English language teaching that ignores its colonial and neocolonial manifestation and embracing more critical consciousness of the field and praxis is necessary if IEP practitioners are to become more culturally relevant, culturally informed, antiracist and anticolonial – something truly at the apex of innovation.

Questions for IEPs to Consider Going Forward

(1) IEPs have historically provided unique, yet limited, research sites for applied linguistics and language teacher preparation. How can they extend their breadth to help inform research that is more applicable globally?
(2) How can IEPs resist and combat the current (and often very loud) trends of isolationism, nationalism and anti-intellectualism that have transformed the profession and the demand for its services?
(3) In what ways can IEPs initiate, foster and sustain more meaningful relationships with the greater host institution community in order to better democratize access to approaches to multiculturalism, inclusivity and an understanding of language acquisition for better support international multilingual learners of English.
(4) How can IEPs engage international multilingual students in meaningful learning of and engagement in their host communities while

also challenging stereotypes towards them often held by community members and facilitating better cross-cultural understanding between the two?
(5) Many institutions of higher education seek our third-party providers for the development of their pathway programs. How can IEPs better work with administrative leadership to position themselves at the forefront of their own in-house pathway program creation and implementation?
(6) How can pre-service and in-service IEP educators get the training they need in not only language-focused technology education, but also in technology problem-solving themselves in order to remain competitive and relevant?
(7) What is the push needed to get IEP administrators and educators meaningfully engaged in critical analysis of how racism, whiteness and native speakerism has shaped their field and informed their teaching methodologies, materials and ideologies? What specifically can IEPs do to acknowledge this history and work to decolonize outside of altered mission statements?

To Innovate is to Change

Calls for change or the desire to innovate within a field are not new, especially in the realm of education. For many, however, the innovation simply comes with being a part of something long enough to see 'trendy' approaches repackaged in various ways and under new buzzwords, something with which it's difficult to not become disillusioned. The change needed to truly innovate in IEPs is a full-on disruption to the status quo, one that more than likely will generate discomfort, resistance, push-back, and perhaps even fall out in the pursuit of maintaining things how they are. Reimaging the partnerships between IEPs and other areas on campus requires units both to step out of their liminal spaces and to become more vocal on the ways they can serve the greater campus community. Challenging the notion of 'native speakers' as an idealized goal takes continued reckoning for which many practitioners may still struggle. Advancing English language educators' skills in relevant applied technology and in embracing more media literacies is a frustrating path to those who do not consider themselves or their practice technologically enhanced. And engaging in the critical anti-racist work needed to radically decolonize this historically colonized field is one that requires a difficult and collective confrontation. In reimagining themselves and their relevance in a post-pandemic world, IEPs are in dire need of breaking free of recycled 'innovation'. In other words, IEPs and IEP practitioners cannot and should not remain stagnant if they are to have a relevant future within the greater context for which they are striving to prepare students.

This volume gives an account of the resilience and innovation that contributed to the development of IEPs and kept them working in a standard model for decades. As we look forward and acknowledge where we are now, it is irresponsible for those of us involved in IEPs and in TESOL to expect suggestions for innovation within the field that do not include critical reflection on our own roles and participation within the system, as well as of the structure of the system itself. Each generation talks about how the world is different *now* then from the seemingly rosier version of how it *was*. What's especially different in our world now is that it is demanding us to think differently about it and its collective history. More precisely, it's asking us to acknowledge exactly whose history has been given the voice and power to cultivate the sociocultural 'norms' under which we in TESOL operate and then use that to knowledge to elicit more radical change.

The introduction to this volume asks us to consider a more conscientious innovation, one in which we slow down, look past immediate solutions to immediate problems of numbers and tuition dollars, and dive deeper into a more sustainable field and practice. It is one where we strive to educate ourselves through a decolonial lens on differing perspectives, knowledges, values, ways of being, and ideas of success for a more globally informed praxis. Conscientious innovation also requires of us to think of the differently, as well as our place as professionals and educators within that world. This alternative approach to innovation is no doubt 'tedious, interminable, and challenging' (Litzenberg, this volume: 9). With it, however, comes the reward of a more meaningful, equitable, culturally relevant, and truly globalized field, one that's especially important as IEPs and IEP practitioners seek to situate themselves more sustainably among a shaky and uncertain future.

Note

(1) Although the labels of native and non-native speakers are problematic and colonized (Gerald, Chapter 8), for the sake of contemporary understanding, I have chosen to use those terms here.

References

Andrei, E. (2017) Technology in teaching English language learners: The case of three middle school teachers. *TESOL Journal* 8 (2), 409–431.

Beavis, C. (2013) Young people, new media and education: Participation and possibilities. *Social Alternatives* 32 (2), 39–44.

Berry, T.R. (2017) The intersections of Africana studies and curriculum theory: A counter-Western narrative for social justice. *Journal of Curriculum Theorizing* 32 (1), 53–66.

Bhattacharya, K. (2016) The vulnerable academic: Personal narratives and strategic de/colonizing of academic structures. *Qualitative Inquiry* 22 (5), 309–321.

Chan, E.L. and Coney, L. (2020) Moving TESOL forward: Increasing educators' critical consciousness through a racial lens. *TESOL Journal* 11 (4), e550.

Ethnologue (2022) English. See www.ethnologue.com/language/eng (accessed October 2022).

Filipčić, S. (2022, May) Web3 & DAOs: An overview of the development and possibilities for the implementation in research and education. In *2022 45th Jubilee International Convention on Information, Communication and Electronic Technology* (MIPRO) (pp. 1278–1283). Online: IEEE. https://ieeexplore.ieee.org/xpl/conhome/9803295/proceeding.

Henry, A. (2019) Online media creation and L2 motivation: A socially situated perspective. *TESOL Quarterly* 53 (2), 372–404. https://doi.org/10.1002/tesq.485.

Howard, T. and Rodriguez-Minkoff, A.C. (2017) Culturally relevant pedagogy 20 years later: Progress or pontificating? What have we learned, and where do we go? *Teachers College Record* 119 (1), 1–32.

Kubota, R. (2001) Teaching world Englishes to native speakers of English in the USA. *World Englishes* 20 (1), 47–64.

Kubota, R. (2002) The author responds: (Un) Raveling racism in a nice field like TESOL. *TESOL Quarterly* 36 (1), 84–92.

Kubota, R. (2019) Confronting epistemological racism, decolonizing scholarly knowledge: Race and gender in applied linguistics. *Applied Linguistics* 41 (5), 712–732.

Litzenberg, J. (2020) "If I don't do it, somebody else will": Covert neoliberal policy discourses in the decision-making processes of an intensive English program. *TESOL Quarterly* 54 (4), 823–845.

Morrison, L. (2016) Native English speakers are the world's worst communicators. *BBC Worklife*, 31 October. See https://www.bbc.com/worklife/article/20161028-native-english-speakers-are-the-worlds-worst-communicators (accessed November 2022).

Mortenson, L. (2021) White TESOL instructors' engagement with social justice content in an EAP program: Teacher neutrality as a tool of white supremacy. *BC TEAL Journal* 6 (1), 106–131.

Mustafa, B. (2022) Analyzing education based on metaverse technology. *Technium Social Sciences Journal* 32, 278–295.

Olmanson, J. and Falls, Z. (2016) New media literacies. In M.A. Peters (ed.) *Encyclopedia of Educational Philosophy and Theory* (pp. 1–3). Singapore: Springer Singapore. See http://link.springer.com/referencework entry/10.1007/978-981-287-532-7_300-1 (accessed October 2022).

Peace Corps (n.d.) www.peacecorps.gov (accessed October 2022).

Scheurich, J.J. and Young, M. (1997) Coloring epistemologies: Are our research epistemologies racially biased? *Educational Researcher* 26 (4), 4–16.

Sweeney, E. and Hua, Z. (2010) Accommodating toward your audience: Do native speakers of English know how to accommodate their communication strategies toward nonnative speakers of English?. *The Journal of Business Communication* 47 (4), 477–504.

Tondeur, J., Scherer, R., Baran, E., Siddiq, F., Valtonen, T. and Sointu, E. (2019) Teacher educators as gatekeepers: Preparing the next generation of teachers for technology integration in education. *British Journal of Educational Technology* 50 (3), 1189–1209.

Tour, E. (2020) Teaching digital literacies in EAL/ESL classrooms: Practical strategies. *TESOL Journal* 11 (1), e00458. https://doi.org/10.1002/tesj.458.

Index

9/11 63, 212

Accreditation 13, 16, 48–9, 68, 77, 142, 180, 182, *See also* CEA
Advocacy xvi, 15, 32, 54, 112, 117
Agent(s) 175, 177, 183, 215
America
  Central 96
  Latin 20–1, 160, 163, 171
  North v, 1, 23, 28, 160–61, 164–67
  South v, 96
America Language Institute (ALI) xiv–v, 39–41, 43–6
American Council on Education (ACE) 45, 101–02, 104
American Council on the Teaching of Foreign Languages (ACTFL) 92
Applied Linguistics ix–xiv, xvi, 1–2, 6, 10–13, 15, 17, 23–5, 34–8, 42, 48–9, 52–3, 56, 64–9, 78, 82, 105, 105, 117–21, 124, 129, 149, 183, 208, 210–11, 221
Approach xi, 3, 11–3, 16, 21–2, 25–6, 31–2, 34, 48, 80–2, 88, 94–6, 98, 105–08, 128, 136, 142, 150, 152, 160, 164, 167, 170–01, 179, 187–88, 193, 196, 198, 204, 216–17, 219, 221–23, *see also* Deficit
Asia x, 23, 79
Azar (Grammar Text) 59, 68

Bonfiglio, Thomas Paul 16, 133, 137–38
Brazilian Teachers Program 14, 162–3, 167

California State University (San Marcos) 155
Cambridge Education Group 178
Capitalist 163
CEA (Commission on English Language Program Accreditation) xv, 14, 48, 64–6
Center for English Language Training (CELT) 40–41
Colonial v, 103, 107, 160, 165, 169, 172, 220
  Anticolonial 102, 105, 217–18, 220–21

Decolonial ix, xii–vi, 11–12, 14, 160, 163–64, 171–72, 223
  Neo-Colonial 220–21
Community College xi, 55, 69, 72–3, 77–8, 81–2, 146, 160, 164–65, 167, 200
Community Service 93, 96–8, 146, 214
Complex Dynamic Systems Theory (CDST) 48
Content-Based Instruction (CBI) 61, 93–4, 107, 124–25
Covid-19 2, 31, 72, 79, 82, 92, 126, 155, 178, 192–93, 199, 201
  Pandemic xv, 2, 16, 31, 69–76, 92–3, 112, 126, 155, 178, 187, 192–93, 199, 201–03, 212, 214, 218, 222
Credentialing
  TEFL xi, xv–vi, 15, 54, 56, 59, 64, 78
  TESL xi, 15, 74, 78
  TESOL ix–xv, 1, 4, 11, 13, 16–7, 25, 30, 34–49, 55, 58–9, 64–70, 74–5, 78, 89, 103–06, 118, 121, 126, 135–36, 142, 144–45, 156, 163, 165, 185–86, 192, 201–02, 208, 210–11, 215–17, 220–23
Credit
  Credit-Bearing 28, 47, 76, 88, 111, 122, 175–84
  Non-Credit 4, 15, 76, 90, 121–2
Curriculum xi, 1–10, 13, 32, 35, 53, 59–62, 67, 69, 71, 75, 81, 107, 110–11, 113, 118, 123–27, 144, 149–50, 164, 169–70, 178, 181–82, 184, 195–96, 203, 214, 223

Decolonial *see* Colonial
Defense Language Institute (DLI) 44, 192
Deficit
  Approach 102, 108
  Model 109
  Orientation 150
  Perspective 108, 113, 138
DEI (Diversity, Equity, Inclusion) 32, 102–09, 113, 135, 216
DePaul University 176

225

Index

Development xii, xv, xvi, 11, 13, 15, 21, 23, 27, 31, 35, 39, 47, 82, 90, 98, 104–06, 108, 110, 118, 125–26, 135, 144–47, 149–50, 152, 155, 160, 164–65, 167, 171, 175, 177, 183–84, 202, 204, 210–11, 213
    Assessment 23, 27–8, 82, 184
    Career 93, 95
    Community 156
    Course 13, 26,
    Curriculum 2, 111, 124
    Faculty 5,
    Intercultural *See* Intercultural
    ITA 88
    Language x, 1, 23, 48, 89, 102, 107–10, 113, 145, 149
    Linguistic x, 146, 162
    Materials xiv, 13, 20, 22, 27
    Personal 216
    Professional x, 4, 95, 105, 159–60, 166, 168, 170, 180–83, 195, 201
    Program 1–2, 166–67, 184, 189, 209–12, 222–23
    Project 151–52, 164
    Skills 76, 91, 96, 108, 112, 123, 145, 147, 149, 217
    Studies 52–3, 61
    Teacher ix, 13, 35, 121, 177
Diversity 11, 15, 32, 37, 81, 87, 90, 98, 101–03, 110, 136, 147, 150, 155, 183, 213, 220 *See also* DEI (Diversity, Equity, Inclusion)
Diversity, Equity, Inclusion *See* DEI (Diversity, Equity, Inclusion)
Drexel University 176
Duolingo 75, 126

English
    Department 55, 86
    Language Learner 30, 71, 73, 80, 109, 114, 144–46, 150, 180, 183–84
English as a Lingua Franca (ELF) xii, 35
English for Academic Purposes (EAP) xi, 13, 26–9, 31–2, 47, 53, 60–1, 68, 106, 116–19, 121, 129,177–78, 210, 212
English Language Institute (ELI) 12–3, 20–32, 36, 39–41, 43–8, 184, 209–11
English Language Program (ELP) 13, 15, 38–41, 43–8, 98–9, 105, 112
English without Borders Program 162
EnglishUSA xv, 47
Enrollment 2, 4, 6, 11, 15, 63, 71–4, 79, 86, 92–3, 95–6, 98, 104, 126, 175, 178, 181, 184–85, 187, 210, 213, 216
Epistemology 133, 137, 216–17, 220–21

Equity xi, 15, 32, 86, 97, 102–03, 107, 136, 141, 185, 213, *See also* DEI (Diversity, Equity, Inclusion); *See also* Inequity
Europe x, 96, 163

Flexibility 4–5, 13, 32, 46, 53, 58–60, 62, 82, 126, 128, 208, 217
Fries, Charles C. 1, 20–3, 27, 32
Fulbright 159

George Mason University 176
Global North 106, 160, 165, 170
Global South 160, 165, 170

Hybrid xv, 79, 155, 204, 212

IELTS 89, 126, 183
Inclusion xi, 15, 32, 39, 87, 98, 102–03, 108, 110, 113, 127, 139, 155, 202, 212; *See also* DEI (Diversity, Equity, Inclusion)
Inequity; *See also* Equity 117, 221
Institute for International Education (IIE) 45, 48, 71
Intercultural
    Awareness 148
    Challenges 80
    Communication xiv, 81–2, 105, 149, 214, 217
    Competence 102
    Development 15, 105
    Dimensions 159, 161, 166
    Education 112
    Experience 30
    Instruction 32
    Interactions 150
    Knowledge 16
    Learning x, 98, 112
    Opportunities 149
    Pedagogies 163
    Project 149
    Sensitivity Measures 147
International Performance Test (IPT) 89–90
Internationalization xiii, xiv, 11, 14–5, 86, 97–8, 101–03, 113, 162, 164–66, 171–72, 176
    Campus 4, 101–03, 112, 211
    Curriculum 112
    Decolonial 160, 171
    Education 159–61, 165, 169, 171–72
    Efforts xii, 4, 103–04, 107–10, 113
    Framework 102
    Goals 101, 102, 188
    Initiatives 86, 160
    Planning 104

Practices 159
Priorities 86
Strategies 98
INTO 69–70, 76, 176, 178

K-12 (PK-12) 2, 16–17, 30, 38, 68, 74, 82, 122, 183, 200
Kaplan International 176, 178
King Abdullah Scholarship Program 70
King, Martin Luther 138
Kings Education 178

Language Learning (journal) xii, 1, 12–3, 23–5, 31, 34, 36–48, 210
Language Policy xiv, 3, 9–11
Languaging 139–40
Liminal Space 16, 116, 123, 129, 209, 217, 222
Linguistic Imperialism 103

Matriculated xvi, 47, 76, 87–9, 92, 97–8, 104, 121, 198
  Non-Matriculated 47, 85
  Pre-Matriculated 38–48, 85, 213, 217
Minnesota English Language Program (MELP) ix, xi, 112
Mission (Statement) 10, 20, 32, 37, 50–2, 60, 67–8, 77, 88, 118, 123, 126, 151, 154, 156, 181, 210, 216, 222
Modern Language Journal (journal) 13, 34, 36–8, 40, 42, 45, 48
MOOC (Massive Open Online Course) 32, 93–5
Multicultural 4, 11, 13, 15, 102–03, 108, 111–12, 136, 213–18, 220–21
Multilingual(ism) x, xi, 15, 108–09, 111, 113, 136
  Competence 111
  Education 217
  Skills 108, 110
  Students/Learners ix, xi, xvi, 74, 101–05, 107–11, 203, 209–10, 212–13, 218, 221
  Support 97, 213
  User(s) 104–05, 108, 111–13

NAFSA xv, 47, 56, 58, 63–4, 66, 68, 70
Native
  Native Speaker 16, 24, 52, 106, 108, 132–39, 215–16, 222–23
  Native speakerism 16, 132 –34, 139, 215, 220, 222–23
  Nativeness 17, 132–42
  Non-native speaker 48, 52, 55, 89, 91, 96, 109, 218, 135–36, 138, 140–42, 216

Navitas 178
Neoliberal 7, 46, 208–09, 211, 213, 216
Northeastern University 177

Open Doors 71
Open Educational Resource (OER) 94–5, 197, 202
Oregon State University 178

Pandemic *See* Covid-19
Pathway Program ix, xvi, 14, 76–9, 82, 105, 175–89, 205, 211–14, 217, 222
  Bridge Program 76, 175–76, 184
PK-12 *See* K-12
Plurilingual 106–07, 169
Professionalization 64–5, 189
  Deprofessionalization 189
Profit 79, 81, 86, 178, 186, 189, 216
  For-profit 14, 69, 73, 179, 188
  Non-Profit x, 69, 149

Race ix, xvi, 16–7, 107, 133, 137–42, 216–17, 220
  Antiracist 32, 103, 140, 220–21
Rampton, Ben 16, 133–37, 140
Recruit/Recruitment xiii, 1, 5, 11, 28, 62, 85, 101–02, 119, 175, 177, 180, 183–89
Redden, Elizabeth 189
Remote (Classes) 16, 78–9
Rowan University 177

September 11 *See* 9/11
Service Learning xiv, 14, 29, 123, 144–56, 188, 214
Shorelight 69–70, 76, 178, 186
Social Justice xvi, 10, 107, 146, 150, 152, 160
Soft Power 20, 161
Stakeholder 5, 7, 14, 17, 77, 92, 98, 116, 119, 127–28, 149–56, 178, 188, 192, 199, 208, 211
Standardized Test 85, 89, 92, 147, 154, 216,
Stoller, Fredricka 59, 68
Strategic Priority 87, 98
Student and Exchange Visitor Program (SEVP) 76
Study Group (educational service provider) 178

Task-Based Language Teaching (TBLT) 7, 25, 61, 168
Teaching Assistants/assistantship xii, 26, 68, 89–90, 118
  Graduate 53, 62, 68

ITA x, 13, 26, 52, 68, 88–90, 98, 199, 210
TEFL *See* Credentialing
TESL *See* Credentialing
TESOL Quarterly (journal) xv, 13, 34–42, 45–6, 48, 135
Third-Party (Provider) 14, 70, 126–27, 175–89, 177, 212, 214, 222,
TOEFL 60, 89, 126, 162, 183
TPACK (Technological Pedagogical and Content Knowledge) 193–94, 196, 199–200, 202–03, 205, 215
   Sociocultural Layer 198–200
Translanguaging 81, 106, 110
Translingual xiv
Tuition 4, 77, 86–7, 92, 95–7, 176, 184, 187, 212, 223

University of Delaware 176
University of Michigan xii, 1, 12, 20–1, 23–26, 28, 31–2, 36, 44, 47, 57, 59, 209–10
University of Minnesota ix, xi, 24, 111–12

Virtual xv, 78–80, 96, 144, 155, 177, 202, 214–15, 218–19
Visa
   F-1 96
   J-1 88, 91–2, 98–9

Widdowson, Henry 135
World Englishes 107, 218

Zoom (Classes) 79, 117, 199, 203

For Product Safety Concerns and Information please contact our EU Authorised Representative:

Easy Access System Europe

Mustamäe tee 50

10621 Tallinn

Estonia

gpsr.requests@easproject.com

www.ingramcontent.com/pod-product-compliance
Ingram Content Group UK Ltd.
Pitfield, Milton Keynes, MK11 3LW, UK
UKHW021823220426
5349IPUK00003B/52